J.K. LASSER'S

CHOOSING THE RIGHT LONG-TERM CARE INSURANCE

Benjamin Lipson

John Wiley & Sons, Inc.

Published by John Wiley & Sons, Inc.
Published simultaneously in Canada.

This publication is designed to provide accurate and authoritative information in regard to the
subject matter covered. It is sold with the understanding that the publisher is not engaged in
rendering professional services. If professional advice or other expert assistance is required,
the services of a competent professional person should be sought.

The material presented in this publication is based on the experience and interpretation of the
author through his experience as an insurance columnist and an insurance broker. Although
the information has been carefully researched and checked for accuracy, currency, and
completeness, the author does not accept any responsibility or liability with regard to errors,
misuse, and misinterpretation. It is not the intention of the author that any reader shall rely
upon any of the information here for any specific medical, legal, or tax advice.

ISBN 0-471-15205-6

Printed in the United States of America

10 9 8 7 6 5 4 3 2

This book is dedicated to my grandaughters Janie and Amy with the fervent wish that when they become seniors traditional doctoring will be the accepted norm for the delivery of health care and they will be able to live independently with dignity in their golden years.

Acknowledgments

My internist, Dr. John Goodson, of Massachusetts General Hospital, prodded me for years to write a book about long-term care insurance. This work would be a natural extension of my *Boston Globe* columns and opinion pieces, where I have always advocated for health care reform and patient rights. This book reflects Dr. Goodson's concern with the plight of seniors and their families who often confront the loss of independence in addition to the need for specialized care that accompany growing older. I am grateful for the doctor's encouragement.

When I sat down to write the text, I depended on my 50 years of experience in the industry and upon the information I uncovered writing for the *Globe*. But no book of this importance can be based on one person's knowledge. Many people contributed to this effort.

I am indebted to several insurance industry experts who generously shared their insights and their time during extensive interviews. Thank you, especially, to an exemplarily corporate citizen, Richard Wolfe, senior vice president of field operations for UnumProvident Corporation. As a result of his efforts I was furnished with reams of invaluable data to help consumers make informed choices. He and those under his direct supervision gave me straight answers to all my questions—even those that were irritating and involved sensitive issues. Their candor reflects the way a first-class insurance company does business.

Those who study the industry outside corporate offices were also central to this effort. Marc Cohen, Ph.D., vice president of LifePlans, Inc., in Waltham, Massachusetts, provided me with industry, academic, and government sources, as well as an honest, detailed interview. Lisa McAree, managing general agent for nine long-term care insurers, offered an inside look at long-term care policy provisions and practices. Meredith Beit Patterson, elder care consultant, explained the role of professional care managers in long-term care. Joseph Belth, Ph.D., publisher of *The Insurance Forum*, outlined a clear explanation of ratings firms. Richard Albert, regional sales director of MetLife Individual Long-Term Care Sales Group, provided encouragement. June Saltzberg, Bodimedex president, let me in on the truth about the cognitive impairment test. Diane Paulson, managing attorney, Medicare Advocacy Project of the Greater Boston Legal Services, gave helpful insights for beneficiaries wishing to access their long-term care rights. Jay Menario, former head of long-term care product development for UnumProvident Corporation, for supplying underwriting and statistical data, and Chris Goetcheus, communications officer of the Massachusetts Division of Insurance for providing important consumer information.

Several people helped me with the writing of this book. David Pugh, my editor at John Wiley & Sons, Inc., assisted me in the development of the manuscript. Judy Budz provided editing and encouragement along the way; and Geraldina DeBenedictis put up with my lengthy typing assignments and deciphered my tapes.

My daughter, Judy Lipson, good-naturedly sacrificed her few leisure hours to help me with last-minute typing and e-mailing.

And, of course, my wife Ellie supported my hectic schedule even though it meant time away from our activities during the summer. She tolerated my preoccupations, listened to my concerns, and praised my efforts.

Contents

Foreword

Yung-Ping Chen, PhD
Frank J. Manning Eminent Scholar's Chair Professor of Gerontology
University of Massachusetts Boston, Boston, Massachusetts

J.K. Lasser's Choosing the Right Long-Term Care Insurance by Benjamin Lipson fills more than the proverbial gap in information; it is a valuable addition to J.K. Lasser's long list of practical guides for financial needs.

How to pay for long-term care services is an issue that promises (or more accurately, threatens) to become increasingly challenging in the next several decades as a result of the aging of the elderly population. By comparison, funding long-term care will be even more daunting than funding Social Security and Medicare, partly because long-term care entails issues more complex than supplying retirement income or providing acute health care, and partly because, although Social Security and Medicare's funding model needs reform, it is still functioning, whereas the system of funding long-term care is widely acknowledged to be in a state of serious disrepair.

The need for long-term care services is a risk that is best protected by insurance, yet the current funding for these services relies heavily on personal out-of-pocket payment and public welfare (Medicaid) but only lightly on social insurance and private insurance. This method is akin to sitting on a two-legged stool that is unlikely to be stable and sustainable, because it tends to impoverish many people and thereby severely strains the Medicaid budget nationwide. Some regard it as a catastrophe waiting to happen.

To incorporate insurance as a key component of funding and to mobilize public and private resources more effectively, an argument may be made for a three-legged-stool funding model, with social insurance providing a basic protection that would be supplemented by private insurance and personal payment. When these measures do not provide sufficient protection for some individuals, Medicaid as public welfare would serve its traditional role of helping the poor. But the implementation of this funding model must await the alignment of many stars. Meantime, private insurance should be promoted.

However, private long-term care insurance has many strikes against it. This insurance is perceived to be for the purpose of staying in a nursing home, because policies in earlier days were designed to cover nursing home expenses. People do not want to think about being in a nursing home, so they do nothing that makes them think of it. Today's long-term care policies cover almost all forms of services including home care and assisted living, but this market, though slowly growing, has not taken off. Why not?

A long-term care policy is expensive when people buy it at older ages; they do not buy it while younger, when premiums are lower, because at that time they are not concerned about the problem. Sometimes people do not buy it because they dread the thought of "use it or lose it," and even when they use it they can win (receive benefits) only when they lose (become disabled—a less than fulfilling proposition.) Sometimes people do not purchase it because they don't think they will ever need such care, and should they do, Medicare or Medicaid will pay or they can self-pay. Sometimes they just plain put it off because it is too complicated a product that brings no joy from spending; with enough procrastination people eventually become uninsurable. In addition, sometimes people are wary about buying because some companies deny payment due to fine-print exclusions. Long-term care insurance also poses problems for the insurance agent, who may find it difficult and time-consuming to convince customers to buy. Then there are those agents who use sales approaches, however well-intentioned, that tend to frighten people away. There is also occasional deliberate misselling, as in other trades or professions.

Here is where Benjamin Lipson comes in. In clear, nontechnical language, he explains a great deal of technical information that will help people understand their needs and options. To the extent he makes it easier for consumers to decide, he also helps the insurance agents. To the extent he helps the insurance agents, he also helps the insurance industry. To the extent private insurance can supplant public funds, he helps reduce costs to government, thereby benefiting taxpayers. To the extent insurance payments replace the out-of-pocket personal payments, he helps people conserve their income and savings. Finally, because any illness is a family affair, especially those disabilities that require care in the long term, he helps individuals and their families acquire peace of mind when he makes it easier for them to learn how to protect themselves through insurance. For all these reasons, I believe Mr. Lipson is making a valuable contribution.

Preface

All the proceeds from this book are going to the Marjorie E. Lipson Memorial Fund within the John D. Stoeckle Center for Primary Care at the Massachusetts General Hospital. I donate these proceeds in gratitude for Dr. John Stoeckle's treatment of my daughter, Marjorie, and in her loving memory.

Marjorie died at age 35, after a 20-year battle with anorexia and bulimia. My struggle to support Marjorie during her illness reinforced my recognition that the medical system in this country is breaking down under the weight of bottom-line medicine that puts profits before patients.

I was not a naive advocate; I knew my way around the giant insurance bureaucracy. But I am an insurance man, not a physician. On my own, even my very best efforts seemed to achieve little. I found myself turning more and more to Dr. Stoeckle, Marjorie's primary care physician.

Margie was denied treatment by many physicians who were then unfamiliar with eating disorders. But Dr. Stoeckle accepted her as a patient, he connected with her, and was able to establish a treatment plan for the unique characteristics of her illness.

Dr. Stoeckle helped us through the heartbreaking maze of treatment decisions and insurance requirements. Dr. Stoeckle was my family's rock, supporter, and nurturer—a true caregiver.

Thirty years ago we would have called a physician of this type a family doctor. Today we call them primary care doctors. Thirty years ago, our family doctor would have come to our christenings, Bar Mitzvahs, graduations, weddings, wakes, and funerals; today they hardly recognize us in their examining rooms.

Our society needs a return to the values of traditional doctoring, in which the physician focuses on patients and their families, not the regulations of the health care or insurance bureaucracies.

I couldn't save Marjorie, but I vowed that for the rest of my life I would work for other patients.

Supporting the John D. Stoeckle Center at Massachusetts General Hospital is the cornerstone of this vow.

Dr. Stoeckle, who retired in 2001 after more than 50 years as a primary care physician, centered his practice of medicine on the notion that "the secret to caring for the patient is to care for him." He believed that the best doctoring happens when the physician brings the family into the planning process. His career, both practice and research, addressed the vital interactions among doctor, patient, and family.

The Massachusetts General Hospital has established the Stoeckle Center for Primary Care to honor Dr. Stoeckle's contributions and perpetuate his philosophy. The Center "seeks to improve the general care of patients by promoting the professional ideals, values, and behaviors in which medicine's science and art, the technical and the personal, are conspicuously joined in the care of the individual patient."

The driving force behind the Stoeckle Center is his associate, Dr. John D. Goodson, who says, "There must be an unwavering focus on the health of each individual. . . . Traditional doctoring skills, the humanistic application of science with full and complete mutual sharing of decision-making, must be sustained, nurtured, and supported in the modern health care environment."

The Stoeckle Center for Primary Care "focuses on the decision-making process with the clear and explicit mission of guaranteeing that each and every decision is in the individual patient's best interest."

To this end, the Marjorie E. Lipson Memorial Fund within the Stoeckle Center will be used to promote patient advocacy and patients' rights within health care and insurance bureaucracies. The Fund will support physician training through seminars, lectures, publications, and other sources for physician and staff awareness.

My daughter, Marjorie, was fun loving, smart, athletic, and popular. Her mother, sister, nieces, and I will always miss her. We choose to remember her in life, not in her illness. We are happy to support the well-being of other patients through the work of the Stoeckle Center.

If you would like more information, write to:

John D. Stoeckle Center for Primary Care
c/o The Development Office
Massachusetts General Hospital
100 Charles River Plaza, Suite 600
Boston, MA 02114
Phone: 1-877-644-7733
E-mail: mghdevelopment@partners.org

Introduction

Informing the public about the facts of long-term care insurance is a personal mission for me; and this book is my informed and personal statement. During my 50-year career in the insurance business, I have been a broker, a consultant, and always an ardent advocate for patients' rights and senior health concerns. For the past 20 years, my columns and opinion pieces on insurance have appeared in the *Boston Globe*. My earlier book, *How to Collect More on Your Insurance Claims*, told consumers exactly how to manage the multibillion-dollar insurance industry before it managed them right out of their homes, cars, and bank accounts. Today consumers need to scrutinize their long-term care insurance options just as carefully.

Except for making a will, there may be no other financial or insurance decision that comes with the same emotionally loaded preconceptions and unpalatable alternatives as does planning for our old age, not to mention our very, very old age. The insurance industry complicates our decision making by producing jargon-ridden, statistically complex, and flashy brochures and complex policies. It encourages its sales representatives to push products in the agent's best interest, and to arouse potential customers with doomsday scenarios about institutional nursing homes and dripping bedpans.

As a son, an adviser to senior citizens on health care matters, and a senior myself, I understand the fear of losing one's independence and the concern over financial impoverishment. But these darkly legitimate fears and concerns pale in the face of our ignorance about what our long-term care needs may actually be. While the consumer sweats, scrambles, and spends, the insurance industry develops more and more complex long-term care product lines. After all, insurance companies are businesses, pushed by shareholders and accountable for their bottom lines. Meanwhile, their product development is being pulled by a rapidly expanding customer base of aging baby boomers and mid-career children caring for parents in decline.

Health care insurance on its own is not a long-term care solution. Dad's Medicare coverage will not keep him in the hospital a few extra days so that his broken hip can set. Health insurance policies dole out hospital days like gruel, using complex formulas to justify sending poor Dad home in a wheelchair if he is barely able to make an independent transfer from his wheelchair back into his own bed.

Where is the government in all of this? Often, we wish that Congress and our statehouses would simply stay out of our business. Federal entitlement programs like Medicare and Social Security weigh down the national budget. Who remembers the overreach of Clinton's universal health care task force? Tax law is already so complex that most of us hire an expert to decode and deduct dollars on our Form 1040s.

In fact, the Health Insurance Portability and Accountability Act of 1996, known as HIPAA, indirectly made a statement about the federal government's role in long-term care insurance. The answer: That role will be as small as possible. If you are unfortunate enough, or maybe fortunate enough, to spend virtually all your annual income on food, rent, and clothing, you may expect that Medicaid will foot your long-term care needs, subsidizing your nursing home bed or home health care professional.

This book is for the rest of us, since long-term care will be our problem and no one else's. We are the ones who have 7 percent of our income left over at the end of the year. We are the qualified customers who are being courted by the insurance industry.

I hope you use this book to become a truly qualified customer. Take it to the beach, read it in your bedroom, share it with your spouse, your parents, and your children. Give it to your wedding attendants. Everyone must learn to make sensible and rational decisions about long-term care, to cut through the complexity of brochures, competing policies, and persuasive sales pitches. Plan properly now, and you'll have the "dollars to stay at home" when you are ready to do so. Plan poorly, and your very old age will not be the golden years you anticipate and deserve.

CHAPTER 1

Independence for All

This book is not intended to scare you. On the contrary, when you've finished reading you will be equipped to make wise choices about the long-term care you want. You'll understand where long-term care coverage stands in your financial planning universe, how taxes impact your decisions, which type of policy might be best for you, what secrets lie buried inside your policy, and how to deflect an emotional sales pitch. You'll know what to expect if you have preexisting conditions that might disqualify you from coverage, and you'll understand the implications behind the dreaded cognitive impairment test. You will have a hard-hitting list of questions for yourself and your insurance agent, along with a set of guidelines to follow as you make your long-term care planning choices.

This book, then, is based on four assumptions, which have been the basis of my 50-year career as an advocate for patients' rights and senior health insurance concerns:

1. We recognize that government dollars for health and long-term care are shrinking. We know, without being constantly reminded by the insurance industry, that our long-term care costs might impoverish us.

2. We expect to plan carefully for our futures, whether we're just out of college or just into retirement.

3. We are educated consumers, already expert at reading computer specifications, comparing colleges, and analyzing mortgage rates. We know how

to read the fine print and are not impressed with bells and whistles designed to confuse us.

4. The most important goal for our very old age is to preserve our priceless independence and dignity.

Many of us are unsettled by the thought of aging, but life rewards the forward thinker. Long-term care planning effectively starts on the first rung of the career ladder, often as a benefit of employment. In midlife it becomes intergenerational, as adult children worry about advising their parents and assessing their own options. In later years, long-term care considerations become a foundation of preretirement financial planning, and the cornerstone of a senior citizen's well-being.

This book offers you, your parents, your children, and your advisers the tools to make rational and prudent decisions about long-term care options. It will steer you away from a prescription for long-term pain and suffering and lead you toward the preservation of your most valued assets, dignity and independence.

Those Misleading Statistics

The insurance industry has taken its time recognizing the intelligence of its customers. One promotional brochure now stresses that the company's goal is to "help you maintain your independence."[1] Another offers "facts that can help you understand the risks associated with long-term care and our solutions for helping you maintain your personal and financial independence should you need long-term care."[2] But often these promises about "independence," whether by design or not, tend to be misleading. The insurance brochures are not promising to keep you out of a nursing home. Rather, the brochures are careful not to offend the nursing home industry, which itself wants people to buy long-term care coverage. This way, when they are admitted to a home as private pay or insured residents, they will be subjected to a higher room rate than those supported only by Medicaid.

If you are over 60, chances are that you have been repeatedly bombarded with lunch and seminar invitations from insurance agents selling long-term care policies. If you're under 60, your dinner is frequently interrupted by phone calls with the same appeal. Despite their apparent interest in helping you maintain your independence, these insurance agents are intent on letting you know what you can expect in your old age: inevitable impoverishment.

It's enough to make you lose your appetite.

The pitch goes this way: Don't worry about fire insurance; your risk of making a claim on your homeowner's insurance is 1 in 88. A car accident? Overall, your probability for a car accident is about 1 in 47, which is why you bought an automobile liability and collision insurance policy when you purchased your first car.[3]

Take a deep breath, says the insurance agent, and listen to these much more ominous predictions and statistics about your old age. If you make it past 50, you have a one in five probability of eventually needing long-term care.[4] If you reach 65, your chances of spending time in a nursing home increase to 43 percent.[5] Make it past 80, and you have a one in two chance of joining your remaining friends and neighbors in a long-term care facility.[6]

This frightening pitch became so troubling for the executive director of a large trade association that he wrote to the CEO of the insurance company. Long-term care coverage was meant to be an attractive perk of membership, said the director, but the agents who were presenting the plan during home visits were scaring the members right out of the association. Why should the insurance company salespeople be the agents of such woe? Who anointed them the bearers of such bad tidings? Why would anyone want to hear that because of the high "statistical probability of ending up in a nursing home" they could expect to see their "life savings wiped out" and their caretakers debilitated?

What did the CEO say? Granted, these dinner-hour visits may not be pleasant, but such predictions are necessary to explain the risks of aging.

The executive director explained to the CEO that such "scare tactics" insulted the intelligence of the association's membership, already accustomed to prudent, thoughtful decision making. The executive director had lost his appetite along with his members.

Long-Term Care Insurance Meets the ER

My neighbor, Jane, called me one day from the local emergency room. Her father had fallen, and Jane might be facing another care crisis. Jane was an only child; since her mother's death she had been responsible for her father. Above all, she did not want him to be forced to go into a nursing home prematurely.

Her father had worked hard all his life as a laborer, and her mother had cleaned houses. They had lived from paycheck to paycheck, scrimping to send Jane to college and to drop the remaining dollar on the collection plate each Sunday. Jane wanted her father to live his last years at home, with dignity and independence.

For three years, Jane had been the personal assistant to the regional manager of a home furniture chain. Jane's boss was very sympathetic to her role as a multitasking caretaker, allowing her to leave work to tend to her father's emergencies, take her kids to soccer practice, attend their dental appointments, and confer with their teachers. In turn, Jane was very conscientious about her job, coming in early and often skipping lunch hours to make up for the hours she had to take for her personal commitments.

Katie, the boss, understood Jane's situation because she had been there. Years earlier, Katie herself had been forced by the demands of her job to move her own mother, who previously lived alone, to a nursing home. The nursing home placement felt premature, but Katie had no choice. Her job required that she travel her region regularly, and she was on track for an executive position in the home office.

The day Jane called me, her father had slipped, fallen, and cut his head. He was dizzy and bleeding. Jane was swamped at work; the annual reviews for the store managers were due. She couldn't leave immediately to attend to her father so she told him to call 911. She would meet him at the hospital in an hour.

Rush hour traffic slowed her further, and she arrived to find that her father had been seen by the triage nurse. Now he was sitting in the ER waiting room, expecting to be called for an X ray. He had been waiting alone for an hour and a half, and the ER secretary warned Jane that the X ray department was so backed up that she might as well pick up a hamburger since they would be sitting for another two hours.

Jane was frustrated, but she was also relieved. When she called me, she said, "I'm lucky this time. They think Dad is okay, and nothing seems to be broken. I guess the X ray is a precaution. But what if he slips again? I'm afraid that Dad is going to need round-the-clock care fairly soon. I'm worried that he'll fall out of bed, or get lost and disoriented in the neighborhood. I don't even know how I'll manage to help him dress in the morning or get to the toilet."

She paused, then said, "What am I going to say to my mother when I visit her grave? I promised to take care of Dad."

For Jane, payback time had come. She wanted desperately to help her father live the rest of his life as he deserved to, in his own home and surrounded by familiar cronies. But Jane simply didn't have the money. Besides, her husband, who had been patient about the time Jane gave to Dad, gently pointed out that she was spending hours away from her kids. The boy was already in middle school; he needed his parents at home in the evenings to help with his homework. Her husband also asked where they would find the extra money to pay for a caregiver for Dad. They would be looking at colleges for the kids in three years.

What a painful double bind! Her father was a proud man who did not want to go on what he called the "public dole." Dad and Mom had never accepted charity, and Dad had proudly resisted spending down his assets to qualify for Medicaid nursing home coverage. He did not qualify for admission to a VA hospital, either. For the time being, Jane could help her dad manage his costs. Together they could probably cover 90 days of home care. They might even be able to squeeze out another few months of paying for a nighttime companion, in case he fell out of bed. After that, Dad would have to spend the money he had left. He would end up in a nursing home paid for by Medicaid. He didn't need that level of care, but there was no alternative to the premature placement.

"I suppose it's too late to buy long-term care insurance for him," she said to me.

It was, and too bad. The $4,000 premium per year for long-term care coverage now looked like a bargain.

As worried as she was, Jane realized that her situation was not as bad as it could be. When she had started working for Katie, she had signed up for the company's long-term care coverage plan. "I'm starting to realize that my company-paid long-term care insurance policy is the best fringe benefit I have!"

Protecting the Independent Senior

My job is to plan for catastrophe, yet Jane's story was an echo of my own. My mother, a fiercely independent and proud woman, worked until she was 86 years old; but after she was forced into a nursing home at age 93, she died within weeks. Ethel enjoyed a long life. Its end was certainly not a direct result of the loss of independence and personal dignity she experienced in the nursing home. But if I had helped her plan for her very old age, she might have spent her last months surrounded by neighbors and friends, instead of professional caretakers.

Ethel knew what she was worth. She returned to Filene's department store, the employer of her teen years, when she was widowed at 59. She broke sales records, but the store's management retired her when she was 67. Not ready for television and afternoon bridge, Ethel applied to Lord & Taylor. "Ma," I warned her, "you're wasting your time. You're going to be demeaned and then rejected by some kid who could be your grandchild."

Ethel was undeterred. "Ben, I'm not going to listen to you. I'm going to have my hair done, and I am going to apply for the job."

My mother sold handbags at Lord & Taylor until she was 86, never missing a day. Or wasting a dollar. When, on a steamy August day, I sent a prepaid taxi to bring her home, she expressed her disapproval to the driver. "You tell my son not to waste his money." Her work ethic as well as her life ethic prescribed independence coupled with frugality.

Ethel had her first extended experience with nursing care after abdominal surgery at age 86. We negotiated with her: "Please, Ma, promise to stay just one week in the recuperative care center, and then we'll get you back to your own place." Convinced that recuperative care was a one-way ticket to the nursing home, Ethel outsmarted us. Against medical advice, despite jeopardizing her Medicare coverage, she called an ambulance and left the care center after staying one night. The center's social worker officially scolded her, but privately admitted that the entire staff stood "behind the plants and cheered her as she climbed into the ambulance."

My mother maintained that freedom until she was 93. In many respects, she was lucky. She stayed in her own apartment. Her neighbors loved her homemade cookies, showering her in return with flowers, candy, and Mother's Day gifts. She refused to consider long-term care, even when we suggested a live-in companion. "Let me understand this," Ethel said with disdain. "You want to have someone come to live here, watch my television, eat my food, and still *pay* her?" Pointing her finger at me, she cried: "Shame on you!"

I didn't feel shame, but I certainly felt guilt when she finally moved to a nursing home. The placement was a good one, but no nursing home has the staff to provide sensitive care 24 hours a day, seven days a week. Inevitably, patients are at risk, left occasionally untended, sometimes unsupervised, and always deteriorating. My mother's worst fears came true. She lost her independence, her dignity, her privacy, her days in the warm sun, and, worst of all, her contact with the world outside the home. From the first minute of her confinement, my mother and I each mourned her loss.

Despite struggling with the pain of losing two of my three daughters, the end of my mother's life is still one of my saddest memories. I feel guilty that although I am an expert in insurance, I did not do more to explore ways to keep her at home until she died.

Pledging Your Bottom Dollar

Long-term care options have come a long way since the 1950s, when people were often forced to promise all their assets in exchange for a nursing home bed. My mother was frugal. Her independence was the sticking point, not the nursing home costs. But in the 1960s my client Ted watched his grandfather have to pledge his house for collateral for a room at the "old folks' home."

Ted's grandfather lived with his son and daughter-in-law for 25 years, but then the "kids" began to have health problems of their own. Struggling with arthritis and diabetes, they couldn't physically manage Grandpa's needs. If they overslept, he was trapped in bed for hours. If they had doctor's appointments of their own, they needed an adult baby-sitter. Feeling abandoned and bitter, Grandpa was moved from the family home. He branded his daughter-in-law "callous" and his son "ungrateful," despite their years of tender care.

What happened to Grandpa? Ted remembers that Grandpa died unexpectedly within a week. Grief-stricken, his children had to bury their father, suffer their guilt, and hire lawyers to recover the assets they had pledged for his care. Today, careful long-term care planning might have allowed Grandpa and his children to experience a more peaceful farewell.

What Is Long-Term Care?

The chances are that without realizing it, you might in fact have already tapped into the long-term care system, although not into a nursing home. We like to think of long-term care as the concern of senior citizens, but the term has a broader legal meaning. Long-term care involves becoming cognitively impaired, or the expectation that you will be unable to manage at least two of the six activities of daily living (bathing, dressing, toileting, transferring, continence, and eating) for 90 days or more. The government and the insurance industry call these activities ADLs for short.

Have you broken an ankle on the slopes or gotten beaned at the softball game? If those injuries required three months of help moving from chair to bed, changing out of your pajamas, or using the toilet, you might have qualified as a long-term care recipient. Nevertheless, for most younger patients, absent a terminal illness or debilitating physical ailment, long-term care actually lasts for only a short term (but at least three months), since the patient recovers the ability to carry on the activities of daily living. The need for long-term care, in other words, is a legal determination, based on guidelines set out by law and interpreted by Medicaid and your private insurer.

Most of us associate nursing homes with long-term care. Ethel's nursing home admission was her sad last stop. In fact, nursing homes are at the far end of the continuum of care. There are also skilled nursing care facilities or assisted living centers, rehabilitation units, short-term geriatric centers, and, ultimately, home-based care from a variety of community, medical, and religious agencies. Let's consider the differences that exist in these settings.

Nursing Homes

The old folks' home of Ted's story is now called a nursing home. Every person over the age of 18 has at least one image of these facilities, with wheelchairs lining the halls, residents staring vacantly, staff harried and sometimes abrupt. However, we like to think that in the new millennium nursing home life has come a long way—but still not far enough. Think of the facilities this way: A nursing home offers around-the-clock care that goes beyond the physical and emotional capabilities of a single caregiver. Often a licensed nurse manages a staff of assistants who provide the actual custodial care. Nursing homes may cost as much as double the price of assisted living facilities.

And the typical profile of a nursing home resident? According to a report prepared for the U.S. Department of Health and Human Services, between 75 percent and 86 percent of nursing home residents have some degree of cognitive impairment. These residents typically are married and qualify for support from either Medicare or a private insurer, since they are usually limited in 4.7 out of the six ADLs.[7] Their thinking may be fuzzy, that is, and they may be able to use the toilet but not bathe, dress, eat, or transfer from bed to wheelchair. Sixty-three percent of these residents have moved from another form of long-term care, either an assisted living facility or a home care situation. Twenty-five percent of the residents have come directly from a hospital.[8] When the nursing home residents are publicly funded by Medicaid, they "require" as many as five different types of services, including more medical care, more skilled nursing, and more social services.[9] Privately funded nursing home residents enjoy fewer paid services,[10] perhaps because their insurance policies are not comprehensive enough to cover them.

Assisted Living

Assisted living communities range from those which are a step away from full-time nursing home care to ones that encourage independence while providing meals, housekeeping, and personal care. If your Aunt Doris moved into an apartment that had maid service, an emergency call button in the bathroom, and daily room checks by one of the staff, she was probably in an assisted living environment. Sometimes such facilities are called adult congregate living facilities or personal care homes.

Like Aunt Doris—and my mother, Ethel—these residents usually see themselves as much better off, both physically and cognitively, than their friends in the nursing home next door. While their diagnoses might be similar to those in nursing homes, assisted living residents often needed help with only 2.8 of the six ADLs.[11] Doris, for instance, had difficulty dressing and bathing herself in the morning, but once she got moving, she played a high-level game of bridge. Here she was not typical, since between 47 percent and 81 percent of assisted living residents are cognitively impaired.[12]

Continuing Care Retirement Communities

Not every Florida condominium complex built around a golf course is secretly a continuing care retirement community, but some may be. This type of community may offer options that range from completely independent living all the way to round-the-clock nursing home care, with a variety of possibilities in between. Sometimes this housing arrangement is called a life care community. To join, residents must buy their unit and also pay a monthly fee. The community may provide transportation to the grocery store, the mall, or the concert hall, amenities that residents pay for through a hefty up-front fee and significant monthly dues. At least financially, the life care community resembles an updated version of the residence where Ted's grandfather died. You can be assured of lifetime care, but you'll be pledging significant dollars to get it.

Dollars to Stay at Home

All my mother, Ethel, wanted was to spend her last years in the apartment she loved. She would have been able to do so if she had been willing to pay a home health aide to live with her. Ethel was not ready for extended skilled nursing, anyway, even after her surgery. The people in the recuperative center, as she put it, were sicker than she was, but they were all, at least theoretically, headed back to their own homes.

Who delivers long-term care at home? The short answer is "just about anyone." It depends on the patient's level of need. Nonmedical personnel may handle the simple tasks, while the more complicated procedures often require skilled care, even a nurse. If you cannot leave your house, but need a medical professional to measure your glucose levels, change the bandages on an ulcerated leg, or provide physical therapy for your broken ankle, a trained professional will probably be your care provider. If you need help fetching groceries, going to church or synagogue, and doing your laundry, your spouse may do the caretaking job. In turn, the cost of care varies enormously. Your neighbor may charge a pittance to pick up your groceries, and you can give the kid down the street a dollar a week to bring in the mail. Medicaid will foot the bill for your visiting medical professional if your income level qualifies you for that program. The key point is that each of these levels of care, from meal preparation to physical therapy, is part of the long-term care environment.

What Long-Term Care Is Not

Long-term care is not health-care. It is not covered by your medical insurance. If you meet certain conditions, Medicare and your supplemental health care coverage (Medigap) will pay for some skilled nursing, rehabilitation, physical, speech, or occupational therapy in your home. But if you fail to meet conditions that include home confinement, a physician's prescription, and the use of certified providers, both Medicare and the private insurer will bow out of the scene. Furthermore, if your progress plateaus, expect to battle the bureaucracy for your benefits. For your protection and peace of mind, have ready in the wings an insurance policy, your savings, or the love of your family.

Whom Do You Trust?: The Claims about Long-Term Care Needs

If you accept the word of the insurance companies and some industry studies, many of us over 65 are headed straight for long-term care. One industry study suggests that after 65, we each have a 43 percent chance of checking into a nursing home.[13] The vast majority of us will stay in the nursing home three months or less, but an unlucky 10 percent of us will remain in that nursing home bed more than five years, according to *Long-Term Care: A Dollars and Sense Guide*.[14] One study prepared for the U.S. Department of Health and Human Services and the Robert Wood Johnson Foundation says that my mother's fears about her rehabilitation stay were well founded: "The probability of entering a nursing home from a hospital is twice as high as entering an assisted living facility."[15]

There *is* good news. Nursing home use is actually declining. A recent AARP paper suggests that about 7 million people over age 65 needed long-term care services of some sort in 1997, most of which was provided by family members on an unpaid basis. In 1998, 1.5 million persons "received long-term care services in over 17,000 certified nursing facilities. An estimated 600,000 were living in 28,000 assisted living facilities and 8 million people received home health care.[16]

But the cost estimates are frightening. Insurance agents almost always tell the story of Dr. Benjamin Spock, writer of child-rearing books that hold a place of honor on the bookshelves of many parents. By the end of his life, at the age of 94, Dr. Spock could not afford the cost of his long-term care. His family admitted they struggled to pay for his care at the end of his life, despite the millions he earned with his books. Maybe Dr. Spock did not anticipate the cost of living to his very old age. The AARP study estimates the cost of a year of nursing home care in 1998 to be $56,000.[17] Of course, prices will vary depending on where you live, but these 1998 cost figures are a real bargain by today's rates. How could Dr. Spock have known that he would require such extensive financial resources to fund his last years?

Here are more astounding numbers about the cost of long-term care. In the late 1990s, according to a report prepared privately for the insurance industry and based on data from the Health Care Financing Administration (HCFA) now the Centers for Medicare & Medical Services (CMS), "annual long-term care expenditures approached $125 billion."[18] Medicaid's share declined to 39 percent of that total, while the cost to private insurance companies doubled from 1991, to about 7 percent. "Long-term care continues to be the single largest out-of-pocket expense faced by the elderly and their families."[19] One-hour home-care visits for nursing or physical therapy have been estimated to cost as much as $78 each; a program of three visits a week costs $12,000 a year.[20] In 1998, the average daily cost for assisted living was $60, or $21,000 a year.[21] Today you would pay even more for the same services.

Before you panic, however, take another look at these statistics. An Agency for Healthcare Research and Quality study, "Long-Term Care: Elderly Men and Women Are Fairly Accurate in Predicting Their Need for Nursing Home Care in the Next Few Years" says that a "typical 75-year-old person in good health has only a 6 percent chance of entering a nursing home in the next five years. For those in worse health, the probability ranges from 17 percent for major illness to 44 percent for chronic impairment."[22] In fact, according to this study, we might do well to trust our instinct as we read those tea leaves. We are reasonably accurate predictors of our own futures, at least as far as nursing home admission is concerned.

What's the Price of Peace of Mind?

At least initially, it might seem sensible to suggest that, assuming we can make the payments, we add long-term care coverage to our insurance portfolios. If you're under 65 and have considered such a purchase, you have a lot of company. One-third of all policies are now being bought by people under 65.[23] These consumers are usually more wealthy than the general population and usually have not been afflicted with the disabilities that frequently come with the aging process. They tend to be more highly educated, and they are usually married. The goal of these consumers of long-term care coverage is twofold: to leave something for their children and to take care of themselves, both worthy goals.[24]

What are these younger oldsters getting for their dollar? For one thing, higher and higher premiums. The Life-Span Institute study commissioned by the insurance industry says that the average premium for long-term care insurance coverage has increased 11 percent in the past five years.[25] These buyers select a variety of coverage types, but it is clear that older buyers, especially those with fewer assets and lower incomes, more often select nursing home coverage if it is available. Many also tend to be women, who are often poorer than men are but expect to live longer. Insurance salespeople may particularly target this single female group simply because of their perceived need. Like my mother, Ethel, they often do not have insurance protection that would allow them to age peacefully at home by providing them with homemaking assistance and personal care support.

Perhaps the most complex and threatening aspect of long-term care planning today involves the dreaded diagnosis of cognitive impairment, especially Alzheimer's disease. We've heard stories about people who got lost driving home from the market or didn't recognize their children. Alzheimer's requires increasingly intense levels of supervision to protect the safety of the person and those around him or her. The condition may demand an attendant to stand "within arm's reach" in case the person spills hot coffee at breakfast. Unfortunately, the insurance industry has developed elaborate, sometimes deceptive mechanisms for measuring a potential buyer's cognitive abilities, quickly eliminating those who appear to be poor risks. The industry's official diagnosis of Alzheimer's is a fuzzy one. Read further for a detailed description of the cognitive impairment test administered by insurance companies and suggestions about how to handle it.

Who Gets a Piece of the Action?

You may be able to judge a book by its cover; but buying long-term care insurance requires X-ray vision. The insurance industry has, perhaps deliberately, made a basically simple product into a "Where's Waldo?" kind of optical illusion. The insurance company is concerned with covering its own risk and collecting its premiums, and the careless customer may pay out but risk missing out.

Spend a couple of hours—no, spend a week—reading advertisements, brochures, and insurance policies for long-term care products. Even the most alert of consumers realize immediately that they have no idea what the policies are saying. Who but the company president is able to decipher the bewildering explanations of tax-qualified versus nonqualified plans, the actuarial predictions, and the nonspecific language? Insurance companies know that most buyers, no matter how well educated, merely default to the suggestion of their agent, who, according to the LifePlans survey, is believed to be "knowledgeable, adept at the available coverage options, and a good listener."[26]

Studies show that most buyers assume that the agent "recommended the policy best suited to their needs."[27] Most often, those of us in the insurance business believe this to be the case. No legitimate insurance professional wants to sell a product that does not truly benefit the customer. Too often, however, our hearts drown out our heads when we study long-term care protection. Few insurance decisions carry as much emotional load and require such dramatic outlays of cash as long-term care policies. Baby boomers are often reluctant to think about this aspect of their futures. This group, perhaps less eager than their parents were to assume daily caretaking obligations for Mom or Dad, see buying a personal long-term care policy as a forecast for years of nonproductivity, lost independence, and being a burden. Weighed by memories of Grandpa in the nursing home, we run from the insurance agent even faster than from the tax collector.

It does not help that most consumers are victims of unconscious incompetence. They do not know what questions they should be asking. Buyers duck away from considering the "triggers" or disabilities that need to exist before benefits are payable and miss the details inherent in the waiting period. They cannot fathom providing proof of their own weaknesses.

My old friend, Bill, called me to ask if his mother's long-term care policy might help pay at least some of the costs of her assisted living residence. Bill bought the policy through the Internet, and he was confident that it would cover her costs in full. But when we looked at the policy closely, we realized that there were multiple provisions that delayed his mother's coverage. Yes, she was now in assisted living, and yes, she needed the meals provided, but she really didn't require assistance while bathing or dressing. Certainly Mom did her own "toileting," as the policy delicately put it. She was hardly ever incontinent. Bill was wrong in thinking that assisted living was part of Mom's coverage. His mother had to qualify for admission in order to move across the street to the affiliated nursing home, or else Bill needed to raid his own retirement savings to help her out.

Bill was stunned. He had done his homework when he helped his mother select her coverage. Unfortunately, what happened was that the brochure made promises that the policy itself didn't keep. The company brochure looked great, but it was aimed at a group of seniors who were more comfortable with 3 percent savings accounts than with day trading. This target market could still calculate in their heads the prices of clothes on the sale rack, but they were helpless before the jargon of insurance underwriters. Bill and his mother had made a poor choice; and now, one way or the other, they would pay.

The Insurance Industry's Strategy: Rate Fluctuation

Fortunately for consumers, federal and state governments have become more active in policy regulation and oversight. Consumer activism, the compliance departments within each company, and the intense competition for business have also helped clean up the long-term care product. Still, you might as well look for certainty at the roulette table or just pick up a lottery ticket if you need to be concerned about fixed premium rates. Insurance lobbyists are at work in states where such regulation is not yet in place to prevent its enactment.

Few policies carry a complete lifetime guarantee of premiums. Why should any company offer this policy, since all prices go up and go down? We know a gallon of gas that today is $1.35 tomorrow may be $1.75. Remember, however, that the insurance company, itself worth billions of dollars, does not want to assume the risk of fixing premiums for long-term care. The industry prefers to pass that risk on to the consumer, rich or poor, in the form of rate increases as dictated by the company actuaries.

The specter of buying a policy, carrying it while you're healthy, and then canceling it before you need it is a haunting one. As premiums increase, that specter takes on a ghoulish reality. Some states have enacted legislation that provides rate stabilization, so that the initial premium is guaranteed for four to five years and future increases are limited by guarantees. These extended rate guarantees can actually be a trap. The company knows that if you have successfully paid premiums for up to 10 years, the likelihood is that you will never find a policy for the same cost. You literally can't go anywhere else and will probably pay any increased premium the company establishes.

Don't take comfort in the familiar promise that "once you're accepted for coverage, your premium will never increase because of your age or any changes in your health." These words sound good, but don't mean what they seem to mean. Actually, what the company is promising is that you will not be singled out for a rate increase, no matter how your bone density or your tendency to forget your phone number change. Count on premium increases, but they will apply to your entire class of buyers, not to you alone.

Sometimes the agent will tell you that his or her company, which has been in business for 10 or 20 years, has never had a rate increase. Don't be misled. The premium for the particular policy type may have been stable, but the insurer will frequently come out with a new policy form, add a few inexpensive bells and whistles, and then charge a higher rate for the new policy series. Insurance companies want to increase the rate with every new policy form as a way to accumulate the dollars to pay for claims made from the old policy series.

In fact, insurers sometimes tighten their underwriting standards to make sure their ratio of premiums to claims is under control. The difficulty is that some companies never inform their agents and brokers that the underwriting standards have gotten tougher. Without using internal memos or revisions to the sales manuals, the actuaries and the underwriters agree tacitly to be more selective in accepting consumers who have troublesome physical conditions. The company's claims ratio improves, but the slightly overweight applicant, the cancer survivor, or the colitis patient must accept longer waiting periods and perhaps higher premiums.

Selling in the Boomer Marketplace

Years past its toddlerhood, long-term care insurance is now a raging adolescent. The consumer has many options for buying long-term care protection. Want a quick choice? Type the phrase "long-term care" into your favorite Internet search engine and see how many offers pop up on your screen. The AARP, whose birthday card invariably appears in your mailbox at age 55, markets these insurance products. So do such respected companies as TIAA CREF (Teachers Insurance and Annuity Association College Retirement Equities Fund), UnumProvident, MetLife, GE Capital, Conseco, CNA Financial Corporation, and John Hancock, the most familiar names in the industry.

Some consumers like to throw business to their high school buddy, who has taken over Dad's agency. Others enter the market when the lawyer they ask to draw up their wills brings a pal, the insurance salesperson, along to discuss annuities and long-term care. Financial planners, stockbrokers, insurance brokers and agents, banks, and national associations sell long-term care products.

Unlike Medicare, backed by the resources of the federal government and required to insure all risks if they qualify financially, long-term care insurers carefully screen their applicants, often silently disqualifying them during the first phone inquiry. These companies operate much like health maintenance organizations (HMOs), courting younger and healthier participants and discouraging older, sicker patients. They skirt the pressing issues of privacy during interviews, qualifying clients by uncovering the financial underpinnings of their lives. You'll need to look carefully at the benefits included in your policies and think hard about what you want to achieve when you sign your name.

What We Really Want

My contention is that the actual issue for buyers of long-term care protection is the concern over future freedoms. Making long-term care decisions for yourself, your parents, and your spouse may not be fun, but the payoff is more certain than playing a multistate lottery. Prudent consumers can make decisions today that will ensure dignity and independence for themselves, their parents, and their children. Making a personal long-term care decision is a gift to yourself that frees you from worry. Making long-term care decisions for your family is a gift to them, freeing them to return the emotional and loving support we all desire in our old age.

Endnotes

1. GE Capital. *Long-Term Care Choice (Massachusetts).* 1999.
2. UnumProvident. *Now Is the Time to Plan for Long-Term Care.* May 1999.
3. Conseco Insurance. *Facts about Long-Term Care Insurance.* p. 5.
4. Ibid.
5. John Hancock. *Long-Term Care Marketing Guide.* December 1994. p. 29.
6. United Seniors Health Council. *Long-Term Care Planning: A Dollars and Sense Guide.* Washington, DC: United States Seniors Health Cooperative, 1997. p. 4.
7. LifePlans, Inc. *The Use of Nursing-Home and Assisted Living Facilities among Privately Insured and Non-Privately Insured Disabled Elders.* Final Report to the Department of Health and Human Services' Office of Disability, Aging, and Long-Term Care Policy and the Robert Wood Johnson Foundation for Home Care Research Initiatives, April 2000. p. 7.
8. Ibid.
9. Ibid.
10. Ibid.
11. Ibid.
12. Ibid.
13. United Seniors Health Council. *Long-Term Care Planning.* p. 42.
14. Ibid. p. 65
15. LifePlans, Inc. *The Use of Nursing-Home and Assisted Living Facilities.* p. 8.
16. Tucker, Natalie, Enid Kassner, Faith Mullen, and Barbara Coleman. *Long-Term Care.* AARP Public Policy Institute, May 2000.
17. Ibid.
18. LifePlans, Inc. *Who Buys Long-Term Care Insurance in 2000: A Decade of Study of Buyers and Non-Buyers.* Prepared for the Health Insurance Association of America, October 2000. p. 5.
19. Ibid.
20. *Report, Findings, and Recommendations of the Working Group on Long-Term Care.* U.S. Department of Labor, Advisory Council on Employee Welfare and Pension Benefits, November 14, 2000. p. 13.
21. LifePlans, Inc. *Who Buys.* p. 5.
22. "Long-Term Care: Elderly Men and Women Are Fairly Accurate in Predicting Their Need for Nursing Home Care in the Next Few Years." Agency for Healthcare Research and Quality. Publication HS09515.
23. LifePlans, Inc. *Who Buys.* p. 1.
24. Ibid. p. 28.
25. Ibid. p. 2.
26. Ibid. p. 32.
27. Ibid. p. 32.

CHAPTER 2

Alternatives to Long-Term Care Insurance: Doing It Your Way

Some industry literature suggests that insurance companies sell long-term care policies as a public service. The thinking goes like this: The federal budget is overburdened by entitlements. The taxpayer is going broke while he or she supports medical care for those over 65, subsidizes people who didn't save enough for retirement, and pays for nursing home beds used by the poorest among us. We must reduce the burden of these entitlements! Hence the insurance industry's greatest public service is to teach consumers to anticipate the most significant financial crisis of their lives, paying for their long-term care needs. When insurers sell long-term care policies, they hope that we believe they are helping to balance the federal budget, reduce the national debt, and reserve public money for the people who need it most: the truly poor.

To some extent, the insurance industry is correct—we do owe it thanks. Paying for long-term care is an overriding national concern. While those between 65 and 74 have a relatively low disability rate, the rate more than doubles between 75 and 84 and then dramatically increases after age 85. If we live that long, our chances of needing assistance for more than two activities of daily living increase to more than 50 percent.[1] As medical technology and research advance, more of us than ever before will require substantial assistance. Both Democratic and Republican administrations have investigated ways to shift this public burden back to the individual by encouraging privatization of Social Security and long-term care coverage.

Nonetheless, insurance companies know that private long-term care policies are not always the answer.

Spending Money You Don't Have to Buy Insurance

One afternoon, I was listening on my car radio to a so-called financial wizard giving advice about long-term care. I heard this dismaying story:

The caller began, "As a 60-year-old nurse, I have seen what happens to people when they need long-term care. Unfortunately, I chose to work in nursing homes and recuperative centers that didn't offer pension plans, so I can't look forward to having a retirement income besides Social Security and my meager savings."

"Ah," responded the financial wizard, "you have been rewarded by your own good work."

"True," the caller continued, "but I've also taken steps to protect myself in my old age. I have given my daughter a few thousand dollars to buy a condominium and hopefully when I'm ready to retire in a few years I'll have about $20,000 in cash saved in addition to my Social Security to live on."

The caller added: "But what really makes me feel good is that I have bought a $2,000-a-year nursing home policy. At least I know that I'll be taken care of in my old age and not burden my daughter."

Mr. Wizard congratulated the nurse on her foresight.

However, a competent elder law attorney would have said, "Wait! Your limited assets put you in line for Medicaid coverage. You might as well spend the $2,000 you're using for premium payments each year to improve your quality of life, keep your car running, and keep your health insurance current. If you have a few thousand dollars in savings left by the time you need to go to a nursing home, you'll pay for the first months of your care and then Medicaid will pick up the tab. In any case, you ought to have a consultation with an attorney who specializes in elder law to determine your eligibility."

The call was a painful reminder that most people don't understand the financial supports in place for their care. Reputable insurance agents would have told this nurse that she did not fit the financial profile of someone who would benefit from coverage, because she did not have 7 to 10 percent of her income left after paying her bills. Worse, if she paid the premium and skipped buying medications, she'd need that nursing home much sooner than she expected. Here was a long-term care worker who did not know the facts about Medicaid.

Decisions involving Medicaid planning, as in any financial planning, must consider your personal situation and your emotional preferences. I am not a lawyer, and you will not find legal advice in this book. What you will find is an overview of alternative funding strategies. The legal details are complex, and I strongly recommend that you arrange for an individual meeting with an elder law attorney when you are ready to decide on your long-term care options.

Your HMO Won't Take Care of You

It's no surprise, then, that people who educate themselves about mutual funds, health care options, and medical advances often misunderstand their long-term care options. Many people, especially those under 40, believe erroneously that their health insurance will also cover long-term care. People have paid insignificant medical deductibles at their yearly physicals, and then all the diagnostic tests and consultations have been covered by their health insurance. They've been spoiled. And they assume that, somehow, managing long-term care costs will be just as easy.

Let me say it unequivocally: In most if not all situations, your long-term care will *not* be funded by your health insurance—whether you're 35 or 85.

What Choices Do You Have?

Crystal ball gazing is a challenge, but we can make some rational, intelligent, educated guesses about our long-term care options. In addition to buying a long-term care policy from an insurance company, there are other mechanisms to help you remain independent in your very old age, despite any health deterioration that might occur. These alternatives range from providing the money all by yourself to letting the government help you out.

Pay for It Yourself: Self-Insure

Yes, the insurance industry scares us with doomsday statistics. We'll spend our food money on our spouse's caregiver; our hoarded retirement savings will fill the nursing home's coffers. But that's not always the case. You can pay for your own long-term care in a number of less drastic ways.

Work As Long As You Possibly Can

The organization once known as the American Association of Retired Persons has officially changed its name to AARP. The current name reflects a national shift in attitude toward retirement because many Americans now work beyond age 65. For those over 50, the AARP recommends a four-part financial plan: Social Security, pension and savings, health insurance, and earnings.[2] The organization believes that we need to keep working because we'll need the extra cash that comes from gainful employment, we'll reduce the strain on the federal budget, we'll reserve our savings for the time when we really need the dollars, and we'll avoid boredom and unproductive inactivity. If we keep working, we can help our spouse with his or her long-term care costs.

Save Your Money

Your pension plan will keep the roof over your head and the wolf from your door. But have a pool of money dedicated to your long-term care needs, just as you have saved for your retirement. When I hear "retirement experts" describing the anticipated "income streams" of their clients, the ways they will pay for their Florida condos and maintain their city houses, I wonder where the planning for long-term care comes in. The figures always sound good on the radio, but they ignore the very real possibility of extended, expensive long-term care and interest rate fluctuations.

Buy Annuities

You may have set up individual retirement accounts (IRAs) or 401(k)s for your retirement. But I'm talking here about buying annuities designated solely for long-term care costs. You pay into this annuity plan the way you pay into your 401(k), but without the tax benefits. When you need long-term care, you have the satisfaction of knowing that you've put aside the money and that you won't force your spouse to reduce his or her standard of living to pay for your care.

An interesting version of this strategy is the Medicaid annuity. This annuity is a twist on a federally approved plan that was designed to pay for retirement, but is now, so far legally, being applied to long-term care.[3] The buyer essentially sells his or her assets to the insurance company as payment for an annuity. Thus the annuitant owns nothing, but has an income stream. The person is "artificially impoverished" and eligible for Medicaid, should he or she need nursing home care. Stay tuned, though, because some states, including Ohio and Washington, are scrutinizing Medicaid claims that reveal this strategy, identifying them as questionable tactics to spend down assets.[4]

Set Up Trusts

The wealthiest among us often assume that we needn't buy long-term care coverage because we have enough money to pay the cost ourselves. Use this argument with an insurance agent, and he will respond, "Yes, you are really rich. But suppose you become cognitively impaired or unable to make your wishes known. Granted that your kids and your spouse love you, but they may decide to maintain you in circumstances you would not have wanted, simply because they assume that you won't know the difference."

Sad but true. A carefully constructed trust can reserve and preserve money, designating that it may be used only for your care. It will include your wishes for your old age. Add a trustworthy trustee, and you can move confidently into your final years, knowing you'll be cared for as you desire.

Use Your House

For most of us, our house is our largest asset. We expect to pass this inheritance along to our children. In some cases, you can keep your house and still have long-term care; but more often, you may need to use the real estate equity you've accumulated through your lifetime to pay for your very old age.

Hire a Companion

More than one college student has funded their housing by living with and helping care for a homeowner with long-term care needs. Find the right person (or couple), trade a bedroom and kitchen privileges for help with your meals and your laundry, and look to friends, family, and community resources for other needs. Even if you need help with the instrumental activities of daily living, you may be able to stay in your home for many years.

Reverse Your Mortgage

Many people today have more money tied up in their houses than liquid in their bank accounts. One way to tap into this money but stay in the house is through a reverse mortgage. Think about the mortgage you took to pay for the house originally. You paid the bank monthly, your equity built up, and at the end of 20 or 30 years the house was all yours. A reverse mortgage, as the name implies, works in reverse. The bank is basically buying the house back from you a month at a time. Each month you receive a check. You own your house, are responsible for its upkeep, and pay fees and interest on the loan, and you are guaranteed that you will be able to stay there for your lifetime. After you die, the bank can claim the house, or at least the equity that it has contributed, as payment on the loan.

There is a comforting feeling of independence when one considers these options, since none of us likes to think of being forced to dip into the national kitty to care for us. But it might be wise to warn your heirs that the house they grew up in will return to the bank, or that they'd best not count on using your savings to fund their kids' private school education or wait for an inherited 401(k) payout to buy a summer place.

Tell them you are following the advice on the bumper sticker and "spending your children's inheritance."

Your insurance representative will say, "You don't self-insure against cancer or against a fire; why are you self-insuring against the potentially ruinous expense of long-term care?" Tell the agent that you believe in the American dream, which values independence above all. Tell your insurance representative that you want to do it all by yourself, and that you can.

Use Your Life Insurance

Some people over 60 decide to "self-insure" their lives by giving up their life insurance policies. But let's assume that you still have life insurance. There are ways to use the money in these policies to pay for your long-term care costs.

Check Out Your Cash Value

If you have a whole-life or universal life policy, you probably have accumulated cash value in it. You can pull this money out of the policy, either by canceling it outright or by taking a loan against it. If you cancel the policy, however, you may find you are uninsurable if you want to sign up for another one. And if you take a loan against the value, you'll reduce the benefits that your beneficiaries receive.

You're spending money you've put away for another purpose. For the kids, you're sparing them the inconvenience of paying for you now by spending the money they anticipated receiving after your death.

Tap into Living Benefits or Accelerated Death Benefits

Your insurance policy may include a provision for living benefits or accelerated death benefits. These benefits allow you to begin receiving life insurance payments while you are still alive, assuming that you meet the eligibility standards, which typically include having a year or less to live as well as confinement to a nursing home. This option is not automatic. You have to select it when you take your policy, although some insurers have provided accelerated death benefits as a no-cost enhancement. If you claim these benefits, however, you may not be able to use Medicaid benefits.

Consider Viatical Settlements

In this case, you essentially sell your life insurance policy to a company, which then becomes the beneficiary of the policy. In return, the company sends you a lump sum payment while you are living, and receives the insurance proceeds when you die. Do your homework very carefully if you are considering this option. Few states regulate these viatical settlement firms, and you need to be sure that the firm doesn't disappear with your irrevocable insurance trust before it pays you what it promises.

These funding sources are complex variations on the life insurance your grandparents and great-grandparents bought. Grandpa paid the premiums and named the beneficiaries; and when he died, the company paid the heirs. The kids were sad that he was gone, but they appreciated the financial boost he provided.

Great-grandpa and Grandpa, however, did not typically live until the age of 85. Medical advances did not prolong their last years beyond their ability to stay independent and enjoy them. Great-grandpa and Grandpa did not need the long-term care that you may be anticipating.

Grandpa might have borrowed against his life insurance, however, or simply cashed it in. You're considering the same option. If you opt for this funding source, your forebears would understand. It's the kids who will miss the money they expected, even as they appreciate your ability to care independently for yourself if you need care.

Let Your Kids (or Your Spouse) Do It

Parents often say that children are a "gift." But should the gift giver demand a present in return?

Part-Time Caregivers

Unlike Grandma, who cared for her mother—not to mention her husband—until they died, your kids may not be eager to take the old folks (you) into their homes. They might not have a spare room and might be unable to give up career mobility to see you through your old age. The kids may ask you to tap into the financial reservoirs mentioned here, and then would supplement your paid help with their own efforts as part-time caregivers. Look in Chapter 11 for a discussion of caregiving and caregivers, but for now remember that your children or another relative may truly want to support you physically as well as emotionally during your old age.

Full-Time Financial Givers

Your kids may want to support your long-term care needs by paying for your insurance policy. This gift will keep on giving; and if you qualify as their dependent the payments may be considered a medical care expense and be deductible to them. Even if you do not qualify as a dependent, the medical expense payments will be exempt under the federal gift tax laws, and therefore, no matter the size of your premium, neither you nor the children need to report the premiums as a gift.[5]

To determine how this concept may be applicable to your situation, it is strongly recommended that you consult with your tax counsel.

Finally, Explore Government Programs

Are you expecting Uncle Sam to support you in your old age? In fact, you may be surprised at how little the federal government does to support its elderly citizens and how difficult, if not painful, it is to qualify for government help.

Social Service Block Grants

These programs, also known as home care programs, are limited to what one state calls "frail elders" who "live independently in their own homes." Frail elders must meet income requirements established by the state in which they live. They may then qualify for case management services, home health aides, homemakers, delivered meals, respite care, and other benefits. Thus far, this program is so small that, combined with the benefits provided for veterans, it accounts for only 2 percent of total nursing home and home health care expenditures. Subtract the cost of supporting veterans in nursing homes, and you can guess at how few dollars actually go to the frail elder community.

Veterans' Benefits

Every veteran is assured of a package of benefits, including rehabilitative, home health, respite, and hospice care. But the package and eligibility, like all health care coverage, is being studied by Congress and is liable to change. If you think you might be eligible, call your local Veteran's Administration (VA) counselor to discuss the details.

Here are some topics to ask about.

NURSING HOME CARE

If there's space and if you can prove medical need, you may be able to get nursing home care. However, if your income is high enough, you may also be required to pay a deductible and co-payments. There is also a chance that you will be transferred, at VA expense, from a veterans' facility to a community nursing home.

SERVICE AND NONSERVICE DISABILITIES AND ILLNESSES

Whatever the cause of your illness, the VA may limit your funded nursing home stay to six months. In the past, there have been benefit distinctions between service-related and non-service-related illnesses, a complicated subject indeed for Gulf War and Vietnam vets. Talk to your VA representative.

Medicare: Don't Count on It

Medicare is health insurance, not long-term care insurance. It pays for only precisely defined services such as a skilled nursing facility and skilled home health care.

SKILLED NURSING FACILITY

After you have been hospitalized for three days or more, Medicare will pay for your stay in a certified skilled nursing facility. You'll be funded for only 100 days and only if you were admitted within 30 days of leaving the hospital for the same condition. You'll also have to pay a daily co-payment for day 21 through day 100. In 2002, the daily deductible is $101.50.

Clearly, Medicare is not the answer to your long-term care. One problem lies in the three-day hospitalization rule. Given the modern emphasis on day surgery, procedures that might have guaranteed you three hospital days are increasingly uncommon. Also, according to a U.S. Department of Labor study, the average length of a Medicare-paid stay in a skilled nursing facility is 30 days. Medicare was not intended to pay for extended long-term care needs.[6]

Secondly, don't confuse skilled nursing care with custodial care. The patient who just needs help bathing and dressing requires custodial care. Medicare says a service is skilled if it is furnished either by or under the supervision of a registered nurse or physician. Some examples are found in the next section's discussion of Medicare's home health benefit.

HOME HEALTH BENEFIT

If you require skilled care for an injury or illness while being confined to your home, you may collect from Medicare if these services are provided by a certified home health care agency. If your daughter delivers them, she won't get paid. Also, your doctor must prescribe these services, but you do not need a prior hospitalization to claim them.

Fortunately for the Medicare budget, but unfortunately for patients, so few people understand this portion of their Medicare coverage that they often fail to access these benefits. Federal Medicare guidelines call for skilled care, which includes nursing, physical, occupational, and speech therapy, home health aides, and social services, so long as your ability to leave the house is restricted to infrequent, supervised excursions either with an attendant or with a cane or walker.

However, you can't expect Medicare Home Health Benefit to provide around-the-clock skilled care. The benefit available is limited and is intended to cover only skilled nursing care and home health aide services on a part-time or intermittent basis.

The statute states that the term "part-time or intermittent services" pertains to combined services that total less than eight hours per day and 28 or fewer hours each week. In special circumstances with physician documentation these limits can be increased up to less than eight hours each day and 35 or fewer hours per week.

The statute further defines "intermittent" as skilled nursing care or home health aide services that are needed or given on fewer than seven days each week or less than eight hours each day over a period of 21 days (or less).

There is no sunset to these services; as long as the need is documented, and you have the willpower and resources to claim the care. Nor is there a deductible or co-payment for these services, although this is another area where you should stay tuned for developments.

Only a few state legislatures fund advocacy projects for citizens who have trouble with their Medicare coverage. The managing attorney for the Medicare Advocacy Project at Greater Boston Legal Services in Massachusetts, Diane Paulson, told me that even patients who know about the home care benefits may find them difficult to access. Paulson says that qualifying for the coverage is "very hard." It may also be difficult to find certified agencies to provide skilled services, especially since the Medicare reimbursement for patients who demand considerable care is often considered inadequate by the agency. She adds that since Medicare only pays for care once it's administered and does not give prior approval, the patient may be financially liable for the care if the federal program does not pay the bill. According to Paulson, "Many people can't afford that assumed financial risk," and since the only way to "challenge" Medicare is to submit a bill, they forgo the service. These patients go to family members or to noncertified agencies, or they go without.[7]

Home care is expensive, and Congress seems in no hurry to encourage people to use this portion of the Medicare benefit. By shifting the burden to the providers, forcing them to turn away needy clients, take a chance of going unreimbursed, or accept the onerous paperwork involved in getting paid, Congress deliberately made home care less available to seniors who have paid with their taxes for the right to access this benefit.

PERSONAL CARE SERVICES

You're on your own: Medicare doesn't pay for them. This means it won't pay your lawn service, your hairdresser, or to have your car washed. If you need help with one of the ADLs, for instance dressing or bathing, it may cover you for custodial services if you are also getting skilled care.

Medigap Insurance

Your Medigap insurance, the policy you bought to supplement Medicare, will not pay for most of your long-term care, either. Indeed, Medigap programs do not usually pay for services that Medicare doesn't cover, although some insurance companies sell supplements that cover the nursing home co-payments for the Medicare-approved days 21 through 100. There have also been reports that HMOs and other Medigap sellers have resisted paying legitimate home care costs, so stay alert in that regard, too. And remember that the yearly price increases for Medigap plans, particularly those that provide coverage for prescription drugs, show no signs of abating. Still, although there are differences in premiums among Medigap plans, if you can afford it, buy the broadest plan available.

Medicaid: You Probably Can't Count on It

Medicaid pays for almost half of all nursing home patients. It is the payer of last resort for people who do not have the resources to pay for their own care. This group includes disabled children and adults as well as seniors, but for the purposes of this discussion, we'll concentrate on those who need long-term care for their old age.

QUALIFYING FOR MEDICAID

No treatment of the subject of long-term care insurance is complete without some reference to Medicaid. This book is no exception.

Unfortunately, too many sales of long-term care insurance policies are fueled by the overwhelming fear that the insurance applicant will become a Medicaid recipient if long-term care insurance is not purchased.

However, I must emphasize in the strongest possible terms that because of the number of issues involved, which include not only eligibility but also the determination of different kinds of assets, transfers, protection of the spouse, and the various kinds of trusts, a consultation with an elder law attorney is strongly recommended. Do not rely completely on any information or recommendations for Medicaid planning from any insurance representative.

Medicaid is a welfare program shared by the federal and state governments. The federal government has mandated basic income and resource requirements and levels of care. Each state determines the applicant's specific eligibility and services available. Therefore eligibility and benefits vary according to where you live. You must check with your state to see what its asset limits are and the benefits it will provide for nursing home stays and home health care services.

Medicaid can be complicated. That's why William J. Brisk, an elder law attorney in the Newton, Massachusetts area, says it's important to recognize the distinction between advance planning and crisis management.

Clients in the first category, he says, are reasonably healthy but are concerned about the possibility that they may require long-term care in the future. Planning options are more restricted for them since the best way to protect their assets is to give them away. If they are sufficiently healthy and can afford the cost, such clients may want to consider purchasing long-term care insurance policies.

He adds that for clients whose health does not pass underwriting requirements for long-term care insurance, who are already institutionalized, or who cannot afford such policies, other steps may be taken well in advance of any particular need. Older clients may be encouraged to execute new wills (which under certain circumstances might create a testamentary trust for a spouse requiring long-term care) as well as broaden an agent's authorities under durable power of attorney. Advance action may be taken by initiating prudent planning strategies, which are a part of crisis management.

There are options, Brisk says, for those facing imminent nursing home placement or who are already institutionalized especially if a "community" spouse still resides at home. The most common options include gifting assets to family members and establishing trusts.

Although each state determines Medicaid eligibility, the federal government has established some guidelines. The following are generalizations meant to serve as a general guide to financial eligibility. Physical eligibility is based on the level of care you need and must be separately certified by the individual state. You must contact your state Medicaid office (which might go by another name) to find out the specifics that will actually establish your eligibility.

Boston estate attorney Alexander A. Bove Jr. provides several points to help you determine your eligibility for Medicaid benefits.

If you are single:

- If you have less that $2,000 (this varies from state to state) in countable assets (the resource test) and your income is within the allowable limit (the income test discussed next), you will likely qualify for Medicaid benefits.

- Income requirements vary, but most states will make you use your income before they will kick in Medicaid dollars, even if your income exceeds the allowable limit. States that allow this are called "spend-down" states, as they allow you to qualify for benefits by applying (spending down) your excess income for your care. They will then pay the balance of the care cost.

  Other states (approximately 18 of them) are referred to as "income-cap" states and do *not* allow a spend-down. In other words, if you apply for benefits in an income-cap state and your income is even $1 over the cap, you simply cannot qualify for benefits unless you arrange to qualify by placing (legally assigning) all your income to what is called a Miller trust. This is a special type of trust allowed under federal law, that will pay out to you no more than your allowable income limit for the particular state and accumulate any excess, which will later be paid to the state on your death.

- You will be able to keep your burial plot as an exempt asset, a segregated bank account of up to $1,500 for burial purposes, and most exempt assets married couples are allowed to retain.

If you are married and only one spouse needs nursing home care:

- For a married couple in 2002 the at-home spouse is allowed to keep as much as $89,280 in countable assets, and the institutionalized spouse may have $2,000 in assets. It should be noted, however, that there are circumstances where the at-home spouse is allowed to keep considerably more.

- The at-home spouse is also permitted an income allowance that varies depending on his or her needs and living circumstances, according to a formula based on federal poverty level standards. In 2001 the spousal income allowance ranged from a minimum of $1,425 to a maximum of $2,175 per month. It is also important to note that the separate income of the at-home spouse does not affect the Medicaid eligibility of the institutionalized spouse, regardless of the amount of income, even in an income-cap state. For instance, if the at-home spouse is receiving his or her own separate income (e.g., a pension) of $3,500 a month, this will not affect the eligibility of the institutionalized spouse, even though the income exceeds the maximum allowance. The at-home spouse would be able to retain all of it.

- You do not have to count your principal residence, its contents, your car, or your (individual) prepaid burial contracts as assets.

- The nursing home resident receives only a small monthly "personal needs" allowance (usually $50 to $65 per month) since his or her income goes either directly to the nursing home or in some cases to the healthy spouse.

- Don't forget to plan for the at-home spouse as well, after the ill spouse becomes eligible for Medicaid benefits.

The description of the guidelines for purposes of this book is necessarily brief and incomplete. The definitions and restrictions in this area are extensive, and it would take an entire book to provide all the details and exceptions. One of the best in that regard is *The Medical Planning Handbook* by estate attorney Alexander A. Bove Jr. (Little, Brown, 2000).

For now, the important point is that Medicaid will not be the solution of choice for most readers. Watch out for clever schemes to artificially impoverish you. One example of an annuity scheme that doubtless has a short life expectancy is the Medicaid annuity discussed earlier. Furthermore, you must be careful about transferring assets to Junior, Sis, or anyone else. If these gifts are transfers that occur within 36 months of entering a nursing home, you may be ineligible for Medicaid benefits. If you transfer your money to a trust, a look-back period extends to 60 months. "You just can't fool Uncle Sam," and the responsible citizen doesn't want to, either.

PARTNERSHIP POLICIES

Several states have recognized that many middle-income citizens lack the money to pay for long-term care insurance but will have too many assets to qualify for Medicaid. These people face the prospect of spending all their money on nursing home care.

For these people, a partnership policy is one answer. The client buys a long-term care policy that he or she can afford, perhaps covering $50,000 a year for three years. In this way $150,000 is sheltered from Medicaid. That is, the client need only spend down to $150,000 plus the $2,000 asset limit to receive Medicaid benefits. The few states (except New York) that participate in this plan set limits on the assets that can be sheltered. And the sheltering applies only to assets, not to income, which must go toward the cost of care once you qualify for Medicaid.

As of this writing, partnership plans are not available nationwide. If you move from the state where you bought yours, you'll probably have to move back to qualify when you want the Medicaid benefits. And you'll have to go through the underwriting process, just as you would with any long-term care insurance.

The partnership program is likely to grow, because the cost of long-term care will increase along with the aging population. The individual states especially are pushing for some kind of public/private partnership to ease the Medicaid burden and enable citizens to retain more of their assets should they need long-term care. UnumProvident remains cautious about such plans. Their spokesperson anticipates increased tax incentives to encourage the purchase of long-term care insurance, but suggests that the many restrictions of formal partnership programs make them unlikely to proliferate. This insurance executive says the reporting requirements alone may "infringe upon the privacy requirements placed on the insurance companies." Therefore, UnumProvident does not participate in these programs.[8]

In short, stay tuned.

Expect to Take Care of Yourself

Wouldn't it be reassuring if the federal government assumed responsibility for everyone's long-term care, regardless of assets or income?

Maybe not. Consider the costs: huge tax increases, a mind-boggling national debt, bankrupt generation Xers and Yers.

Would you feel more reassured if you assumed that your children would maintain you as your grandparents, willingly or not, cared for their elderly relatives? But clear thinking suggests otherwise. The vast majority of us must rely on our own resources to fund our long-term care. We've read our crystal balls, anticipated the costs, recognized the likely absence of government support, rolled up our sleeves, and taken responsibility for our own futures—after all, that's the American way!

Besides, it's your money. You earned it, and you have a right to spend it any way you deem appropriate.

Endnotes

1. *Report, Findings, and Recommendations of the Working Group on Long-Term Care.* U.S. Department of Labor, Advisory Council on Employee Welfare and Pension Benefit, November 14, 2000. p. 9.
2. Kong, Dolores. "A Penny Saved Is Not Enough." *Boston Globe*, May 23, 2001. p. D1.
3. Davis, Ann. "Suddenly Poor: Insurers Help Elderly Get Medicaid to Pay for Nursing Homes." *Wall Street Journal*, June 6, 2001. p. 1, A10.
4. Ibid.
5. *New England Financial, Legal and Tax Trends, Long Term Care Insurance*, Vol. 7, Issue 1 (April 2001). p. 9.
6. *Report, Findings, and Recommendations of the Working Group on Long-Term Care.* p. 11.
7. Interview with Diane Paulson, managing attorney, Medicare Advocacy Project of Greater Boston Legal Services, June 6, 2001.
8. UnumProvident memo, June 21, 2001.

CHAPTER 3

Reading the Fine Print: How to Buy the Coverage You Want with the Dollars You Have

Ever since you reached for the blue block instead of the red one, you've been a comparison shopper. By definition, we constantly choose between alternatives, but we make our selection by design. Choosing the right long-term care policy works the same way. Insurance companies offer you a lot of choices, assuming your health is good and you have 7 percent of your income left over after you pay your bills each month. You're too rational to be swayed by flashy sales tricks, and you're thoughtful about your future without buying into doomsday scenarios. Now you're ready to learn as much as you can about the nuts and bolts of long-term care coverage, so you'll make the right choice if you decide to buy.

You and the insurance company are partners. The company wants to sell you a policy that will suit your needs (so you'll continue to renew it) and won't bankrupt the company (so it can stay in business). You yourself want the company to stay in business, or else how will it pay your benefits in 20 or 30 years, when you need to make a claim?

Also, the insurance industry acknowledges that its long-term care product is a relatively new type of coverage. Recognizing that many consumers are confused by the coverage, companies publish clearly written brochures and maintain web site pages to help consumers navigate through the decision-making process.

Insurers like to make the case that long-term care policies resemble life insurance more than health care insurance. The idea is that long-term care insurance is planning for a future 20 or 30 years off, and one which, ideally, will never happen. Insurers recognize that they are designing a product that raises a broad range of psychological, medical, and economic issues. One way to look at the value of a long-term care policy is to consider the interaction of price, service, and access to quality care. Let's consider these variables as a series of six choices you'll need to make:

1. *What model of insurance do you want?* Would you prefer a policy that will reimburse your billed expenses out of a pool of money? This model is called a reimbursement policy. Or do you want your policy to pay you a fixed daily benefit, no matter what your daily bills happen to be? This model is called an indemnity policy.

2. *What settings and what levels of care will you need?* Do you think you'll want to move to a nursing home? Stay at home? Use assisted living? Do you anticipate, from your family history, that you will need specialized care or only custodial assistance?

3. *How will you prove you're eligible to receive benefits?* The insurance industry calls these proofs triggers; your policy will specify which disabilities you'll need to prove to qualify for your benefits.

4. *What financial safeguards would make you feel comfortable?* Can you pay for a period of care out of your own pocket? Do you want a company-paid care manager? Will you buy inflation protection? Should your daughter be given a check for taking care of you? How much are you willing to pay for these added benefits?

5. *How much claim negotiation are you willing to do?* Do you feel able to negotiate the maze of collecting benefits? Will someone else help you? Do you want to write checks to each service provider you use?

6. *Can you pay the premium?* Do you want to buy a policy at age 45? Would you prefer to pay premiums only while you're working? Will both you and your spouse buy coverage?

Yes, this list is daunting. That's why I am writing this book and why you're reading it! Stay with me through the decision making, and when we're finished you'll feel confident that you can prudently and unemotionally shop for long-term care because you know exactly what you want, how to talk about it, and how to get it.

Choice Number One: Reimbursement or Indemnity

Long-term care policies come in two basic models: reimbursement and indemnity. Insurers may use other labels to muddy the distinctions, but your agent will likely present you with one or the other of these types of coverage.

A reimbursement policy pays for the actual services you receive from the pool of benefit money you have bought. The agent who sells such a policy, perhaps from a company like MetLife or GE Capital, will explain the policy like this: "You are buying $200 a day for three years as a benefit. Your total pool of money is $219,000 for the policy, and the only limit is the daily or weekly limit. That is, your policy limits how much money you can draw a day or week for services. If you don't use all the money in the first three years, you can draw from the pool in future years until the pool of money is exhausted."

Naturally this is not the whole story, but we'll get to that.

An indemnity policy works differently. In this case, once you are certified as eligible, if you use a licensed provider, you will get the entire daily benefit each day, whether or not you have actually spent it all. This model for long-term care resembles a disability policy. Even if you pay the service providers you use only $50 a day for their help, you'll get the full $200. If you pay a higher premium—typically 20 to 50 percent higher—you can receive care at home from anyone you choose—a family member or friend, or through a licensed home health care agency.

UnumProvident sells this type of policy. The agent will probably say, "You are buying a $200 daily benefit for three [or more] years. Once we certify your disability, you'll go through the waiting period, and then we'll give you the money each day. It's yours, and it's up to you how you use it. If you want to pay a relative or an unlicensed provider, that's okay. If you are willing to pay up to an additional 50 percent for your policy, we can write that provision into it."

There's more to this story, too. We'll get to that.

A Tale of One Family in Two Versions

Here is an alternative reality view of how the two types of policies might work in practice.

Jack and Betty Wallace purchased long-term care policies from Jack's nephew, Will. Will had been a MetLife agent for 25 years and was an outstanding community leader. He treated his parents to a 50th anniversary wedding cruise, a gesture highly appreciated by the older generation. Every time Uncle Jack saw Will at a family party he would say, "Thank you for making us feel secure in our old age." Will's father, Tom, smiled with pride: "That's my boy."

A year after buying the long-term care policy, Jack had a stroke. He could no longer drive or take a shower by himself; he had difficulty walking, and needed help eating and toileting. He was certified as ADL-dependent in more than two activities and thus qualified for his long-term care benefits once the 90-day waiting period had elapsed.

At first everything went well. The MetLife policy paid for a nurse/care manager who worked for the insurance company. Her job was to plan Jack's care, and the couple was happy with her compassion and concern. They found making the claim easy.

The nurse arranged for an agency to send a professional to Jack's house each morning. This professional helped him bathe, dress, and eat, checked his vital signs, and stayed until noon. After that, it was Betty's turn. Since Jack napped every afternoon, Betty managed fairly well until dinner. If she wanted an afternoon out to go grocery shopping or have her hair done, she hired a neighbor to sit with her husband.

But after six months, this fragile arrangement broke down. Jack began to have difficulty getting out of bed and to the bathroom in the middle of the night. More than once he fell, and Betty had to call the on-site condominium manager to help her lift him into a chair. The manager was patient at first, but by the sixth call in one month, he had clearly had enough.

"Please come quickly," Betty cried. "Jack has fallen again!"

"Sorry, Betty. You'll have to wait. I'm doing some work for Mrs. Smith in the next building that can't stop."

"I need you right now!"

"Sorry. You'd better call 911."

Frightened, frustrated, and exhausted, Betty exploded. For one of the few times in her life, she used gutter language, telling the manager exactly what she thought of him.

The manager was sympathetic to Betty's plight, but he told the condo trustees what had happened. They in turn told Betty that the complex was not an assisted living environment and that the condo staff was not on 24-hour call.

Betty was desperate. She called her daughter, Bernice, who lived on the opposite coast. Bernice came the next morning and saw immediately that her parents needed more help than they were getting. Jack's falls, not to mention his toileting accidents, would only become more frequent. Betty was nearly frozen with panic. She told Bernice that their long-term care reimbursement policy limit of $200 a day paid only for actual expenses incurred up to the daily limit for covered benefits.

Bernice checked out the policy. "I'm sorry, Mom, but it looks like you're right. You have a $200 plan, which will pay you up to $200 a day whether you're at home or in a nursing home. Dad's covered care is averaging $100 a day, but he needs 24-hour care supervision, which is not covered. That $200 would pay for a nursing home, where he would get 24 hours of supervision and there would be medical personnel around if he pressed a button."

Reluctantly, the family placed Mr. Wallace in a nursing home. The end result: another premature nursing home placement.

Wait. It didn't have to be this way! Let's rewind to an alternative view of the situation. Same characters, different policy—this time an indemnity plan.

Betty and Jack bought an indemnity plan written by UnumProvident corporation; their agent was Betty's niece, Jill, a successful, well-loved citizen and family member. A year later, Jack had a stroke. Jack qualified under the ADL guidelines; he and Betty made it through the waiting period, after which Jack started to collect his benefits.

The indemnity policy also paid $200 per day, but here's the difference: As long as he employed the services of one certified provider a day, Jack was able to collect all of his daily $200 benefit. One service meant full payment, no matter the size of the provider's daily bill. The indemnity plan paid him the total benefit, without inspecting a record of daily expenses. It assumed that Jack, with Betty's counsel, could determine the best use of the money.

The good news was that the couple had money left over from the daily benefit to pay a college student to spend the night. When Betty needed a break, she could pay someone to sit with Jack. The couple even had enough left over to pay for their daughter's trip from the West Coast and to cover the cost of their uninsured prescription medications.

Today more than one insurer, including MetLife, that heretofore had been offering only reimbursement policies and had aggressively highlighted the disadvantages of indemnity coverage to prospects is starting to offer the indemnity model as a policy option.

It might appear that one version has a happy ending and one does not. Don't be fooled. Choosing between these two types of policies is not nearly so simple. Consider these four questions:

1. How are your benefits paid?
2. Who provides the service?
3. Which model costs less?
4. What about care managers?

HOW ARE YOUR BENEFITS PAID?

Assume you have a $200 daily benefit. Reimbursement pays for only the covered service. If you spend $70 on a provider, you get $70 in reimbursement. The other $130 remains in your pool of benefits. As long as you have a documented service, indemnity will pay you the full $200 even if you spend only $70.

If you take the indemnity plan's full $200 every day, you may run out of your money while you still need it. Your pool will run dry. A reimbursement plan keeps the money that you don't spend in your pool of money, thus effectively stretching out the time limits on your benefits until you spend whatever is left.

The indemnity seller asks the customer, "Why should the insurance company tell you how to spend your money?" The reimbursement seller asks the customer, "Did you actually buy long-term care insurance to pay for airline tickets?" Reimbursement sellers argue that the insurance money was never intended to pay for services that any caring family member or friend would do for love and for free.

WHO PROVIDES THE SERVICE?

Reimbursement policies insist that you use licensed caregivers, although you may be able to purchase a rider to allow you to pay family members. (But see the preceding discussion for the reimbursement seller's take on this option.) An indemnity plan may let you pay family members or informal caregivers who cost less than licensed providers.

Why buy a reimbursement policy, especially if you think you'll have trouble finding a licensed caregiver? Because the policy usually allows for these conditions, and besides, the companies have developed networks of providers for practically every area of the country.

WHICH MODEL COSTS LESS?

Indemnity sellers say that their claims don't cost much to process, there is less overhead, and the premiums should be less.

Sellers of reimbursement policies make the opposite case, arguing that premiums for reimbursement are lower because the claims costs tend to be lower; indemnity policies may cost more because claims costs are higher for indemnity insurers. In fact, as of this writing, the premium costs are almost the same. But a LifePlans consultant anticipates that this will shift as the indemnity insurers begin to play catch-up as their claims start to come due in 10 years.[1]

WHAT ABOUT CARE MANAGERS?

The indemnity seller says that since you were smart enough to select that policy, you're prudent enough to set up your own long-term care arrangements or else hire an objective professional to arrange things for you. The reimbursement seller provides you with a company-paid care manager.

Ah, says the indemnity representative, these paid care managers are actually gatekeepers unwilling to certify the care you need. Wrong, says the reimbursement seller; no care managers, on our staff or subcontracted, have any motive other than to help you in this troubled time. You can also ask them to negotiate a reduced fee with their licensed providers to save money for your pool.

Within this debate you may detect echoes of the change in health care insurance, specifically the distinctions between indemnity coverage and HMOs. Here are the familiar conversations about lower premiums at the expense of access, and freedom of choice versus the potential wastefulness of foolish consumers.

How do you choose between the two models? One industry consultant told me that he uses the "mother" test. He advises people to look at the price differences, consider the choices, and choose what's important to them. "If you think you'll have trouble finding a licensed provider, avoid the reimbursement model. Use your health as a guide. What do you anticipate needing in your older age?"[2]

Some insurers are starting to blur the line between the reimbursement and indemnity models. One company, Prudential, a relatively new player in the long-term care market, offers an indemnity option, which it calls a cash benefit rider, on its reimbursement plan. As long-term care insurance matures as a product, the lines will blur even more. The consumer will be able to find the most appealing and productive benefits for his or her situation so long as the agent or broker attempting to make the sale is knowledgeable regarding the ins and outs of both models and is willing to discuss the pros and cons of both.

Choice Two: Choose Your Setting and Your Level of Care

A somewhat less subtle but even more important decision follows the choice between reimbursement and indemnity models of insurance. Before you speak with an insurance representative, you need to anticipate what kinds of care you might want (or need) in your old age. And where would you want to live while you receive that care? These considerations are what the industry calls levels of care and settings.

Insurers are talking about levels of care when they offer a range of services from skilled nursing care through intermediate care to custodial care or even chore care. "Setting" is more self-evident: Are you willing to go to a nursing home or to an assisted living community? Will you want to stay at home as long as you possibly can? Does your family history suggest you may need adult day care, respite care, even hospice care?

A recent report for the U.S. Department of Health and Human Services found that buyers of longer-term care tend to underestimate both the cost of their long-term care and their need when they buy insurance. The study found that benefits for residents of nursing homes amounted to only 67 percent of the total cost of their care. They needed to make up the rest from their pockets.[3] Furthermore, the study found that there is not a predictable progression from home care to assisted living to nursing home. Instead, the assisted living residence may be a substitute for home health care. The old model of hospital to nursing home is no longer typical.[4]

What Settings Deliver Care?

The consumer is buying a policy that might not pay off for 10 or 15 years, if at all. How should he or she think about settings of care? Even the insurance industry acknowledges that new and innovative long-term care facilities are continuing to emerge: Few insurers anticipated assisted living possibilities in 1985. Chapter 1 looked at the settings that serve long-term care needs. These include home care, assisted living, continuing care retirement communities, nursing homes, and any combination of these types. Your long-term care policy may reimburse any or all of these settings, alone or in combination. While each insurer may define the settings in slightly different terms, you're still essentially talking about the nursing home, assisted living residence, congregate housing, and home you now occupy. But the devil is in the details.

Consider geography. Are there service providers in your neck of the woods? Will an assisted living residence be available near your current home, or near the homes of your kids? What about the nursing home down the street? Are you willing to live there? Will there be room? Remember, some insurers treat these settings alone or in combination. You must read the definitions in your policy and avoid labels such as "alternative care facility" since these may be nursing homes in disguise, as well as forward-looking undefined settings.

And how do you ensure that you will have the choice of living out your last days in your own home? By paying for the coverage and getting it in writing.

Home Care

The GE Capital general agent I interviewed told me that companies are most competitive in their coverage for home care.[5] GE Capital, for instance, is currently offering a home care policy with no waiting period; the customer must have the anticipation of being disabled for 90 days or more to be able to claim benefits, which cover as much as 100 percent of costs. Naturally the policyholder pays for this coverage in higher premiums. The typical home care benefit covers approximately 36 hours a week of care, even though the average beneficiary needs 59 hours.[6] Payment for the rest of the care comes out of the client's pocket.

One problem for those with older policies is the way the benefit is calculated. Jack and Betty experienced a version of this catch-22. Another version caught Bob, who thought he was well covered when he made a claim for home care. His benefit allowed him to spend $600 a week on his care. He needed help three days a week when his wife went to work. Bob needed help transferring, dressing, and eating on these days; the other four days, his wife was around to help him. The thrice-weekly caregiver cost Bob $300 a day. Unfortunately, his policy paid only $200 a day, so Bob had to scratch out the other $100 from his pension payments. Had Bob's policy been enhanced to a weekly benefit, he would have had more than enough to handle the cost of the three-days-a-week helper. Many insurance companies have now changed this provision, at no charge to their policyholders.

To avoid potential litigation, many insurers are reluctant to offer home care only coverage. They fear that at claim time the insured who may need nursing home coverage will contend that the agent actually sold the client an integrated policy covering nursing home care as well as home care. In an integrated policy, insurers offer home care coverage as a percentage of nursing home coverage; typically, the home care benefit amounts to 50 percent of the nursing home benefit.

For the extra premium involved, increasing the home care benefit to 100 percent of the nursing home benefit makes tremendous sense. Having that extra money may help you avoid premature placement in a nursing home. That's why insurance representatives often recommend that when you buy an integrated policy covering both nursing home and home care, your home care benefit be 100 percent. You'll be happy you paid the extra premium when you are able to stay out of a nursing home.

Levels of Care

What makes the analysis of insurance provisions even more complex is the interaction between setting and levels of care. Let's look at how these levels are defined; then we'll see how they might be used in a nursing home, assisted living residence, or your own house.

CHORE CARE

As defined by UnumProvident, these are services that help individuals remain in their homes and keep the homes habitable. Such chores include vacuuming, washing floors and walls, defrosting freezers, cleaning attics and basements to remove hazards, lawn care, and minor home repairs. These are also called household services.[7]

You may want this service if you have home care, but not if you are in an assisted living residence or in a nursing home.

CUSTODIAL CARE

These are services delivered on an extended basis to a chronically disabled person; they are chiefly maintenance, and do not include transportation or personal convenience or companionship services.

HOMEMAKER CARE

These services help maintain independent living. They include shopping, menu planning, meal preparation, light housekeeping, vacuuming, dusting, and changing beds.

You'll want this service for home care.

PERSONAL CARE

UnumProvident ties the services to the ADLs. A different insurer might define this help as services by a home health aide who assists in the activities of daily living, including bathing, bedpan, foot care, dressing, care of dentures, shaving and grooming, assistance with eating, ambulating, and transferring. In other words, the definitions differ, so read the policies carefully when you shop.

You may want this level of care at home, in a nursing home, and in an assisted living residence.

INTERMEDIATE CARE

This category includes occasional nursing or rehabilitative care that can only be performed by or under the supervision of skilled medical personnel and under a doctor's orders. Note the word "occasional" here; what counts is that the services are not provided daily.

You may want this care at home, in an assisted living facility, or in a nursing home.

NURSING CARE

These are services requiring the professional skills of a nurse, performed by a nurse, under the orders of a physician, and to improve or maintain your health.

If Medicare doesn't cover these service, you'll need them at home and pay for them out of your own pocket.

SKILLED CARE

These services, sometimes also covered by Medicare, include nursing care, occupational or physical therapy, blood pressure monitoring, and so on.

Medicare may cover these services at home. You may have to pay for them in any other setting.

Insurers like UnumProvident treat the intersection of setting and care level by combining settings and treatment levels. You may choose a policy that will allow you to receive care in a nursing home or your own apartment, from a licensed home health care professional or a family member or friend. UnumProvident anticipates that your home care needs will include health care, personal care, nutrition, homemaking, and social and safety needs.

In addition to dollars to stay at home, your dollars should work in flexible ways. One of my neighbors learned this the hard way. His mother, at 85, lived happily in an assisted living residence. She played bridge daily, watched her soap operas, and liked the staff and residents. The problem was that Mom needed to take her medications on a regular basis, but sometimes she became so caught up in the game or the story that she missed a pill. The assisted living staff, however, was not paid to attend to Mom's pill schedule, so didn't. My neighbor had to pay a personal care attendant to deliver the pills to Mom three times a day and to make sure she took them. Unfortunately, Mom's tax-qualified long-term care insurance policy didn't cover this contingency.

Choice Three: What Will Trigger the Benefits?

Medicaid law and the IRS's distinctions between tax-qualified and non-tax-qualified long-term care plans have clarified what you need to prove in order to claim your long-term care benefits. Marketplace competition has also gone a long way toward making at least this part of buying long-term care coverage simpler.

These disability triggers fall into two categories, activities of daily living (ADLs), which are established by government regulation for tax-qualified plans, and instrumental activities of daily living, which are defined by each insurance company.

The ADLs:

Bathing: Washing oneself by sponge bath or in either a tub or a shower, including the task of getting into or out of the tub or shower.

Dressing: Putting on and taking off all items of clothing and any necessary braces, fasteners, or artificial limbs.

Eating: Feeding oneself by getting food into the body from a receptacle (such as a plate, cup, or table) or by a feeding tube or intravenously.

Toileting: Getting to and from the toilet, getting on and off the toilet, and performing personal hygiene.

Transferring: Moving into and out of a bed, chair, or wheelchair.

Continence: The ability to maintain control of bowel or bladder function; or when unable to maintain control of bowel or bladder function, the ability to perform related personal hygiene (including caring for catheter or colostomy bag).

Insurers now add the disability of severe cognitive impairment to this list. UnumProvident says a severe cognitive impairment is a "severe deterioration or loss in a) your short- or long-term memory; b) your orientation as to person, place, and time; or c) your deductive or abstract reasoning."[8] This deterioration must be measured by clinical evidence and standardized test. Another insurer might add the condition that the patient must be at risk of harming him- or herself or another person, hence requiring substantial supervision.

Tax-qualified plans use these triggers exclusively. Non-tax-qualified plans may also include triggers built around the instrumental ADLs. These activities include taking medicine, telephoning, cooking, housework, laundry, grocery shopping, and paying bills. Other non-tax-qualified plans use "medical necessity" as certified by a physician. Again, the wise buyer reads the fine print, especially the definition of medical necessity, before signing the policy application.

Give the Triggers a Really Close Look

How many triggers do you need to satisfy? The Health Insurance Portability and Accountability Act of 1996 (HIPAA) requires that once a claimant is unable to perform two of the six ADLs for 90 days, he or she must be certified as disabled and eligible to receive benefits from his or her tax-qualified plan. Furthermore, if a client satisfies the cognitive impairment trigger, the tax-qualified plan must begin to pay benefits even if he or she can still bathe, dress, and carry out the other ADLs. Many plans are tax qualified, but what about those which are not? In this case, each state may establish its own criteria. Some states may allow insurers to impose as many as three triggers, while others begin to pay after one.

Does the policy count all six triggers? Insurers know that the ability to bathe independently is often the first activity of daily living a client is unable to perform. Some eliminate this trigger from the list in their non-tax-qualified plans. Let's assume you are unable to get in and out of the shower by yourself. Do you think you will also want to wait until you can't toilet on your own or feed yourself before you can claim your long-term care benefits? You may be waiting longer than you expect for the money.

The cognitive impairment trigger deserves especially close scrutiny. Most policies now pay for Alzheimer's or other organic brain impairments, but many will not pay for nervous or mental conditions that might be disabling. Note also how the policy distinguishes among "substantial assistance," "hands-on assistance," and "standby assistance." Tax-qualified plans must pay if the person needs substantial assistance, which includes both standby assistance and hands-on assistance. Standby assistance means the necessity of having another person within arm's reach during the activities of daily living. Read your policy for the details.

Choice Four: Policy Provisions

Now we're down to the really fine print. Think of these provisions as a kind of old-fashioned balance scale. If you are willing to have a longer waiting period, you can pay a lower premium. If you want a larger daily benefit, you will pay proportionally more in premiums. A $200 daily benefit costs twice as much as a $100 daily benefit. However, if you extend the benefit period from three years to four years, the cost is less than 30 percent for that additional year because the actuaries realize that the probability that you will need the care decreases for each year of the policy. That is, they are betting that you won't live long enough to use that fourth year of benefits.

The process works similarly to the way you selected your automobile deductible. You are negotiating the balance between the risk you will assume and the payout you want, weighing cost against value. The bad news is that many provisions you can buy are not really worth the cost; the good news is that the marketplace is so competitive you have leverage in your negotiations. If you think one insurer is charging too much for an important set of provisions, shop some more. And many times you will be rewarded with enhanced provisions at no cost, to ensure your willingness to renew the policy.

How Your Premium Is Determined

The amount of your premium is calculated by the benefit amount you select, the waiting or elimination period you want, any inflation option selected, your marital status, your insurability, the length of time for benefits selected, and any bells and whistles chosen.

DAILY OR WEEKLY BENEFIT AMOUNT

This is the dollar amount your policy will pay for each day of covered services. As we have seen, most insurers can cover home care, assisted living, and nursing home care in one policy. Coverage for assisted living and home care can be purchased as a percentage of nursing home coverage. The extra premium required to purchase the same benefit for all settings is well worth the expenditure. You can now buy up to $500 a day in coverage, and if you have selected the reimbursement model, you may save the excess and extend the life of the policy.

How can you figure out the best daily benefit amount for you? Check with your local nursing homes and assisted living facilities. Talk to people who have paid for home care. Consider your age and inflation (see upcoming discussion). Then make a good guess, considering the income you think you will be able to throw into the long-term care pot from your savings and other assets. And don't forget that if you stay at home, you'll still have to heat and maintain the place.

Whatever benefit amount you choose, the insurer agrees to give you a specified number of dollars for each day that you qualify for long-term care benefits. If you spend over that amount, you'll have to come up with the difference. The amount will be fixed, whether it is calculated by the day or, more desirably, by the week.

WAITING PERIOD

Just as there are optional deductibles in your comprehensive fire, theft, and collision automobile insurance that make available reduced premiums, so, too, there are various waiting periods in individual long-term care policies that you can choose to determine the length of time before you can access your long-term care coverage. During the waiting period, you'll have to pay for your own care. The longer you can pay your own costs, the lower your premium will be. Your choice, depending on the jurisdiction in which you reside, can be from zero days to 365 days, with the norm being 90 to 100 days.

Just like a number of benefits found in long-term care insurance policies, the provisions for waiting periods vary from company to company.

The deductible period or elimination period, as it is called by insurers, means the number of days during which you are disabled and either you are receiving services in a nursing facility or an assisted living facility for which no benefit is payable or you are receiving professional home and community care and no benefit is payable.

With some companies, each calendar week that you receive at least one day of professional home and community care will be counted as seven days toward completing the elimination period.

The determination of just how each insurer determines your applicable credit toward completing your waiting period is a very complicated one.

In order for you to understand the relative value of the waiting period in a particular company, you should ask these questions:

- *How many days during the week do I have to receive at least one day of professional home and community care that will be counted as seven toward completing the elimination period?* With some insurers you only have to receive care at least one day to qualify for a seven-day credit.

- *How long a period do I have for completing my waiting period?* If, for example, you chose a 90-day waiting period and you have the type of illness that in the initial stages does not require care every day some companies require that you have at least your 90 days of care during a 180- or 360-day period. If you do not qualify and have the appropriate number of days during that period of time your clock starts all over again and you must sustain treatment during your 90-day period during another 180- or 360-day period. This feature is becoming highly competitive and some companies are about to offer the ability to accumulate your waiting period during a 720-day period.

- *How often do I have to satisfy an elimination period to access benefits?* Some companies provide that any elimination or waiting period longer than 30 days must be satisfied by you only once during your lifetime.

Just how different insurers treat this feature could be a significant factor in determination of the appropriate company to select for your long-term care insurance.

BENEFIT LENGTH

This is the amount of time that George's indemnity policy would pay him his full benefits. He could have collected full daily benefits for every day that he was disabled, as long as he required at least one visit from a licensed health care provider. Let's say George collected these benefits for the entire benefit period, every day for three years. He still cannot transfer from his bed to his wheelchair, and he still can't shower on his own; now he's out of long-term care money and out of luck.

Opponents of the indemnity plan maintain that in this scenario George or his family would have unwisely used the excess dollars, those left over when his actual daily bills were paid for goods and services unrelated to George's care, comfort, and supervision. They also warn that George was at risk of receiving inferior care because his expenses were not being managed by a company-paid care manager.

If George had a reimbursement policy, his benefit would have worked differently. He would have been reimbursed only for the actual expenses he had each day. If these were less than his daily benefit, his pool of money would remain at least partially full. He might have been able to stretch out his benefits beyond the three years specified in his plan, because the daily cost for the services he required during the three-year period never reached the policy's daily limits.

INFLATION PROTECTION AND YOUR AGE

It may be relatively easy for you to establish how much a day you think you'll need in long-term care benefits if you are disabled. But that's only part of the question.

What about the effects of inflation? George could remember when gasoline cost 31 cents a gallon and not $1.60, so he understood inflation. The question for George, as for every buyer, is whether to add inflation protection to a long-term care policy. Inflation protection is a policy option that provides for an increase in benefit levels to help pay for the expected increases in long-term care services.

The Shopper's Guide to Long-Term Care Insurance published by the National Association of Insurance Commissioners offers the following look at the potential effects of inflation:[9]

A nursing home that costs $110 per day today will cost $292 per day in 20 years, assuming the rate of inflation is 5 percent. If the inflation rate is higher, you'll pay even more in 20 years. If you buy a policy that will pay $110 today and does not include inflation protection, you'll be getting $110 in 20 years and too bad about the inflation rate.

You don't expect to live for 20 years in a nursing home? You probably won't. But that's not the point.

What if you are buying your long-term care insurance policy at age 60, but don't use it until you are age 80? You're back into the $292 per day ballpark.

The sticking point is that inflation protection will significantly increase the amount of premium you pay. The cost varies according to your age, your insurer, the maximum yearly benefit you elect, and the type of inflation protection you select—simple or compound.

A simple inflation protection rider increases the daily benefit amount and lifetime maximum by 5 percent of the *dollar amount originally issued.* A compound inflation protection rider increases the daily benefit amount and the lifetime maximum amount by 5 percent of the *previous year's* dollar amount. Some states now require that the insurance companies use compound inflation increases, and all individual and some group policies offer them as an optional benefit.

Your insurer may offer inflation protection on either a periodic or an automatic basis. Automatic inflation protection is just that; your benefit is automatically increased each year. If the offer is made on a periodic basis—for example, every three years—you may accept or reject it. If you accept each offering, you can avoid new medical underwriting. Your premium will increase because you have increased your benefits. If you turn down the inflation option, you may not be able to buy it in the future or you may need new underwriting if you decide you want inflation protection later.

Should you spend the extra money for inflation protection? Here are the ways some experts think about it:

- If you are under 72 and think your need for long-term care will come sooner rather than later, maybe in five years, buy a higher daily benefit. If you are 72, think about your medical and family history to make a guess about your longevity.

- If you think your need will come sooner rather than later because you're over 72, consider simple rather than compound inflation protection. It will save you money. But you'll also lose ground against rising inflation, especially if you surprise yourself by living a long time.

- If you're a young buyer, consider compound inflation protection. You probably have many years before you need to use the long-term care benefits, and your youthful premiums keep your costs manageable.

Midsized Ticket Items

There are other provisions that will add to the cost of your policy.

NONFORFEITURE BENEFITS

What if George forfeited his policy by letting it lapse? If he deliberately let the policy lapse, he would have to do so in writing. If he had paid additional premiums, he might be able to get some of the money back through a *return of premium benefit*, which would provide him with reduced payout based on the amount of premium he had contributed, assuming he hadn't used up the pool of money. He could have bought a *shortened benefit period*, so that the insurance company would pay him reduced benefits equal to the premium he has paid.

What if George didn't mean to let his policy lapse? He just forgot to send a check. In this case, George had 30 days to pay the premium without losing the coverage. As a fail-safe measure, he could also have designated someone else be notified if his payment was late. Finally, if it could be shown that he had not paid because of cognitive impairment, he would have up to five months, by HIPAA mandate, to reinstate his coverage.

RESTORATION OF BENEFITS

Let's say that hip surgery for Uncle George made him eligible for 45 days of benefits and his hip healed quickly. After a few months, he went back to square dancing. Seven months later, while he was swinging his partner in a do-si-do, he reinjured the hip. George was back in the hospital. But he had a clause that assured him that the amount of benefits he collected as a result of his hip surgery would be restored if he went six months without treatment on his hip. Since he hadn't used up all his benefits, the clause seemed to promise that his benefits would be restored to their original conditions. Unfortunately, when the claims inspector looked at George's medication record, he saw that George had been taking prescription-level anti-inflammatories for hip pain. The inspector concluded that George had indeed continued his treatment, and his claim for restoration of benefits was denied.

WAIVER OF PREMIUM

Waiver of premium is a provision found in long-term care insurance policies that relieves the insured of paying the premiums while receiving benefits. Unfortunately, that's only half the story.

Depending on the insurer you choose, you will find one of three different methods by which insurers treat the waiver of premium benefits.

The waiver of premium benefit that commences the day you are eligible for benefits is perhaps the most readily understandable.

The broadest benefit is the one that comes into play when you are eligible for benefits and is retroactive to the inception of your disability. This means if you have a 90-day elimination period and you become disabled under the terms of the contract on January 1, your benefits will not be payable unless you are still disabled 90 days later on April 1. When you become eligible for benefits, any premiums paid since January 1 are refunded.

The least desirable form is the kind of waiver of premium where the clock starts running once you become eligible for benefits after your waiting period. If you have a 90-day waiting period, you will have to be disabled for 180 days before your waiver of premium will kick in.

Waiver of premium is usually automatic for nursing home coverage, but it is not available with some insurers for home care. Some of those that do not provide the benefit on an automatic basis for home care make that policy benefit available for an additional premium.

Nickel-and-Dime Options

A last group of options cost less, but still may not be worth the money. It's up to policyholders to decide if they want to buy these options or the others that the insurers will develop over the next few years.

Settings: Add some of these to your list of choices: adult day care, respite care, hospice care, bed reservation if you are hospitalized from a nursing home, transitional care (from home to assisted living), care outside the United States.

Ancillary health services: Ambulance, emergency alert system, equipment purchase, house remodeling, prescription drugs.

Social supports: Care manager, caregiver training.

Home care only: Chore care, transportation, housekeeping, caregiver training.

Choice Five: Claiming Your Money

Having long-term care insurance won't do you much good if you are so stymied by the claims paperwork that you don't collect your benefits. More than one senior citizen has cajoled a relative or paid a professional to fill out their medical insurance forms so that their insurance carriers could reimburse them.

Insurance companies, recognizing that by definition their claimants are disabled, have made the claim filing process easier. The LifePlans study found that 70 percent of beneficiaries had no trouble collecting their benefits. The number was even higher for nursing home residents, 90 percent of whom said they were happy with the way their claims were managed by their insurance companies.[10]

Do you doubt these numbers? The same survey found that between 75 percent to 86 percent of nursing home residents had some degree of cognitive impairment.[11]

The LifePlans consultant told me that the ease of making claims should be a central reason for choosing one policy over another. He suggests looking for an 800 number and being sure that a representative is available 24 hours a day to answer the phone. Ask the agent how long it takes the company to process the claim and how long it takes to really, truly, put the check in the mail.[12]

The model of insurance you select also affects making claims. If you have an indemnity policy, the money comes to you and you write the checks. Reimbursement sellers have also simplified the procedure by requiring only one claim form a year for each service provider. After that, the provider bills the company, and the client is freed even from checkbook management.

Here is where care managers become valuable. Perhaps the wary consumer suspects that these company-paid care managers are actually gatekeepers, determined to control access to services. Still, your benefits have either daily or weekly limits, so the care manager has little incentive to prevent you from accessing care. A legitimate care manager wants you to have access to the services you need.

In fact, insurers claim that care managers are an inherent protection against provider fraud. They ensure that your provider is licensed, that he or she is not counting a beeper as 24-hour coverage, and that you are being delivered the services for which you are paying.

Choice Six: Affordability

Let's assume that you've selected the policy model you want, chosen the levels of care and settings you prefer, and read the fine print about triggers, features, and claims. Now you must figure out whether you can pay for what you want. If you don't have the premium dollars, it won't matter what special features you choose.

Premium Costs

Being able to deduct some or all of your premiums from your income taxes is enticing, and the feds have instituted this feature to induce us all to buy private long-term care coverage. Each year, Congress makes motions about increasing the deductibility feature. In the meantime, however, much of the cost for individual taxpayers will be out-of-pocket. Yet there are ways to reduce your premiums without giving up the features you want in your policy. Read on.

First a warning: Avoid the so-called "great deal" you may see advertised in a flyer. Who wouldn't want to save 20 percent or even 30 percent on long-term care coverage? It would be like finding money under the mattress. Unfortunately, poor underwriting often supports these great discounts. Think about it; if the company offers deep discounts to every customer, will it have the money left to pay its bill when it becomes due? You'll need to weigh the discount against the stability of the company—look at Chapter 10 for a discussion about evaluating companies.

Rate Stability

Insurers stress that they are offering you rate stability. To some extent, this claim is true. Once you're insured, even the first signs of Parkinson's won't affect your individual premium. Any premium increase will affect the class of buyers to which you belong. You can't be singled out. In other words, let's say you purchased your policy 10 years ago, when you were 60 years old. Now the insurance company deems it appropriate to raise rates. All policyholders who bought their policies 10 years ago at age 60, like you did, will be charged the same increase in premiums.

Some insurers take pride in the fact that they have never raised rates from the time they started to write long-term care insurance. But that's only half the story. Insurers don't tell you that they often offer a new policy series with a few new bells and whistles, then raise premiums because of these added benefits. So long as insurers are writing new business at an increasing rate and new business keeps rolling through the door, there will be funds available to pay claims. The premiums from the new policyholders will be used to pay the claims of the older policyholders.

Don't be lulled into a false sense of security by rate guarantees, then. Underwriters are prohibited from raising the premiums during the rate guarantee period, but what if they sustain poor claims experience and must pay out more benefits than they have predicted? If that happens, underwriters will sock it to the policyholders at the end of the rate period.

Get ready to duck.

Let's say you are 10 years older than your brother, who is now about to buy his own long-term care insurance policy. There is no guarantee that today, when your brother decides to buy the same benefits you bought at his age, his premium will be the same as the premiums paid for your original policy. As we've seen, there may now be a new policy series that requires a higher premium for all applicants age 60. Or the rates for all age groups during the year you purchased your policy may now reflect higher rates—or maybe they've stayed the same because of competitive pressure.

Clearly, it is difficult to speculate on future premiums when insurers do not provide lifetime guarantees. You run the risk of ending up with an increased premium for long-term care when you're retired and living on a fixed income. If that happens you have three options: You can pay the increased premium, you can cancel the policy, or you can continue paying the same premium but for reduced benefits. Most policyholders, but especially seniors, will not want to consider replacement policies since these will be based on their current age at higher premiums and will require current evidence of insurability that could be a difficult hurdle to overcome.

If you look hard enough, you might find a policy that gives you at least a five-year rate guarantee. Why can't the industry guarantee premiums beyond 10 years? The industry response is that they can't see the future, and it would be poor actuarial policy to anticipate the changes in long-term care beyond 10 years in the future. Unfortunately, unless insurers are prepared to offer lifetime premium guarantees the way life insurance companies do with their customers, buying long-term care insurance will remain a risky product for consumers.

Pay Once Yearly

You may not save money by paying only once a year, but you won't be hit with a surcharge, either. Some insurance companies will charge you if you choose a monthly or even twice-yearly pay schedule.

Accelerated Payments

Insurers have developed several ways to encourage you to pay for your long-term care policy during your working years, when you're most likely to have the cash. If you choose this option, you may make as few as 10 payments over 10 years. What if you can't keep up these payments? If you bought the "nonforfeiture" or "shortened benefit period" options, you will still have some benefit credits left if you need to make a claim. However, these benefits are likely to be too small, considering inflation, to do you much good.

Discounts

How else can you save some money up front on your premium? Check out these options:

BUY HEALTHY

Some companies offer a preferred rate to people whose low risk factors qualify them for coverage. Ask your insurance representative about this possibility. If you have a preexisting condition that increases your premium cost, consider a longer waiting period for that trigger. Or keep shopping for a company that will write you a policy at a standard rate because it is looking to increase its market share.

BUY MARRIED

You may also qualify for a spousal discount, offered if both spouses buy long-term care options. John Hancock Insurance offers an option that considers a surviving spouse paid up if the first spouse dies and the policy has been held for 10 years. You may also find a "benefits transfer" option that will shift benefits from the healthy spouse to the disabled one, if one spouse's benefits are already used up. Just remember that you and your spouse are dipping into the same benefits; you're not being given double coverage.

BUY YOUNG

If you buy your policy between the ages of 50 and 60, you'll end up spending far less for the coverage than if you wait until age 75. Look at the math:

Age	Daily Benefit	Annual Premium	Years to 85	Total Paid to Age 85
55	$160	$1,497	30	$44,910
65	$160	$3,034	20	$60,680
75	$160	$7,758	10	$77,580

This chart assumes simple 5 percent inflation and a 90-day waiting period.

Why do you pay so much less when you buy at a young age? To some extent, you're self-funding your policy. Insurers are willing to sell at lower premiums, also, because they calculate that you may let the policy lapse before you need the benefits.

Conclusion

The report of the U.S. Department of Labor's working group on long-term care (LTC) says most people "purchase between $100 and $150 a day worth of coverage. Seventy-five percent of those buyers choose comprehensive plans that would include coverage for both facility care and home health care. Furthermore, more than 50 percent of the people purchasing policies from a major LTC insurer are also purchasing inflation protection."[13] You're free to select your own provisions.

Done step-by-step, selecting the long-term care plan that is right for you is like following a flowchart. You determine the features that matter to you, figure out what you can pay, then shop the options.

Here is one last piece of advice on the topic: Get it in writing!

Insurance representatives are not in business to fool you, but circumstances change. Think ahead: Your agent might retire; the company might be sold and the policy provisions changed; what's "commonly done" may not be what is written in the policy. If you've been promised a benefit that is not specified in the insurance policy, make sure that you have a document, signed by an authorized representative or an officer of the company, which explains exactly what you understand to be the case. Otherwise, no matter how much you insist, plead, and yell, you may not be able to claim the payout on judgment day.

Endnotes

1. Interview with Marc A. Cohen, vice president of LifePlans, Inc., June 1, 2001.
2. Ibid.
3. LifePlans, Inc. *The Use of Nursing-Home and Assisted Living Facilities Among Privately Insured and Non-Privately Insured Disabled Elders.* Final Report to the Department of Health and Human Services' Office of Disability, Aging, and Long-Term Care Policy and the Robert Wood Johnson Foundation for Home Care Research Initiatives, April 2000. p. 8.
4. Ibid.
5. Interview with Lisa McAree, managing general agent, May 23, 2001.
6. Lankford, Kimberly. "Arm Yourself While You Can." *Kiplinger's*, March 2001. p. 98.
7. UnumProvident long-term care policy glossary.
8. Ibid.
9. *The Shopper's Guide to Long-Term Care Insurance.* National Association of Insurance Commissioners. p. 18.
10. LifePlans, Inc. p. 10.
11. Ibid. p. 12.
12. Marc Cohen interview.
13. *Report, Findings, and Recommendations of the Working Group on Long-Term Care.* U.S. Department of Labor, Advisory Council on Employee Welfare and Pension Benefits, November 14, 2000. p. 16.

CHAPTER 4

Current Tax Considerations: Insurability Does Not Always Mean Deductibility

What Does the IRS Have to Say about Paying for Your Old Age?

The Internal Revenue Service has opinions about how some of us should pay for our long-term care. Some of these opinions may surprise you. But if you didn't realize that you might be able to deduct a percentage of your premiums for long-term care insurance, you're not alone. Many long-term care policy purchasers do not think about whether their policies are tax-qualified. Indeed, almost one-third didn't even know about the possibility that premiums might be deductible, according to a study by LifePlans, Inc. for the Health Insurance Association of America.[1] While the feds have not done a terrific job of public relations, they certainly want you to know that your long-term care is most likely going to be your problem, not the government's.

To put it bluntly, free ongoing long-term care is not an entitlement for most of us, despite Social Security, Medicare, and Medicaid. To understand where long-term care fits into your planning, you need to look at the provisions of the Health Insurance Portability and Accountability Act of 1996, called HIPAA, which marked a turning point in the federal government's attitude toward medical and hospital payments. The Act's purpose, at least in part, was to use subtle means to encourage consumers to pay more of their own long-term care expenses so that Uncle Sam could pay less. We are all too familiar with the shortcomings of medical care delivery in the current environment, which includes limitations on lengths of hospital stays, the growth of health maintenance organizations (HMOs) and gatekeepers, and the need for referrals to specialists for the smallest of problems.

Most readers of this book will not qualify for Medicaid. To receive this government assistance, your assets and income must be below a level set by your state; perhaps you may not choose or be legally able to spend down enough of your money to reach the qualification thresholds. Medicare pays for only 10 percent of nursing home care, and this is usually skilled nursing care after a hospitalization. Even if you stay at home in your very old age, Medicare covers only limited services from skilled providers.

Therefore, many Americans, ineligible for Medicaid, must confront the looming future expense of long-term care. Congress included long-term care sections in HIPAA because it was clear that private insurance could help Americans pay for their future care. Congress sweetened the private insurance option for individuals and corporations by tinkering with the tax code. It reasoned that if some or all of the insurance premiums became deductible, and some or all of the benefits were untaxed, more people would buy the product. Grandpa, his children, and his grandchildren could ease their way out from the governmental lap and into long-term self-sufficiency.

Tax laws are by their nature confusing. That is why tax guides are such important resources. This chapter is only a glance at the complexity of the tax laws regarding long-term care premiums and benefits. These laws vary for individual and corporate purchasers, but all include provisions to deduct premium payments, and all offer benefits that may or may not be excludable from income. For guidance and direction as to how current laws can impact your situation you should consult your tax counsel as well.

Individual Long-Term Care Policies

Long-term care policies are either tax-qualified or non-tax-qualified. A tax-qualified policy, as its title suggests, offers some important advantages when you file your Form 1040 every April 15, including the opportunity to deduct a portion of the premium costs and not consider the payments as income when you receive the benefits. There is substantial uncertainty about whether non-tax-qualified policies offer the same benefits.

Deductions? Tax-free income? Why even think twice?

Actually, experts suggest you give your choice careful consideration. Tax-qualified plans, while they allow you to deduct your premiums and will not tax your benefits, may in some cases require that you be more disabled than a non-tax-qualified plan. You'll need to be what the IRS calls "chronically ill" to make a claim for the benefits, and you must use "qualified long-term care services," which might include diagnosis, rehabilitation, treatment, curative or preventive services, that are prescribed by a "licensed health care practitioner."

Table 4.1 gives us a closer look at the differences between the two types of long-term care policies, as suggested in a Commonwealth of Massachusetts pamphlet created for the Division of Insurance in 1999.[2]

A significant difference between tax-qualified and non-tax-qualified plans lies in the definitions of many of the words in Table 4.1. You may think you understand

TABLE 4.1 Two Different Long-Term Care Policies

Tax-Qualified Plans	Non-Tax-Qualified Plans
You may deduct your premium payment if your unreimbursed medical expenses are more than 7.5 percent of your adjusted gross income. Deductibility of these premiums depends on the age of the individual as well as inflation, measured by the consumer price index. A forty-year-old in 2001 may deduct up to $230; his or her 71-year-old grandfather may deduct up to $2,860 for the same policy. The deductible amounts are limits. If the premium is less than the limit, the most that can be deducted is the actual premium.	Forget deducting your premium costs. Premiums are not deductible.
You don't have to claim your long-term care benefits as income on your tax form. In 2001, you may receive up to $200 per day without paying taxes, and more if you can prove that your expenses exceed the cap.	You may have to claim the payments as income.
The triggers that allow benefit payments can be much more restrictive. You must need "substantial assistance" with as many as two of the six possible ADLs to qualify. Read the fine print for the definition of "substantial assistance." There are seven ADLs in California, and one of these triggers may be especially difficult to justify.	There may be varying combinations of benefit triggers, and you may need to satisfy more than two of them. Group policies can use any number of standards.
Cognitive impairment is a trigger if you need "substantial supervision"— again, read the definitions carefully.	You may not need the same level of supervision to receive benefits.
"Medical necessity" is not a trigger for benefits.	Policies may use the term "medical necessity" or a similar measure of disability as a trigger for benefits.
Your disability must be expected to last for at least 90 days.	You may not have to be disabled for 90 days.

what a disability is, what constitutes assistance, or what is indicative of medical necessity. Like most government documents, the word choice matters. Someone with a Ph.D. in English would have trouble parsing HIPAA's nouns and adjectives.

First of all, tax-qualified plans must use definitions for benefit triggers that are established by law, whereas non-tax-qualified plans may define terms in any way the company pleases. While the Glossary at the end of this book defines many of the terms in detail, let's look at an example of the potential for confusion. In a non-tax-qualified plan, to have a disability may mean that due to a sickness, injury, or advanced age, you are cognitively impaired or else you cannot perform two or more ADLs without "standby assistance." These activities of daily living include bathing, dressing, toileting, transferring, continence, eating, and, in California, ambulating. In a tax-qualified plan, disability is defined more strictly, although insurers do not always follow this definition strictly. The tax-qualified plan requires that you be unable to perform at least two ADLs without "substantial assistance." If you have a cognitive impairment, you are eligible for benefits if you require "substantial supervision" to protect you or others from threats to health and safety due to that cognitive impairment.

Collecting your benefits also varies between the two plans. In a non-tax-qualified plan, you might be able to prove "medical necessity" just by presenting a note from your doctor certifying that it is medically necessary for you to receive a service at home that you are unable to perform on your own. Suppose, for example, that you are a diabetic and need daily insulin shots, but are unable to give them to yourself. You have a non-tax-qualified plan that counts "medical necessity" as a benefit trigger. Your doctor writes a letter stipulating that you cannot administer your own insulin, and the insurance company has no choice but to count this inability as a benefit trigger. Medical necessity as the determining factor in receiving benefits is sometimes used as a sales tool to justify the sale of a non-qualified policy, but it should not be the main reason for selecting that type of contract. Company claim departments are hard-pressed to provide significant claims data or scenarios where the medical necessity was the determining factor in paying a claim.

In 2001, sales of non-tax-qualified plans totaled less than 10 percent of policies sold. And since there is no standardization of non-tax-qualified plans, you must do your homework very carefully before you buy, or you could be disappointed when you try to collect your benefits.

The tax-qualified and non-tax-qualified plans may also define "assistance" differently, both in terms of qualifying for benefits and in including them as part of your benefit package. Distinguishing between "substantial supervision" as required for tax-qualified plans and "standby assistance" in non-tax-qualified plans requires a steady eye and patience.

Tax-qualified plans require substantial supervision for at least two ADLs to qualify for benefits. Some insurers have liberalized that requirement to include the term "standby assistance," which means having a person within arm's reach while you are bathing, dressing, or carrying out any of the other ADLs. There are some insurers who make the "standby assistance" benefit available for an additional premium, while others do not make it available at all.

A "licensed health care practitioner" may also be somewhat different in the two plans, since a tax-qualified policy requires certification by any physician, any registered professional nurse, licensed social worker, or other individual who meets such requirements as may be prescribed by the Secretary of the Treasury. If your spouse is not a close friend of the Treasury Secretary, his or her passionate avowal that you need long-term care may not qualify you for treatment under a tax-qualified plan.

Grandfathered Policies

If you bought a long-term care policy before 1997, you're in luck, since these policies were grandfathered by HIPAA. They automatically receive the favorable treatment of the tax-qualified plans. However, beware making any changes in your policy if the tax deduction is a major motivator for you. HIPAA lists a carefully structured set of "permissible changes" to your existing long-term care policy; if you go beyond this list, you could lose the tax-qualified status. You may:

- Change the frequency of your payment schedule—from yearly to quarterly, for instance.
- Suffer an increase in premiums across your class or, more rarely, enjoy a decrease.
- Get a discount on your premium when your spouse buys a policy, too.
- Reduce your coverage and pay a lower premium.
- Enjoy a premium reduction if you become entitled to a group discount through an organization or association.
- Add alternative forms of benefits if they do not increase your premium.
- Add a rider to increase benefits if the rider fulfills the tax-qualified requirements.
- Delete a rider that bars you from coordinating benefits with Medicare.
- Convert or continue your coverage under a group contract.
- Change insurers in an "assumption reinsurance transaction."
- Exercise any rights in your contract that were in effect on December 31, 1996, as well as any right required by state law.

Individuals who buy long-term care policies that are tax-qualified and who file a long form tax return (Form 1040) and itemize deductions may deduct a portion of the premiums according to their age. Table 4.2 illustrates the amount of the deductions available in 2001 for tax-qualified policies.

Even the smallest deduction sounds good, but look again. If you don't item-

TABLE 4.2 Deductions Available for 2002

Age of Insured	Limitation on Deduction
40 or younger	$ 240
41 to 50	$ 450
51 to 60	$ 900
61 to 70	$2,390
71 or older	$2,990

ize your deductions, these tax breaks won't be of any help. If, as a senior, you have paid off your mortgage and your other income information is uncomplicated, you may decide to forgo the individual deductions and just take the standard deduction. Hence deductibility won't mean much to you.

And don't forget the 7.5 percent threshold on medical and dental deductions. Hopefully, you will not be sick enough, or uninsured enough, to reach that 7.5 percent threshold, but then you also won't enjoy the long-term care premium deduction, either. In fact, there is a catch-22 for many seniors who have major uninsured costs for prescription drugs. The cost of their prescriptions could put them over the 7.5 percent deductibility threshold. Unfortunately, these prescriptions might also reflect conditions that may make them ineligible for long-term care insurance.

Benefits in a tax-qualified plan are also not considered as income. In 2002, benefits from a tax-qualified indemnity plan are tax-free up to $210 a day, and the figure may be increased in future years for inflation. If you spend more than that on unreimbursed long-term care costs, those benefits are also tax-free. Read the small print in your non-tax-qualified plan carefully, however, because the benefits will be considered income and will be taxable on tax day unless the policies were grandfathered.

Changing the deductibility laws for long-term care premiums may cause a short-term revenue shortfall, but will have the long-term positive impact of making coverage available for many more Americans. That's why lawmakers need to recognize that transferring the burden of funding long-term care to the insurers is vitally important. Some state governments are also offering tax incentives to employers who contribute to group long-term care policies. Stay tuned to the news for future developments.

Charitable Gift Annuity

As we reach retirement, many of us look for ways to give something back to the organizations that supported us throughout our lives. We truly want to support the school, hospital, research project, and civic or religious organization. Yet we must also consider our spouses' and our own potential long-term care expenses, and therefore we are limited to making an annual donation to our favorite cause.

But for those who have a net worth of a million dollars or more and have most of our assets, from stocks to IRAs, invested in fixed-income instruments, there is another possibility: a charitable gift annuity.

A charitable gift annuity is a contract between a donor and a charity in which the donor transfers cash, securities, or mutual funds to a hospital, for example, and the hospital guarantees a fixed income for life. It allows the wealthy donor to support the causes he or she values. Development offices say that this type of annuity works well for potential donors who are starting to express concern that their potential long-term care expenses will impact their ability to support their favorite charities.

In a two-step process, that concern is removed with the charitable gift annuity that can also be used to fund a long-term care insurance policy.

Step one: Let's say that a couple, ages 72 and 70, wants to set up a charitable gift annuity to benefit their favorite cause or charity. They give $500,000 under the provisions of this annuity. During their lifetimes, the funds are under the control of the charitable organization, who often appoints a custodian to fulfill its obligation to the donors.

The donors have the satisfaction of helping a cause dear to them. They are also guaranteed an annual income of 6.7 percent of the gift as long as they live.[3] If one spouse dies, the surviving spouse is guaranteed the same income for his or her lifetime. When the second spouse dies, all the interest payments cease and the designated organization has use of the gift.

Also, when the original gift is made, the donors may take a portion of the gift amount as a tax deduction for that year. For income tax purposes, for a predetermined number of years thereafter on a sliding scale, the fixed amount of income due the donor is allocated between a return of principal with no tax consequences and an amount considered ordinary income subject to income tax.

Step two: A $500,000 total long-term care insurance benefit (that is, $250,000 for each spouse) currently requires an annual premium of 1.1 percent of this $500,000 gift to the organization. Arrangements can be made so that the custodian pays the income from the charitable gift annuity monthly, quarterly, or annually. At the same time, the custodian can directly pay the long-term care insurance premium.

The bottom line: The couple can receive an annual income from the charitable gift annuity of 5.6 percent, while also funding their long-term care insurance coverage. In addition, if either spouse makes a claim, the waiver of premium feature in the long-term care insurance policy becomes operative. In this case, no premium is required so long as the spouse on claim is disabled. Hence the annual income payable to the donor is increased.

What if the donor is single? A similar process occurs, but the rate of return is of course higher, because only one long-term care premium is funded. Also, the organization no longer has to pay interest to a surviving spouse and there-fore enjoys the full benefits of the charitable gift even sooner.

In summary, then, if the donor dies prematurely or even as a result of a long-term illness, he or she will have helped the organization and also taken care of his or her own needs.

As attractive as this type of arrangement appears, it is very unusual. The agent is often reluctant to recommend a charitable gift annuity that supports a long-term care insurance policy or a life insurance policy, for that matter. Agents know that clients often resent being told what to do with their money, especially if the suggestion is not directly related to insurance. Clients may be-lieve that the only reason the agent mentions a charitable gift annuity of this type is to generate an additional commission.

Therefore, it is important that the charity itself encourage its patrons to consider using a charitable gift annuity in this fashion. The arrangement is a win-win. But without an alert from the charity, many donors who might adopt the annuity will not even know of its existence.

Tax Treatment of Corporate Long-Term Care Policies

Tax treatment of long-term care policies purchased by corporations is also fa-vorable, again because Uncle Sam wants to shift the purchase responsibility to the taxpayer and away from the government. To encourage more corporations to offer their employees long-term care insurance, the IRS says that these companies may generally deduct a portion if not the entire cost of the pre-mium as a business expense. Even in these days of stock market uncertainty, most corporations are far more able to assume the risk of premium changes than are the individuals who need the policies.

Long-term care insurance, in other words, is becoming a valued fringe bene-fit even for the youngest employees. While HIPAA does not prohibit preferen-tial treatment for managers and officers, companies with more than 10 employees are frequently offering guaranteed-issue long-term care individual policy coverage even to their employees in staff positions.

Younger employees are starting to learn the value of this benefit. Consider a 32-year-old secretary who already receives life insurance as a perk of her job. She doesn't feel she needs life insurance and probably wouldn't have bought it, but it comes with the job. Now her company, which provides life insurance cover-age for at least 10 people, is providing a guaranteed-issue individual long-term care policy through a company such as UnumProvident. This benefit was initially reserved for senior management, or at least those between ages 60 and 65. Now her employer recognizes that savvy young workers are aware of the long-term care issues facing their grandparents and great-grandparents and recognize that long-term care planning is part of overall financial and retirement planning.

Making the benefit even more valuable in that kind of plan is that it is guaranteed. Covered employees do not need to take a physical exam, answer questions on the phone, or be evaluated for cognitive impairment. As long as they are actively at work on the date of the application for the insurance, they will qualify for the benefits. Granted, had the young employee felt like shopping for her own coverage, she might have selected a long-term care insurance plan whose provisions she liked better. But as her mother taught her, why look a gift horse in the mouth? She is happy to accept the long-term care coverage just as she accepted the life insurance policy.

Tax Treatment by Corporate Type

In the cases of self-employed individuals, sole proprietors, partners, and more than 2 percent shareholders in S corporations, a percentage of the eligible premiums may be deducted as a business expense, with the same age variables as in individual policies. And the rest of the premium may be combined with medical expenses and then deducted, as long as the total of these expenses is more than 7.5 percent of adjusted gross income.

A self-employed person is allowed to deduct a percentage of the eligible premiums he or she contributes for a tax-qualified plan. This deduction is subject to the age-based chart in Table 4.2, and falls under the category of a business expense. Again, the percentage increases as the client ages and as years pass.

Here are the premium deductibility limits for self-employed individuals and small businesses. These figures include owners, partners, shareholders, and their spouses:

Year	Deductibility Limit
2001	60%
2002	70%
2003 and later	100%

What this means is that Dr. John, the sole proprietor of his medical practice, may deduct as a business expense up to 60 percent of the cost of his long-term care premium subject to the limits for his age (see Table 4.2). The other 40 percent is deductible if he is unlucky enough to have spent more than 7.5 percent of his adjusted gross income on medical expenses. His wife's coverage and any dependent coverage are subject to the same guidelines when the long-term care insurance premiums are paid for by the practice as a business expense.

If you're an executive in a C corporation, you may enjoy even greater benefits. These corporations may claim the entire premium cost for the employees, their spouses, their dependents, retirees, and retirees' spouses as a business expense. Best of all, the employee does not have to claim the premium cost as income. Let's say that Bob Smith is vice president of Widgets.com, which pays for his long-term care insurance, as well as his wife's. The cost of these premiums is $3,000, all deductible to the company. So Bob enjoys the protection of the insurance without paying Uncle Sam and the IRS as much as 35 percent of the premium cost as additional income. If Bob needs long-term care, the rules applying to individual owners kick in.

This long-term care insurance benefit is so attractive that many employers have devised creative bookkeeping strategies to entice valuable employees to stay on the job. Take a look at this example:

Jack, a 62-year-old systems analyst at Widgets.com decided to opt for early retirement, but his company did not want him to go. From Jack's point of view, the timing was perfect. The values in his pension plan combined with his 401(k) totaled more money than he had ever dreamed of earning. Now, though, he was concerned that the company's money managers were so aggressive that the bottom would fall out of his portfolio before he could enjoy the money. He wanted to be more conservative with his retirement funds by turning them into IRA rollovers.

Besides, Jack had some personal dreams. Ever since he was a youngster, Jack had dreamed of attending a baseball game in the home park of every major league baseball team in the country. There was no better time to do it than now, while he was healthy and wealthy. Jack told his bosses that he was determined to retire.

The company did not want to lose Jack's expertise. The human resources manager offered him a deal. Jack could resign his position as a system's analyst. The company would then rehire him at a salary of $25,000 a year to be available for special projects. Since he would then be on the company payroll, the firm would pay 50 percent of his health insurance not only to age 65, but beyond.

There was one catch. For the past three years, Jack had contributed to the care and support of his mother-in-law, who had suffered a stroke. So far, Mom had stayed in her own home, but Jack knew a nursing home admission was coming. He also knew how much this care would cost. Jack did not want his wife or himself to be in the same position someday. He planned to buy a long-term care insurance policy that would give him generous benefits and inflation coverage, but it would cost $3,200 for both spouses. Could the company contribute to this expense, too?

Before Jack signed on and agreed to the deal, the company controller came up with a creative answer in a new contract for his new status, which made everyone a winner. She told Jack that the best strategy was for the company to pay the $3,200 long-term care insurance premium and pay Jack an annual salary of $21,800. If the company paid the annual premium for Jack's and his wife's long-term care insurance, Jack would have to pay income tax on only $21,800 because under current tax law he did not have to report the $3,200 premium benefit. The company still had a $25,000 deduction, counting Jack's salary and the cost of his policy.

Jack's employer learned a valuable lesson from these negotiations with him. The controller knew that senior executives typically enjoyed long-term care insurance as part of their benefits packages, but the feature had not been offered to other employees. She urged management to make long-term care coverage a standard feature for most employees. However, in arrangements of this nature care should be taken so that the transaction is not considered a cafeteria plan whose tax benefits do not extend to individual long-term care insurance policies.

Ideally, the best way for a corporation to give an existing employee a clear tax benefit is to pay the entire long-term care premium as an additional fringe benefit without any reduction in salary. The law does not require that all company employees enjoy the same long-term care benefits, so management can pick and choose the employees it wants to cover.

When a limited liability company, a partnership, or an S corporation offers long-term care insurance, it may deduct the cost as a business expense. If the employee is not a partner or owns less than a 2 percent interest, the entire premium is deductible to the company. But if the employee is a partner or owns more than 2 percent, the deduction is limited to the rules for self-employed people.

Overall, the point is that that consumers must be sure of the advantages of a tax-qualified long-term care plan before they purchase one. If, when consumers do their homework, they discover that the plan's provisions are so stringent that they fail to qualify despite their perceived need for long-term care, the policy may not be a good one for them. Only someone who knows the complexity of the tax laws and is also familiar with the consumer's individual financial situation and long-term health prospects may be able to give the buyer advice that leads him or her to make an informed decision.

Meanwhile, the insurance industry, which has generated billions of dollars of corporate life insurance, is fast realizing the hidden potential for the sale of corporate-paid long-term care insurance. That's why their advanced underwriting departments are working overtime to develop creative strategies and marketing campaigns aimed at that lucrative market.

Corporate America, get ready. You are the number one prospect of many long-term care insurers.

Hopefully, in the meantime you will realize that there are provisions in the current tax law that might be applicable to your particular situation. That is why it is strongly recommended that you seek advice on any tax issue from a qualified professional tax expert of your own choosing to discuss your eligibility for any potential tax benefit.

Endnotes

1. LifePlans, Inc. *Who Buys Long-Term Care Insurance in 2000: A Decade of Study of Buyers and Non-Buyers.* Prepared for the Health Insurance Association of America, October 2000. p. 28.
2. Massachusetts Division of Insurance. *Your Options for Financing Long-Term Care: A Massachusetts Guide.* December 1999.
3. Gift annuity rate tables, American Council on Gift Annuities, effective July 1, 2001, for joint annuities covering two lives.

CHAPTER 5

Underwriting for Physical Impairments: Playing Underwriting Roulette

One of the repeated messages of this book is that long-term care insurance is not health insurance. Your health care insurer will not cover your nursing home costs, and Medicare's skilled care coverage terminates with day 100. While your Medigap policy may pick up Medicare's deductible for days 21 through 100, you're on your own after that.

Long-term care insurance is not life insurance, either, although the insurance industry prefers that you conceptualize the products in similar terms. In other words, like buying life insurance, buying long-term care insurance means planning for a distant future, whether you're now 40 or a healthy and wealthy senior citizen. While health insurance covers your immediate needs, both life insurance and long-term care insurance demand that you look 10 or more years into the future.

Insurers recognize that they must educate their consumers, especially since the premiums for long-term care at this time will probably come directly out of the customer's own pocket. While the employer may pay all or part of your health care insurance and sometimes all or part of your life insurance, long-term care insurance is a rare employee benefit, especially for small businesses.

The most important distinction between these two kinds of insurance, however, involves the distinction between morbidity and mortality. The state of your physical health may qualify you for one and not for the other.

Satisfying the Underwriter's Rules

Here is an example. Jim is one of the most careful, cautious shoppers I know. When he shopped for an automobile, he studied *Consumer Reports* and *Road and Track*, while analyzing product literature from every major manufacturer. He visited dealers who sold American cars and those who sold foreign cars. After two months of analysis, comparison, and test drives, Jim chose the model that perfectly suited his needs, put down his cash, and hit the road. No buyer remorse for him.

Jim decided to apply the same principles to shopping for long-term care coverage. He comparison shopped online. He asked his high school buddy, a local insurance broker, to come over with some possibilities for him. He studied the brochures he received from AARP, TIAA CREF, and several competing insurance companies. He was determined to buy exactly the policy he wanted and to have no second thoughts afterward. Three months later, Jim decided on a policy with GE Capital, the country's undisputed largest seller of individual long-term care insurance policies. He called the GE Capital agent to put down his cash and plug into the coverage.

In the end, though, Jim couldn't buy a long-term care insurance policy because of what the underwriters learned about him.

The health report sent by Jim's primary care doctor included a small note that Jim seemed to have the slightest tremor in his right thumb. They had been golfing pals for years, and the doctor wrote off the shakiness to Jim's usual high energy. Jim seemed much too young for Parkinson's, the "old person's disease," and had no troubling symptoms. Only a handful of academic medical centers have brain scans sophisticated enough to provide objective measures of Parkinson's, but Jim's doctor never really considered this diagnosis. He just told Jim to relax.

Still, when the GE Capital underwriters saw Jim's medical records, including office notes from a neurologist Jim had forgotten he had been referred to, his application was immediately declined. He must be in the first stages of Parkinson's disease. It did not matter that medications now control virtually all of the early symptoms of Parkinson's. Nor did it matter that Jim was a good athlete who swam 20 laps daily and loved to play golf. And in the end, it didn't matter that Jim had done such a thorough job of shopping for the long-term care policy he wanted. He had a condition that was considered uninsurable by every major, credible long-term care insurance company. The data in his medical records did not qualify him for acceptance by the underwriters.

The agent from GE had to deliver the bad news, not a pleasant task for someone trained to sell insurance and not to play doctor. The home office also had a message for the agent: Why hadn't he himself seen the tremor and terminated the interview? He could have saved himself some time and the company the cost of the underwriting process.

Jim had long and productive years ahead of him. He participated in his employer's life insurance benefit without being individually screened. But he was rejected for long-term care coverage.

This chapter will take a close look at the differences between long-term care insurance qualifications and life insurance qualifications. We'll see that while the life insurance industry estimates primarily your risk of a premature death, the long-term care insurer is concerned with your functionality and stability.

The life insurance underwriter wants you to live a very long time, pay lots of premiums, and then let your policy lapse. If you must collect the death benefits, the underwriter hopes the check will come to your beneficiaries only after your premiums have contributed mightily to the company's coffers. The long-term care underwriter wants you to buy the coverage when you're between 40 and 60, then to stay functional, stable, and controlled until you are 80, paying premiums all along. Then, ideally, you'll die suddenly, never making a claim.

Death, like taxes, is a certainty; but long-term care needs are not. That's mortality versus morbidity in a nutshell.

Health Insurance: In Sickness and in Health

Let's look again at what you're buying with your health care premium. Whether you belong to an HMO or an indemnity plan, you have coverage for hospitalization, doctor's visits, and other benefits. Some but certainly not all plans will pay a part of your prescription drug costs. (If you don't know whether you have prescription drug coverage, put your bookmark on this page right now and check out your policy!) You probably have a deductible, and you may have had a waiting period before your health care insurance took effect. You may also make co-payments for many services, including hospitalization and doctor's visits.

Your health care coverage may be a benefit of your job, in which case your employer is kicking in some of the cost of the premiums. Or you may have bought the policy through an affinity group, such as your professional association or AARP. In any case, the likelihood is that after a brief waiting period, your family's and your coverage was automatic. The insurance company knows that it can afford to take its chances with you—the company's risk is so widely spread that your particular health issues may not break the bank. Your health care premiums will undoubtedly go up yearly, though, whether or not you are healthy or ill. Neither HMOs nor indemnity insurers (nor, incidentally, the federal government's Medicare or Medicaid programs) seem able to control the rising costs of health care.

Life Insurance: Considerations of Mortality— Till Death Us Do Part

You probably know about health care insurance because you've been managing the co-payments and deductibles for some time. Maybe you're also familiar with life insurance since your employer has shared its cost with you. In this case, you may choose the amount of life insurance you want, perhaps as a multiple of your yearly salary.

If you have life insurance sold through your employer, you may not even have needed to have an insurance physical. You and your dependents were guaranteed coverage, so long as you were actively at work when the insurance was in effect. You didn't need a telephone or a face-to-face interview with an examiner. Just about every insurer who sells group life insurance offers a guaranteed issue benefit.

Individual life insurance policies operate differently. You have to qualify physically. The life insurance underwriters are looking at your mortality; they estimate your normal life expectancy by studying actuarial tables, which relate to your physical condition. If the statistics for your age, gender, and physical condition suggest you have many productive years of paying premiums ahead of you, the company will sell you a life insurance policy.

In practice this means that you may be able to buy life insurance even if you have osteoporosis, because the underwriters assume that the condition won't kill until you've paid years and years of premiums. If, however, you have stage two breast cancer, you may find buying life insurance difficult. But if you have a medical condition that suggests to the underwriter that you have the slightest risk of dying prematurely, expect that your premiums will have surcharges on them. The company must protect itself against the chance that you will leave your heirs a large death benefit before it has collected premiums to cover its payout.

To demonstrate the state of your health to the life insurance issuer, you filled out an application, had a medical examination that involved blood tests for AIDS and other blood chemistries, a urinalysis, and possibly an electrocardiogram, chest X ray, and stress test if the benefit amount is high enough. If the insurer was satisfied that you had a long life ahead of you, your policy was approved for issue.

Long-Term Care Coverage: A Bet on Your Morbidity— For Better or Worse

Just as you have to make an educated guess about the long-term state of your health when you consider long-term care insurance, the insurance company is also taking a gamble. Don't forget: You may not even need long-term care! Even given the direst of statistical estimates, that 60 percent of us will need long-term care at some point in our lives, 40 percent of us will not. Besides, you may not need long-term care long enough to recover the cost of your years of premiums. If you buy the coverage, you're a downside better. A nursing home bed or a home health aide may not be in your future.

Also, as of this writing, few employers chip in for long-term care insurance, although the benefit has tremendous value for even the youngest employees. Why don't more employers offer the benefit? Perhaps because their young workers aren't educated to see its value. For instance, a newly married 23-year-old may appreciate that a group life insurance benefit would help his or her spouse put their future kids through college, but the young adult may ignore the hustling insurance agent who warns about the risk of falling on the ski slope. Why think in depressing terms about injury and even paralysis? Skiing is supposed to be fun.

Besides, there are few long-term care plans that offer guaranteed enrollment for individual policies. Insurers know that there is little actuarial benefit in offering such policies, since the risk is not spread sufficiently to cover every potential claim. With guaranteed issue there are no health questions to answer and no requirements of a physical examination or personal interview. These policies come with strict eligibility guidelines that require a certain number of employees and limit coverage for those from age 60 to 65. Group coverage tends to be more liberal, as either the entire workforce is covered or segments of employee categories with more than 10 employees are insured.

Sickly or Healthy

Now that you understand the distinction between mortality and morbidity, you see why a single insurance company views you with one microscope for life insurance and another for long-term care coverage. In both cases, the company underwriters must figure out what your risk is to the company—how likely it is that you will claim benefits without paying years of premiums.

Even if you've recently had a life insurance physical, you'll need additional scrutiny for long-term care coverage. MetLife, like all the quality insurers who market the product, constantly trains company agents and brokers to do what's good for consumers while at the same time providing underwriting insights to producers. The company wants the producers to be well equipped to expedite the underwriting process and eliminate unnecessary expenditures.

Sandy DeMartino is MetLife's underwriting manager for individual long-term care. A registered nurse, she conducts training sessions that reflect the kind of training that successful insurers employ. Some of these sessions are video-taped, then sent to the field force and used to develop brokerage business.

To help agents and brokers distinguish between the underwriting differences present in life insurance and long-term care insurance, DeMartino says that while MetLife might accept the results of a life insurance screening from its own underwriters, the long-term care division will probably ask the life underwriter for details of the patient's condition.[1]

Get the message here: You have to pass one test for life insurance and another for long-term care.

Insurers do not expect that you will be the bionic man or woman. They know that some people over 40, and most over 60, have chronic health concerns, according to DeMartino. If everyone with any medical concern were eliminated from long-term care considerations, the product would not exist. So, says DeMartino, insurers don't ask, "Is this person totally healthy?" They ask, "Is this person healthy or sickly?"

This is a tricky concept. Your doctor may have one opinion, while the insurance underwriter has another. Your doctor sees you at your yearly physical, gives you a flu shot, and suggests aspirin for your occasional ache or pain. Often he or she just pats you on the shoulder, reassures you that you're fine, and sends you on your way. If that ache in your foot has a 5 percent chance of turning into chronic arthritis, your doctor may mention the possibility to you, reminding you that 95 percent favorable odds are more than pretty good. If your doctor suggests you have a blood test because you are complaining of fatigue, he or she is just being cautious. You're healthy.

Unfortunately, you're "sickly" to the long-term care underwriters. Maybe your doctor told you to forget about the 5 percent chance you are developing arthritis; but the long-term care underwriter says, "Hold on! Our data tells us that a 5 percent chance at 40 means a 40 percent chance later. We can't sell you long-term care coverage." Your blood test turned out to be negative? That's good news to you, but the underwriter says, "Why was that test ordered? Are you supposed to be doing a follow-up test? What is your doctor watching for?" Your application drops into the "pending" file until you take a follow-up test.

It's not that long-term care insurance underwriters expect you to be free of chronic medical conditions. They know that most people think about long-term care if they have a personal experience with the need, either within their own families or through a personal medical scare. Insurers want to be sure that any condition you have is now stable and managed, showing no progression. They are not interested in your life expectancy; they are evaluating your prospects for staying free of care.

The issue isn't how long you live; it's how functional you are while you are alive.

Playing the Odds: Figuring Out Your Functionality

The measure of your functionality isn't left to the whim of the insurance company. Insurance company examiners use a legal set of measures to determine just how near you are to needing long-term care assistance.

The Activities of Daily Living

In practice, insurers determine your functionality by asking about your ability to manage the activities of daily living—bathing, dressing, eating, toileting, transferring, and continence—and cognitive impairment. These activities are ordained by law and set in stone. There is no negotiating them.

They are also the triggers that prompt the payment of long-term care benefits, and you need to demonstrate disability in only two of them to make a claim. DeMartino says that any applicant with one disability in an ADL is automatically disqualified for insurance coverage.

Look at Chapter 2 for more discussion of the ADLs. Since the most subtle and most difficult to diagnose trigger is cognitive impairment, a whole chapter of this book has been devoted to that subject (Chapter 7). The cognitive impairment test is also part of the paramedical survey found in Appendix D.

Instrumental Activities of Daily Living

Insurers also employ a second measure of functionality, the client's ability to fulfill the instrumental activities of daily living. These include telephoning, bill paying, grocery shopping, cooking, doing laundry, taking medicine, and housekeeping. You will also find these instrumental activities in the long-term care paramedical survey.

If you've spent much of your life eating out and avoiding the washing machine, it may seem strange that the ability to carry out these activities is a measure of your physical well-being. The underwriters also acknowledge that the instrumental ADLs tend to be biased toward women, who are of course the majority of nursing home residents and the largest pool of long-term care buyers. Nonetheless, insurers argue that they have good reason for insisting on these assessments of functionality.

Who cares if you do your own laundry or use the telephone? Sandy DeMartino's explanation to the insurance representatives in her class is instructive here. First of all, the instrumental ADLs have significant predictive value; they are "indicators of functionality and predictive of the ability to maintain an independent lifestyle." Long-term care underwriters believe, according to DeMartino, that a client who has trouble with one of the instrumental ADLs is "coming close" to needing assistance with a basic ADL.

The thinking goes this way: Mr. Jones, a widower, doesn't use the telephone much anymore. Either he can't see the keypad, even though the numbers are enlarged, or he can't manage the small motions of hitting the buttons. How will he call for help if he needs it? How will he make a doctor's appointment or make plans for dinner? He's going to stop socializing. He can't even call a taxi. But can he punch a number his son programmed on the phone's speed-dialer? If so, he's still in the game.

Can Mr. Jones write his own checks and balance his checkbook? No? Well, maybe Mrs. Jones always wrote the checks. Mr. Agent, just put that fact on the application.

But why isn't Mr. Jones signing his own checks or looking through the bills that are piling up on his dining room table? Is he now unable to read the print? Does he not understand what the bills say?

Strike one.

Mr. Jones does not go to the grocery store; but then, he never did. His wife always did the food shopping. It's not that Mr. Jones has trouble with the long aisles or that he can't drive himself anymore. When he needs to get a ride, he calls his daughter-in-law. He knows how to get himself to the doctor and he knows how to get to McDonald's. Besides, he does a good job of popping prepared food into the microwave.

He's still in the game.

Mr. Jones is also scrupulous about his prescription pills. He fills the pill boxes lined up on his kitchen table once a week, and carefully takes the day's ration. He still manages his health.

What about laundry? Mrs. Jones always took care of such wifely household tasks. Since she has died, Mr. Jones is letting his clothes go. He looks slovenly and unkempt, and his friends aren't as eager to keep him company.

Strike two.

And now that we're visiting Mr. Jones, we realize that his house is also dirty. The dishes are still on the table, and there are several weeks' worth of old newspapers on the floor in the living room.

Strike three for Mr. Jones.

He is out of the ball game.

Fact-Finding

The agent found it easy to eliminate Mr. Jones. The three strikes were obvious. But typically insurers need more time to evaluate the "health or sickliness" of their applicants.

Each potential policyholder must undergo an established process of medical fact-finding, the stages of which are determined by the applicant's age and personal health history, and the field agent's observations. Some applicants, typically the youngest ones, need only fill out the field application and authorize their doctor's report to buy long-term care coverage. Others may require a focused phone interview to talk about a specific medical condition that has caught the underwriter's attention. If your condition raises more than a minor red flag, your phone interview will be longer and more invasive, as the interviewer tries to clear up discrepancies on your application. Finally, as we have seen, your signature on the application authorizes the insurer to query any cardiologist, neurologist, psychiatrist, or other specialist it chooses to assess your condition. You may have to have additional laboratory tests or another physical examination.

The Field Interview Form

The form is step one, and everyone takes it. In fact, the agent takes this information partly to qualify you as a client, having been instructed by the underwriters not to forward a long-term care application that is obviously not going

to be approved. When you fill out the extensive check-off she[...]
your health, the insurance representative is looking for indicatio[...]
are already disabled in one of the ADLs or instrumental ADLs. The[...]
terview forms may vary slightly, but they all are considered a valuable u[...]
writing tool.

One purpose of the field interview form is to get your take on your health. The company wants to know how you feel today, compared to a year ago. Improving health, after all, will keep you out of long-term care. Do you have medical tests or even surgeries pending? Your insurer wants to know.

The Conseco form, for instance, asks about specific conditions, the automatic disqualifiers that will be considered more fully in the next chapter. Say yes to these, and the underwriter will say no to your long-term insurance. The interview form also looks for indications that you are losing functionality, specifically whether you need supervision with any of the ADLs. A yes answer also means your agent cannot submit your application.

Then the questions move into indirect evaluation. Have you seen a physician for numbness (think stroke), unexplained weight loss (think cancer), fainting or falling (think stroke), skin ulcers (diabetes), tremor (Parkinson's)? Have you had joints replaced (think arthritis)? Have any medical or diagnostic procedures been recommended? Do you have symptoms that have gone undiagnosed? Have you been hospitalized, been treated in the emergency room, stayed in a nursing home? Has another company denied you long-term care coverage? A yes answer to any of these questions will worry your underwriter and prompt follow-up phone conversation.

You'll be asked about your medications, especially if they have changed. Assume that the long-term care underwriter will match your prescription list against your check sheet of conditions and pick up the phone if the lists don't match. Are you taking blood pressure medication although you haven't listed hypertension on your application form? Your call will come.

Don't assume, however, that a yes answer to any of these questions will automatically prevent you from buying long-term care coverage. Remember the rule: If your condition is well managed, stable, and not progressive, you may still make the underwriter smile. Read the next chapter concerning preexisting and troublesome conditions to see what the insurer might say to you even if you say yes.

Your insurance representative is on a fact-finding mission. DeMartino instructs her audience that the more information they can gather about their clients, the more informed will be the decisions of the underwriters. She suggests insurance agents look at the prescription bottles, ask about falls, gather a list of doctors and specialists, and check the house for canes, walkers, or wheelchairs. If you don't fancy this type of inspection, meet the agent at his or her office instead.

Warn your primary care doctor to expect a questionnaire about you. If you

...et describing
...s that you
...field in-
...nder-

your specialists may also get a letter. Every doctor
...formation; but since the premiums for long-term
...life insurance, the long-term care underwriter of-
...primary care doctor.

...ur physicians have a significant influence over
...for instance, the casual notation of a tremor re-
...n care coverage, even though the doctor, his old
...im. Perhaps he did not want to use the dreaded
...kinson's, since Jim was too young to fit the disease profile. Perhaps
the doctor wrote off the tremor as just another symptom of Jim's natural inten-
sity. Perhaps he blamed the tremor on too much caffeine or an unusually competitive game of tennis—and maybe it was. Doctors typically want to be frank
with their patients, and certainly do not want to run the risk of malpractice.
But his doctor's casual notation about the momentary tremor meant he would
be denied long-term care coverage, although the diagnosis is typically confirmed only by putting the patient on a long-term drug regimen and observing
the results.

Chapter 7, which discusses the screening process for cognitive impairment,
tells a similar story, when a doctor's passing reference to his patient's "Florida
moment" almost derailed the fellow's long-term care application. In Jim's
case, a follow-up letter of inquiry might have made a difference.

The Phone Interview

Step two is the phone interview with a nurse specialist who has your application in front of her (or him). You must take this step if you're over 61, or if you
are younger and have a condition that has alerted the underwriters. In her
video training session, DeMartino stresses that this interview should take
place no sooner than two weeks after the initial application to allow time for
physician letters to be received.

The phone interview will last about 15 minutes and has both an explicit
and an implicit purpose. Explicitly, the examiner is reviewing the field application form, checking for contradictions and asking for further information.
The reviewer, often a registered nurse, questions the applicant about a mix-
ture of factual information, including the applicant's Social Security number
and address. Next the interviewer will go through the application, matching
medications to medical conditions, pushing for more detail. The interviewer
may ask about the client's most recent physical, latest blood pressure reading, why he or she is taking medication. The interviewer will ask the client
about his or her daily physical activity and may go back as far as 10 years into
the client's medical history. The implicit purpose is to listen for slurred
speech, which might be an indicator of undisclosed medication or a residual
effect of a stroke.

And, surprise! The phone interview also includes a mini cognitive impairment test. In the MetLife model, the applicant is asked to remember three common words. The interviewer asks a series of intervening questions, including the day of the week, the year, and the name of the president of the United States—each intended to distract the potential policyholder from the memory task.

Even if you have no trouble remembering three random words in a list, there is an even more challenging task in the MetLife phone interview. The client is asked to count backward from 20 by three's. Take heart: Imagine giving this test in 20 years to a generation raised with calculators.

The Face-to-Face Interview

For applicants over 75, there is no avoiding the face-to-face interview, which usually takes place in your own home. The insurance company wants to check your level of cognizance. You won't have to disrobe, although you may be asked for blood and urine samples.

Look at Chapter 7, on the cognitive impairment test, for a detailed description of what you can expect during this 45-minute visit and how best to prepare for it.

Tell Me No Secrets: The Privacy Issue

By now, you doubtless recognize that buying long-term care insurance invites both a physical and a financial inspection of your life. You may well feel invaded by the prospect of sharing your medical and sometimes financial secrets with the agent sitting in your living room, especially if you haven't been forthcoming with your spouse, not to mention your kids. It's not very reassuring, either, to realize that the entire company bureaucracy may be able to access your records. Perhaps only the IRS finds out more about you.

Supreme Court Justice Louis D. Brandeis noted that "to receive the apparent benefits of society we passively, voluntarily and sometimes under pressure, consent to what are essentially intrusions to our right to privacy." Because we want the "apparent benefits of society," we willingly fill out credit card and mortgage loan applications, personnel forms for new jobs, and insurance applications. Credit cards, mortgages, and new jobs are all the "benefits."

The problem is that when you sign the authorization at the bottom of a long-term care application form, you're giving up much more privacy than you may recognize. You are essentially authorizing a search warrant of your medical and financial records. The risk to your privacy is especially great in this computerized, networked age, when any information you share with one company, accurate or not, may turn up in the files of another. Despite your right to the information, you may have some difficulty discovering what these institutions have to say about you.

Recognizing this threat to our privacy, Congress passed and the president signed the Gramm-Leach-Bliley Act of 1999, calling for new privacy standards for consumer financial and health information. The U.S. Department of Health and Human Services is working on specific provisions of the bill. Meanwhile, the National Association of Insurance Commissioners has adopted a model for consumer privacy regulation that requires "explicit consumer permission" before a company may "share, sell, market, or give away health information except for explicit consumer purposes."[2]

Don't feel reassured that your privacy is safe, however, because the model is abstract in phrasing and vague in action. One company, UnumProvident, instructs its producers in a June 1, 2001, letter that "to the extent that the Company discloses nonpublic personal information of any individual to you, you agree that you will not disclose or use the information other than to carry out the purposes for which the Company disclosed the information to you."[3] Obviously this premier insurer, like the other companies, makes every effort to protect your financial and medical records. Still, the possibility that your confidentiality will be breached remains.

In fact, the insurance industry is a major offender in the assault on our privacy. When you sign the authorization at the bottom of the long-term care insurance application, you have effectively signed a search warrant that has no hint of due process. If you don't sign this section of the application, you won't be able to buy the insurance. This two-part statement is a certification and an authorization. When you sign the certification, you are saying that the information you have provided is true. I'll have more to say about that certification later in this chapter.

First, what about the authorization you've signed? Most such authorizations state: I hereby authorize any licensed physician, medical practitioner, hospital, clinic, or other medical or medically related facility, insurance company, the medical information bureau, or other organization, institution, or person having any records of knowledge of me and my health to give the insurance company any such information. A photocopy of this signed authorization shall be valid as the original.

Boil this statement down and what it says in plain English is: I authorize anybody with any knowledge about me to give this knowledge to the insurance company. Good-bye, privacy.

What's more, you've given the insurance company the right to investigate any medical fact it has come across, no matter which doctors you've listed on your form or when the condition troubled you. Consider, for example, Mary, who legitimately forgot that her primary care doctor had once suggested that she see a psychologist to talk about the stresses in her marriage. Mary never followed through on the referral, but her doctor had noted it in her records. Now the insurer calls Mary and her doctor, asking for details on why she might have needed therapy.

Or maybe Mary, 10 years ago, did see the psychologist, successfully completed her therapy, and resolved the stresses at home. Mary never told her husband about the therapy. But now the story is out. The insurance company underwriters want details and write to her psychologist, who moved long ago to a state with better reimbursement rates. What is Mary to do? Her husband is more suspicious than the underwriters. While the lower premiums associated with long-term care coverage often limit this extensive medical scrutiny, such investigations remain a possibility for applicants.

What if the examiner during your at-home physical suspects that you have an undiagnosed medical or cognitive condition? Insurance company policy typically prohibits any "subjective" discussion between the examiner and the potential client. Most examiners will likely tell you what your blood pressure and weight are, since you may already know. But the examiner probably will not share more subjective evaluations, even those he or she writes on the interviewing sheet. Here we are in the age of physician responsibility and record accessibility. Yet I can't think of another medical institution or a worker who is allowed to hold observations about your health or cognitive ability so close to the vest. And these observations are available to every office worker and bureaucrat in the insurance company's computer network.

Let's say that the insurer discovers a physical problem that you don't know about. Take the case of Susan, who was troubled by the unexpected news that she would not be eligible for an insurance company's long-term care policy. She requested that the company send her the medical information on which it based its decision.

Susan was a healthy 70-year-old woman who played doubles tennis several times a week and cared for her ailing husband after his heart attack. She knew that her husband would not qualify for long-term care coverage, so he did not bother applying for his coverage. Susan was in great shape. She weighed barely more than she had in college, and her energy level was high. She dealt a sharp game of mah-jongg and kept up with her grandchildren at the zoo. She figured she would breeze through the insurance company's physical and cognitive screening. Her agent thought so, too. Susan was rejected.

Her agent was surprised by the rejection, but Susan was shocked. She called immediately to find out what could be physically wrong with her, but the company's "privacy considerations" prohibited it from releasing such private information over the telephone. No matter that Susan felt her well-being was at stake or that she was upset by the intimation that she had a potentially dangerous condition. Susan needed to put the request in writing, so she did. Two more weeks passed, during which Susan's anxiety increased. In the third week, the insurer's medical director wrote that her urine sample showed red blood cells, even though nothing from her doctor had indicated any such problem.

Now Susan was truly alarmed. "Send my doctor the lab report immediately," she wrote, "and include all other medical information you have gathered about me." Within two weeks the insurance company had complied, and

Susan's doctor called to determine whether she had been experiencing any symptoms. Susan was grateful for the heads-up about a potential health problem, but regretted the period of painful waiting and the indirect discovery that she had a condition that would demand monitoring.

And I'll Tell You No Lies: The Honesty Issue

In Susan's case, her lab work revealed a problem that disqualified her from coverage. What about less measurable physical complaints? While no reputable insurance broker would advise a consumer to report every headache or sleepless night on an insurance application, none would countenance fraud, either. An alert insurance representative will not forward an application if the client is likely to be rejected on physical grounds.

The applicant who deliberately withholds information about a preexisting condition will be found out, either in the report sent by one's doctor or when making a claim. Sometimes, of course, applicants try to beat the system.

The White Lie

Once I arrived to interview a couple who had asked to explore their long-term care coverage options. When I pulled up to their house, I saw a car with a handicap plate parked in the driveway.

"Whose car is that?" I asked the couple. Why put them through a long interview process and explain the types of policies if they were inevitably going to fail the physical screening?

Margaret, the wife, answered, "It's mine. Why, have you blocked it?"

"No," I told her, "but I couldn't help noticing the handicap plate. Could you tell me why you have it?"

"Oh, that—it's a convenience," Margaret answered. "I used to get asthma attacks from time to time, and I used to need oxygen. But you know, these new medications have been great. They have helped me avoid the type of attacks I used to have 10 years ago."

Why keep the handicap plate?

"Because I get great parking spaces I wouldn't get any other way."

It is highly unlikely that any insurance company would have accepted this explanation at face value.

I told Margaret that before we even talked about long-term care insurance, we would require a letter from the doctor who treated her for her asthma. She could get it herself or authorize me to write the doctor. The letter would need to include a detailed history, her medications, the date of her last attack, and any other medical conditions she may have had.

That was it for Margaret. Upset, she abruptly terminated the interview. I never heard from her again.

My 50 years in the insurance business have given me an instinct for customers like Margaret. Thinking about long-term care coverage, Margaret understated her condition to avoid a physical test.

My 50 years in the business have also taught me any insurance company would insist on documentation of her condition; there would be no putting off a diagnostic test or a specialist's letter. In the end, Margaret would not have passed the underwriter's scrutiny and would have gone uninsured.

When a White Lie Turns Darker

Let's say that Margaret's asthma was being managed very well by a medication acceptable to the insurance underwriters. She told the truth and bought the long-term care policy. But Margaret had not revealed on her insurance application that in addition to asthma, she suffered from increasingly troubling arthritis. Her new doctor, assigned by the HMO and unfamiliar with her chart, forgot to note the condition, too.

Within four months of buying her long-term care coverage, Margaret breaks her hip and becomes wheelchair-bound. She cannot move unassisted from her bed to the chair or make it to the toilet without her husband's help. She has now met the disability conditions of her policy—inability to handle two activities of daily living (ADLs)—and should be able to claim her long-term care benefits. She calls her agent and makes the claim.

No check arrives. Instead, the insurer says to her, "You didn't reveal your arthritis to us on your application. We want to look at the medical records relating to that condition." The young HMO doctor has now moved on to a different company, and Margaret's complete records land in the hands of a secretary who sends them in their entirety to the insurance company. Margaret will not receive any long-term care benefits. Since her policy is less than two years old, it falls within the contestability limit. The insurance company denies her claim; had Margaret been on the level, she never would have been issued a policy.

Contesting a policy, according to a UnumProvident spokesperson, means that the company "question[s] the validity of coverage under this policy by letter" to the policyholder. "The contest is effective on the date [the insurer] mail[s] the letter and refund[s] the premium to you." The NAIC has developed a model version of the contestability clause that is used by most states. The model allows the insurer to contest the policy within six months of its issue upon "showing a misrepresentation that is material to [the client's] acceptance of coverage."[4] This is the clause that caught Margaret.

For a policy that has been in force more than six months but less than two years, the insurer may contest if there is a misrepresentation that is "material both to your acceptance of coverage and which pertains to the conditions of your disability." After two years from the policy's effective date in some states, "only fraudulent misstatements" in the application may be used to contest the policy. If the policy is reinstated, the contestable period starts again with the reinstatement date. Finally, in most states, there is "no time limit to contest this policy for fraudulent misstatements."

As of this writing, several states have changed the NAIC model. Connecticut, North Carolina, and Virginia each required that the fraud wording be removed. Other states have changed the time limits in a variety of ways. For example, Connecticut allows contestability after two years only for nonpayment of premium. Maryland says, "A claim cannot be denied on a disease or physical condition that was disclosed on the application."[5] Texas, Virginia, North Carolina, and Wisconsin have also made changes. Check with your state's office of insurance to find out the contestability limits in your state.

When the Dark Lie Becomes White Again

Interestingly, if Margaret had been able to stay out of the wheelchair for two years, she might have claimed ignorance, not omission, and been able to claim her benefits. After two years, the law in most states is much more forgiving, especially North Carolina, Texas, and Virginia.

In these states, to avoid paying the benefit on a claim when the policy is more than two years old, the insurance company would be required to prove that someone like Margaret had an "intent to deceive." To deny benefits, the company would have to prove that she had committed a major fraud, like sending an imposter to take her physical or diagnostic tests.

In Margaret's case, the policy was less than two years old. All the company had to prove was that the misrepresentation in her medical history was material because she had a form of arthritis that was listed in the company underwriting guide as uninsurable. Even though Margaret believed she didn't deliberately make a material misrepresentation and didn't think her arthritis was a big problem, she obviously didn't know or didn't want to know how insurance companies underwrite long-term care insurance.

To manage their risk and to avoid the issue of fraud, insurance companies conduct careful "front-end" underwriting. They collect as much medical data as they need when you apply for coverage. If the underwriters want you to take a diagnostic test, you'll be asked to do so or refused coverage. If you need a note from your specialist, you'll have to get one. My advice is to choose an insurance company that takes more than 72 hours to check you out. Otherwise, you may be sending premiums to a company that won't be around to pay your benefits when you need them. Or else you'll be subjected, like Margaret, to contest. In her case, the company had a legitimate right to ask for medical records. They suspected fraud.

What about the insurance companies that don't bother to gather medical records before they sell you a policy? These companies are betting that you'll pay your premiums but never make a claim. Ideally you'll die before you need long-term care, or maybe you'll simply forfeit your policy when your job changes. The company saves the up-front cost of asking your physician for a report and figures it'll check you out when and if you make a claim for benefits. This process, illegal in some states, is called post-claims underwriting. It gives you the illusion of coverage but not the reality; it gives the insurance company your premium money but not the responsibility to pay your benefits. Who is the winner in this case? You decide.

If you now believe that the insurance company unfairly scrutinizes your long-term care application before it considers you a suitable risk, think again. Granted, you're exposing yourself to medical scrutiny you might not want. Granted, you're being poked and prodded, on paper and in fact, by agents, examiners, underwriters, and paper pushers in the insurance company. But take your medicine. Underwriting is a vital part of the insurance process, and the company who skips this step will not be around to pay you years from now when you make your claim. Suffer through the physical underwriting, because the long-term care insurance prescription, in the last analysis, may be one you choose to fill. Read the next chapter for some tactics to make the medicine go down in a more delightful way.

Endnotes

1. DeMartino, Sandy. *Long-Term Care Insurance Underwriting.* MetLife training video, February 7, 2000.
2. NAIC News Release. September 26, 2000.
3. Richard A. Wolf, senior vice president, field sales, UnumProvident. Letter to producers, June 1, 2001.
4. Lynn Poore, senior contract consultant, long-term care contracts, compliance and filing, UnumProvident. E-mail, June 27, 2001.
5. Ibid.

CHAPTER 6

Underwriting for Physical Impairments: Changing the Odds in Underwriting Roulette

If you are 40 years old and healthy, skip this chapter. All you will have to do to prove your insurability is to fill out the application, watch the return mail for the policy, and pay the premiums. This chapter is for everyone else, those who are healthy most of the time, but sickly on occasion.

The underlying premise of this chapter is that if your health is not absolutely normal, you should never apply for long-term care insurance in an absolutely normal manner. You must create your own insurability by maneuvering around the underwriter's objections to prove you're medically qualified for coverage.

Automatic Disqualifiers

First, though, an admission. If you have certain conditions, you will not be able to buy long-term care coverage no matter how much you work the system.

Insurers will not sell life insurance to terminally ill clients, and no insurer will offer long-term care coverage to a consumer who absolutely, without question, will need some form of long-term care. That's simply a fact of long-term care insurance; insurers are profit-making institutions, not charities. Therefore, no matter how many doctors' reports you gather or how much money you have in your pocket, if you have one of these conditions, you will automatically be denied coverage.

Here is Conseco's list of automatic declines. It is typical of the industry list:[1]

- AIDS.
- Alzheimer's disease.
- Amputation due to disease.
- Organic brain disease.
- Cirrhosis.
- Dementia.
- Kidney disease.
- Multiple sclerosis.
- Paraplegia.
- Parkinson's disease.
- Senility.
- Psychosis.
- ADL deficits (bathing, dressing, transferring, toileting, continence, eating).
- Home oxygen use.
- Postpolio syndrome.
- Organ transplant.
- Use of medical appliances (excluding cane).

Of course, insurance companies always have the option to review and change this list of conditions. Don't look for any eliminations, however. While underwriters occasionally respond to industry competition or actuarial data by reassessing a condition, they very, very rarely reconsider an excluded condition. The best a consumer may hope for is a case-by-case analysis; but if you suffer from one of these automatic exclusions, you will probably be better off considering an alternative means to fund your potential long-term care needs.

Long-term care applications also include a list of prohibited medications. These medications are tied, not surprisingly, to the automatically excluded conditions. In some cases, dosages below an established level are acceptable, while those above are prohibited. Appendix B includes a sample of this list. Your application will not go forward if you take more than the acceptable dose of any of these medications.

Preexisting Conditions

Automatic declines are clear-cut. But the question of insurability becomes fuzzier when you have chronic conditions not on the automatic exclusion list. Insurance underwriters, as we have seen, recognize that many applicants for long-term care coverage may have some preexisting chronic medical condition. Besides, if you're knowledgeable enough to consider insurance to cover long-term care costs, you're doubtless smart enough to take your prescribed medications and probably even wealthy enough to pay the pharmacy for the drugs.

What generalizations can we make about underwriting standards for chronic medical conditions? Only one: If your preexisting condition is not on the list of automatic declines, you can't absolutely predict how the underwriters will view it.

In tax-qualified plans, unlike either the outright exclusion of coverage for a preexisting condition or a provision that excludes coverage for a limited period of time found in some forms of disability income and health insurance policies, no such exclusion exists.

So long as you are fully candid and provide the long-term care insurer all details relative to your coronary history, if in fact you had one, including all doctors consulted as well as your medication regimen, once a policy is issued any disability related to your coronary history would be covered subject to the terms and conditions and waiting period found in your policy.

Insurers strive for a delicate balance between writing policies and taking risks. In a memo to me, a spokesperson for UnumProvident corporation explained that its underwriting philosophy is "to seek opportunities to expand the market while protecting the integrity of the business."[2]

We're going to look closely at ways you can increase your own insurability, but first we need to understand how underwriters view specific medical conditions. With a few exceptions, the major insurance companies have similar underwriting concerns. According to Sandy DeMartino, a registered nurse who is MetLife's underwriting manager for individual long-term care, there are a number of conditions that most often lead to the need for long-term care. These conditions are uppermost in the minds of all conscientious underwriters when assessing an insured's application file. There are others that occur on occasion, but the following present the overwhelming majority of conditions that may trigger the need for long-term care:[3]

- Dementia.
- Diabetes mellitus.
- Fractures.
- Chronic obstructive pulmonary disorder (COPD).
- Hypertension.
- Stroke, cerebrovascular accident (CVA).

- Bone or joint disease.
- Cancer.
- Atrial fibrillation, arrhythmia.

What counts about these conditions is that they do not automatically exclude you from long-term care coverage. Instead, because these conditions are the ones that most often trigger long-term care needs, they are most carefully scrutinized by underwriters who manage the risk/income balance.

There is no negotiating over levels of dementia. If you have it, you're uninsurable. Underwriters find the road from diagnosis to long-term care so direct for such patients that there's no turning back.

Diabetes mellitus is another matter. Juvenile diabetes presents a number of problems, especially for seniors who have been in treatment for many years. Adult onset diabetes, in contrast, is often controlled by diet or by oral medication. In any case, underwriters assess the risk of eye problems, amputation, kidney disease, neuropathy, and hypertension in diabetes sufferers. Many insurers will offer policies to patients who use insulin without complication and remain well controlled. If you are diabetic, your agent may ask you about a specific list of complications, instead of accepting a blanket response such as "I'm doing just fine."

If you have emphysema or chronic obstructive pulmonary disorder (COPD) you may be uninsurable. Insurers know that if you have difficulty breathing you will not be able to take care of yourself. They'll look at your use of tobacco and estimate your probability for needing oxygen. Very seldom are policies issued with that kind of impairment.

Hypertension, if uncontrolled, may lead to a stroke and concerns underwriters. There are some insurers who decline without exception any applicant with a history of stroke.

Fractures are often the result of dizziness, a fall, or osteoporosis, so underwriters often link these conditions. Some insurers distinguish between minor (non-weight-bearing) and major (weight-bearing) fractures when they assess medical history. You may have a waiting period for a major fracture, but you'll be declined if you've had multiple or recent fractures. If you break a bone, you may need general anesthesia, too, another high-risk factor, especially for seniors.

Bone and joint diseases raise concerns about osteoporosis and arthritis, among other conditions. Either can cause fracture; and prednisone, commonly used to treat rheumatoid arthritis as well as respiratory disease, may cause bone damage if taken in high doses.

Cancer is considered by type. MetLife will sell a policy to a client whose cancer has not spread to another organ and who has been free of treatment for two years. In the case of breast cancer, if the lymph nodes were positive, the client may have to wait as long as 10 years.

UnumProvident adds chronic pain and fatigue to the list of preexisting conditions the underwriters flag. Both pain and fatigue cause limitations in the

ADLs. UnumProvident says that these conditions can be "quite subjective with respect to pain and limitation. Painful backs and major joints (hips, knees, and shoulders) can be indicative of possible future problems. Use of narcotic pain medications . . . is considered uninsurable."[4]

With some of these conditions, who you tell may make all the difference. Harold, for instance, may have had a transient ischemic attack (TIA) two years ago. He was dozing in his chair when his wife woke him to get dressed for their bridge game. When he went into the bedroom, however, he felt momentarily confused, even disoriented. He sat down and recovered after a minute. Harold said nothing to his wife, played a good game of bridge, and forgot about the incident. He never mentioned it to his doctor.

One of Harold's friends had a similar incident at about the same time, but this fellow's disorientation happened in front of his wife. She called her friends, canceled their bridge game, and insisted that her husband see his internist. That doctor sent him to a neurologist, who told him he might have had a TIA and therefore needed a brain scan and magnetic resonance imaging (MRI). The husband refused. "I'm fine. I have no problems now." Maybe the friend's decision was justified healthwise, but it worked against his long-term care insurance application.

The incident remained on the second man's medical record. When they saw that he had refused to take the tests, the underwriters became nervous that he might have had a TIA or a more serious neurological problem. Without laboratory reports, no condition could be ruled out. The underwriters declined his application, and he had to shop around for a company that would at least consider him if he went a full year without incident.

So you think you've had the diagnostic tests you need? Consider this description of the way a physician might think about the preexisting condition of atrial fibrillation, which is an arrhythmia that carries a high stroke risk. It is a model for the way a long-term care insurance underwriter might think.

One internist explains that atrial fibrillation increases sixfold the risk of stroke, so controlling the condition is a major medical concern. Medications may help the heart, a pump, work more efficiently, and adding anticoagulants to the treatment plan reduces the stroke risk by 60 percent.

That still leaves the patient with a 40 percent risk of stroke. It's no wonder, then, that long-term care underwriters whose concern is with morbidity closely examine an applicant with atrial fibrillation.

The major risk factors for stroke include advanced age, high blood pressure, a previous stroke or TIA, or a weak heart. Add to these diabetes, excessive alcohol use, a history of smoking, coronary disease, or vascular artery disease, and the patient's chances for stroke grow further.

The underwriters, therefore, will take into consideration a history of elevated lipids and whether these lipids have been reduced. They will examine any historical or physical evidence of peripheral vascular disease or carotid artery disease, and ask whether through an exam or a scan the primary care doctor has screened for adequate blood flow. If the patient has experienced any dizziness or unexplained speech or muscle disturbance, the underwriter might suspect a transient ischemic attack or an earlier undiagnosed stroke, and will also be looking for any blood diseases such as hemochromatosis or polycythemia.[5]

Whew.

And you never even heard of atrial fibrillation until basketball superstar and presidential candidate Bill Bradley hit the front pages.

Given a Preexisting Condition, What Are Your Options?

Don't be scared and don't give up! You have some cards to play, too.

Even this poor client with the atrial fibrillation may have been able to buy a policy after a year of good health or evidence of good control. The case illustrated in Chapter 12 involving an applicant with a questionable EKG tracing proves that although one insurance company may decline your business, another may be willing to talk to you.

Here are some ways to shift the insurability odds to your favor:

- Don't take anything at face value, not even the insurance field application. There are always alternatives to accepting an insurance company's decision. Medical requirements vary by company, and although you may be a "high risk" to one underwriter, another may not rate you at all. Interpretations of test results, especially those for electrocardiogram, differ markedly. And insurance companies take hard or soft positions on different abnormalities at different times.

- The best defense is a good offense. Regular physicals, fully recorded and safely filed, are an insurance applicant's greatest ally. Most underwriters will be more impressed with a significant history of controlled hypertension or diabetes than with a simple admission that the condition exists. In other words, they will be more liberal in their evaluations if they know an illness is under control.

- Ask for a rating change. You always have the option of applying for a rate reduction after two years. Perhaps the original rate was based on outdated information, or the underwriting criteria have changed because of new actuarial data.

- Consider the competition. If your health hasn't changed, see what long-term care insurance another company might have to offer. You may fail to satisfy one underwriter's requirements yet have absolutely no problem with another's. Even though you're older, you might pay less for similar coverage.

The Insurer Has Options, Too

And if these strategies don't work, the insurance company has tricks of its own to handle your preexisting condition. It may offer you any one or several of these options:

- You could be issued coverage as applied for.
- The insurance company might want you to pay an extra premium that could be from 25 percent more than the standard price to double the standard price.
- The insurance company could limit the benefits it is willing to offer you. If you apply for $6,000 a month in benefits, you may be able to buy $4,000 a month.
- The insurance company could limit the home care benefit. For example, if you apply for an integrated program with $200 nursing home and $200 in home care costs, the insurance company might think there is a serious risk of home care. It counteroffers you $100 a day for home care, and maintains the $200 nursing home benefit.
- There could be a combination of any of these options, including both an increased premium because of your higher rating and a reduction in your benefits.

Being Proactive: How to Influence Physical Underwriting

Insurance companies are in business to sell policies, and their representative is your ally. The broker wants you to qualify for long-term care insurance. He or she needs the commission from your business to pay the mortgage and feed the kids. Sometimes the best strategy for passing the physical screening is to let the agent do the groundwork and to take his or her advice. Other times, you can improve your insurability by taking specific actions.

Prepare for a Home Visit by an Insurance Company Nurse

One client, David, forgot that his face-to-face assessment for long-term care insurance was scheduled for 10 A.M. He overslept, drank two cups of black coffee, and dressed for the insurance examiner. He wanted to look spiffy so he put on a heavy Irish sweater and flannel slacks, finishing the outfit with his best walking boots.

When the examiner took David's blood pressure, she discovered it was elevated despite the medications he was taking to control it. David didn't tell her that he had been skipping the pills because he didn't like their side effects.

With his fancy clothes, he came in over the limit for the company's height/weight charts.

Suddenly, David's ability to satisfy the underwriter was in doubt.

My advice: David might have postponed the meeting until he was psychologically and physically ready for it. The caffeine raised his blood pressure, not to mention his general level of arousal. He had been using too much salt at his meals, and his nightly martinis elevated his pressure, too. David knew his weight was only marginally acceptable, so he could have passed up sartorial splendor for lightweight clothes. The examiner expects that he will look neat and clean, not that he will be a model for *GQ* magazine.

Prepare Your Doctor

When DeeDee told her doctor that she was applying for long-term care insurance, he assured her that he had gathered every necessary diagnostic test at her most recent physical a few months earlier. DeeDee was thrilled that she wouldn't have to give yet another blood or urine sample.

My advice: Just as DeeDee did, give your doctor a heads-up about the insurance application. Perhaps you, too, have had all the tests, and your doctor can prepare them for the underwriters.

Don't Play Actuary

Bertha and Harry spent three months analyzing the long-term care policy they wanted and settled on an indemnity plan. But something went wrong when they tried to buy it.

Bertha told me that the agent she first contacted offered both spouses a preferred rate, feeling certain that both Harry and Bertha would qualify. The couple was happy with the premium the agent predicted for them.

"Why did he make these promises?" Bertha asked me. "I think he really let us down."

It seems that the underwriters, looking at Bertha's weight and seeing it was slightly more than their chart allowed, became suspicious of her daily dose of 20mg of Zocor for hypertension. They refused to offer her a preferred rate for the indemnity policy she wanted. Harry qualified, but the same coverage would cost Bertha $235 more, a standard rate.

Bertha was irate and forgot about all the planning they had done. She called another agent, who offered a reimbursement plan, with benefits that were very different from those of the indemnity plan they had originally selected. In this new plan, she and her husband both qualified for preferred rates. No matter that this reimbursement policy would actually cost her $150 more than the first agent's offer; it was the principle of the thing.

When I talked to Bertha, it was clear her feelings were hurt. What were a few extra pounds? So what about the dosage of her medications? She felt that she had been stigmatized by the insurance industry.

My advice: I explained to Bertha that her original agent had indeed done his homework and was probably sorry that the policy did not come with the premium he predicted. But Bertha had also acted emotionally and should think again. She needed to decide whether it made sense to spend $150 more for coverage, just to make a point about the attitude of insurance underwriters.

Find the Right Company

Suppose you have to take a medication that some insurance companies consider to be an automatic decline. This happened to one of my clients, who was declined by an insurance company because he took five milligrams of prednisone for his colitis.

My advice: Let's check out another company. Experience has taught me that in some cases a second company will be so eager to build its business that it will accept your use of the medication, conduct detailed front-end underwriting, fully understand your preexisting condition, and still sell you the policy. It is true that insurers all recognize the statistical possibility that the steroid my client was taking might cause long-term bone problems. Still, the first company was unwilling to sell long-term care benefits to anyone on the drug, but the second was happy to sell my client his policy. They figured that any dose under 10 milligrams was safe.

Take the Policy As Offered

Jane called me to complain that she was paying 50 percent more than her sister was for the same coverage. "What's going on here?" she complained. "My sister and I have the same medical condition, and she is three years older than I am. We both have controlled hypertension and that's all. Because of her I applied for long-term care insurance. But Sis got a standard policy a year ago and she's raving about the benefits. Why do I have to pay so much more?

"Are you and your sister exactly alike?" I asked.

"Well," Jane admitted, "I am 40 pounds overweight. But why should I be penalized for that?"

"Your doctor has probably told you at every checkup that you have more than one significant risk factor for coronary artery disease," I replied. "And the underwriters may be worried that your extra weight will ruin your knees, your bones will deteriorate, or you'll fall."

My advice: Take the policy even though it comes with the increased premium. It would be nice if underwriters could just trust you to lose the extra pounds, but the people who rate your premium work with statistics, not people. So lose the pounds, stay that way for a year, and then call the company for rate reconsideration.

Assume That Underwriters Are Human, Too

Two months after one client purchased her policy, she pulled out the application to check it over. To her dismay, she realized that she hadn't informed me or the company about a routine Pap smear done earlier that year. Would the insurance company now cancel the policy because she unwittingly forgot to tell it about the test?

My advice: "If your Pap smear was normal, don't worry. From time to time insurance underwriters can be as human as anyone else. They won't penalize you for an after-the-fact notification as long as your test was okay. Besides, the chances are they may have learned about it from your physician. However, if your test was not normal, the attitude of your insurance company may not be your biggest concern. You'll have more than one problem to worry about.

Gather Your Documentation First

One woman told me very confidentially about her special problem. For the past 15 years she and her husband had been in therapy because they had a severely retarded daughter. Now the daughter was a young adult, and they needed professional help to deal with her changing body and unexpected moods. Currently, she told me, they were visiting their therapist only monthly; but in the past, they had gone to therapy as often as twice a week. One parent had also been prescribed medication to get through some rough spots many years before.

I knew the couple wanted to buy long-term care insurance so they could protect their assets for their child. The problem was to convince the insurance company underwriters that they were good risks. I felt honored that the couple trusted me with their story.

My advice: First, I reassured the couple:

"Underwriters," I told her, "do not automatically respond to every psychotropic medication. If they did, half of the population would be deemed uninsurable."

Then we both needed to do some homework.

I suggested that the couple ask their therapist for a "to whom it may concern" letter. This letter should explain the nature of the therapist's intervention with them, detail any medications, and specify that both father and mother were functioning normally, holding full-time jobs, and carrying on all day-to-day activities.

My job was to show the letter and the list of medications to the company underwriters without revealing the names of my clients. If the underwriter agreed that the couple was eligible for long-term care insurance, the company would propose a rate plan and coverage limits for them, and we could go ahead with the policy. "Naturally," I explained to the wife, "the company will want to verify the letter you've given them and reserve the right to contact any other physicians who have treated you. But by doing your homework ahead of time, we'll be a step ahead of any potential objections."

Look at It from Your Parent's Point of View

A client I had worked with for many years called me to see what he could do about his superstitious mother. Mom, 83 years old, was very active and alert.

There was no question that she could pass the cognitive impairment screening. But what if she slipped on the ice or was in a car accident? She would need help with her daily activities.

"My mom says she feels great now, and that's enough for her. She won't tell me anything about her medical condition. She won't consider buying long-term care insurance."

Why not? Mom's objections seemed to be entirely emotional. A good friend had applied for insurance, and the insurance company learned from her physician that she had cancer. She died a few months later. Mom's theory was that no news is good news.

My advice: It's important to respect your mother's wishes, but also to try to help her past this kind of superstitious thinking.

Unfortunately, if she won't give you permission to request her medical history from her physician, you won't even be able to talk to me informally, off the record, about her likelihood of passing the physical screening. You'll probably have to figure out another way to support her very old age.

"I'm not a fan of checking out other people's medicine cabinets," I told the son, "but maybe you have already noticed what prescription drugs your mother is taking. If you know the names of the medications and the dosages, check them against the list of uninsurable conditions. Since the prescribing doctors' names appear on the bottles, you can also look up their specialties. Then if it appears that Mom has no significant medical secrets, talk to her again. After all, she raised you to be a loving, thoughtful, and prudent son. Surely she has those qualities herself."

Don't Believe Everything You Hear

My client, Bob, figured he could never buy long-term care coverage because he had already been turned down once, a year earlier. The underwriters at that time had told him that since he was only six months past his prostate cancer surgery, he wouldn't qualify.

Now, 18 months after his surgery, he was free of the cancer. His prognosis was completely positive, he needed no medications other than 20mg of Zocor for cholesterol, and he worked full time.

"I heard from one of the guys at the gym that once you've been rejected, you'll never be eligible for long-term care benefits."

My advice: "Bob, you're too smart a fellow to believe such an old wives' tale. The insurance companies want to sell policies, and the underwriters want to write them. True that they'll ask you why you were declined in the past. But then they'll evaluate your risk by asking for a copy of your pathology report, your latest prostate-specific antigen (PSA) readings, and your history of chemotherapy, radiation, and other postsurgical medications."

I told Bob, "Go for the coverage! If everything checks out now, you'll probably be able to buy it."

Manage Your Very Old Age by Taking Your Doctor's Advice Now

A 58-year-old client told me that she didn't want to take a bone density test, despite the advice of her physician. "Every year he tells me to get the screening," the client said, "but I don't want to. I've heard from my friends that the pill you have to take will upset my stomach and give me a headache. Besides, I don't want to find out some medical fact about myself that will disqualify me from purchasing long-term care insurance when I'm ready to buy."

My advice: "Your personal health needs always come first. If your physician thinks that you need the bone density test, you'd better take it. The most important way to manage your very old age is to take care of yourself very well before you get there—while you're young. Obviously it's important to plan for your long-term care, but why set yourself up for a physical impairment such as a broken hip if you can avoid it?"

"And besides," I said, "the underwriters probably won't even write you a policy if you need the test and haven't taken it. They'll just postpone your application until you climb on the scanning table and let the technician do his job. It's a quick and painless test, anyhow, so get it done."

Shop Around

Insurance is a competitive business. You never know when underwriters looking to build their business will act favorably on your application. While you don't want to buy a policy from a company that won't be around in 20 years to pay your benefits, it makes sense for you to find an agent or representative who will take the time to do the necessary homework.

But Investigate before You Switch Policies

One of my neighbors consulted with me about his long-term care coverage. He had bought the policy two years earlier, right after he had been diagnosed with hypertension and begun medication. Now his blood pressure was almost normal, and he had reduced his medication dosage, but he was still paying a surcharge on his premiums.

"One of my golf partners told me he could sell me similar coverage for a standard rate, even though I'm two years older. Do you think I should switch to his company?"

My advice: "It's great that your blood pressure is down! Why don't you share the good news with your original broker? It may be that his company will also eliminate the surcharge on your coverage. If they do, you'll actually save money because they'll give you the benefits of standard insurance at a premium rate of two years younger than your golf buddy can offer."

And there was another angle to consider. I continued, "If you buy the new insurance, the clock on your contestability period starts again. That means that if you need to make a claim, the new insurance company has a right to contest it against the chance of misrepresentation. I know you'd never misrepresent your condition, neighbor, but why put yourself through that hassle and delay? Talk to your original broker before you make the switch."

Maybe You'll Get Lucky

One fellow I know applied for long-term care insurance even though he was taking more prednisone than the underwriters liked. The agent didn't notice the dosage level, either. The underwriter missed the aberration and approved the policy.

My advice: Be happy. You've been lucky enough to beat the system. Underwriters make mistakes, and they'll usually stand behind them to maintain their credibility with the field force selling insurance. I know of one time when an underwriter wanted to issue a limited benefit policy, refusing to write the full amount requested by the applicant. But no one told the insurer's issuing department, and the lucky applicant got a full benefits policy. Although the error was eventually discovered, the insurer stood behind the policy as issued.

If you have a new underwriter, or a seasoned professional under pressure to beat his or her end-of-the-year quota, you may also be in luck. But don't go for a policy approved by an overly aggressive underwriter, since you may end up with higher rates down the line—assuming the company remains in business long enough to renew your policy.

Know When to Quit

Sally is 76 years old. She sometimes uses a cane at home, and always takes it with her when she goes downtown to shop, mostly to give herself a sense of security. A recent bad fall served as a wake-up call.

"I think of the cane as my safety valve. I'm always afraid I'll trip over a bump in the concrete or get hit by a car at a crosswalk."

Sally wanted to buy long-term care insurance, but didn't know if she would pass the screening test.

My advice: This time I had to admit to Sally that her expectation of failing the screening was well founded. Because she is 76, she would certainly be required to have a face-to-face screening with an insurance examiner. This examiner would see the cane and ask Sally questions about how often she used it and why. While the insurance examiner does not exactly ferret out the secrets of an applicant's condition, in Sally's case the cane would be an obvious disqualifier. She probably would not be able to buy the coverage.

A Last Word on the Physical Screening

The company wants your premium dollars to flow into their coffers for years and years and years; but they don't want to have to pay you any benefits. The most cynical among us might conclude that the ideal long-term care prospect is one who will live a very long life and die when he is hit by a car crossing the street. The insurance company in this case enjoys all gain, no pain.

At times, conditions that would prohibit life insurance sales will have no effect on long-term care applications. For instance, a relatively advanced, if stable, breast cancer diagnosis may not stand in the way of long-term care coverage. The underwriters have figured out that you won't need much long-term care, then you'll die before you live through the waiting period, anyway.

Does this all seem unfair? It really isn't. Insurance companies are businesses that must report to their shareholders; if they don't make a profit, they won't be around long enough to pay you when you make that claim. In fact, you need to avoid buying from insurers who fail to properly evaluate your medical condition. In their haste to grow their long-term care business and increase their market share, these companies may be signing up too many poor risks. When payback time comes, they'll fold up under the financial pressure. After all, every time you send your premium check, you're betting on the long-term health of your company as much as it has bet on yours!

And incidentally, the "unfair" physical evaluation works both ways. If your hypertension is controlled by diet, you may have no trouble buying a long-term care policy at standard rates. But the same 120 over 100 blood pressure reading taken during a life insurance physical, exactly the time when you're most under pressure, might cost you extra premium dollars when you apply for life insurance.

Automatic physical disqualifiers are a fact of life in the insurance business. They are simply not negotiable, and the insurance company has sound financial reasons for refusing to compromise.

But for those of us without these conditions, the game is far from over. The persistent consumer, together with a hardworking reputable agent, needs to step up to the plate. Even if you have a preexisting condition, make your case before the insurance company underwriters, be open to options and offers, and remember your overall goal: safeguarding the independence of your very old age.

Endnotes

1. *Conseco Risk Guidelines.* At-risk flyer, March 1999.
2. UnumProvident memo, June 20, 2001.
3. DeMartino, Sandy. *Long-Term Care Insurance Underwriting.* MetLife training video, February 7, 2000.
4. *Conseco Risk Guidelines.* At-risk flyer, March 1999.
5. Interview with Ralph A. Sherman, M.D., former assistant clinical professor of medicine and instructor at Harvard Medical School, November 6, 2001.

CHAPTER 7

The Cognitive Impairment Test: No Lifelines Allowed

Just because I can't remember where I left my keys doesn't necessarily mean I have Alzheimer's disease.[1]
—Dr. Dennis Selkoe, Alzheimer's researcher and codirector of the Center for Neurologic Diseases, Harvard Medical School/Brigham and Women's Hospital, Boston

Helen is 81 years old, but passes for 70. Her doctor marvels at her stamina and envies her golf swing. She reads the *Boston Globe*, the *New York Times*, and the *Wall Street Journal* daily; she subscribes to *Time*, *Newsweek*, and *Ms* magazine. Helen misses Dan Rather only when she is busy competing in tournament scrabble events. But her application for long-term care insurance was turned down. What happened?

Helen failed the cognitive impairment test.

Cognitive impairment, in the words of insurance companies writing long-term care insurance, generally means the lack of adequate "awareness and perception, as well as the ability to understand and reason" that will allow an individual to function independently.[2] The term is a legal one, established by the HIPAA as a trigger for the payment of insurance benefits. You may be able to manage the bathing, dressing, toileting, and other basic activities of daily living, but if you have a "severe" cognitive impairment as defined by the law and certified by a licensed "health care practitioner," you are entitled to insurance benefits under a tax-qualified plan.

This means that the insurance company is keenly concerned with how you think and feel, how well oriented you are to the environment, and how well you remember short-term information. They use a face-to-face interview to measure your abilities. This meeting is required for virtually every long-term care insurance applicant over 75 years of age, and sometimes for those even younger, especially if the company suspects there may be problems with cognition. Every part of the interview, even the cursory medical history, is aimed at evaluating your cognizance. If you flunk this test, you'll flunk the course and be denied long-term insurance.

Helen had no lifelines available when the cognitive assessor sent by the insurance company rang her doorbell. She was on her own during the test. While she was competently handling her daily life, she became flustered during portions of the interview. There was no Regis Philbin around to calm her down, either, so she did not make it past the elimination round.

Will This Be on the Exam?

For insurance company purposes, cognitive impairment is defined as "a deficiency in a person's short- or long-term memory; orientation as to person, place, and time; deductive or abstract reasoning; or judgment as it relates to safety awareness."[3] Unfortunately, insurers rely heavily on your risk of cognitive impairment based on a face-to-face interview that lasts about 30 minutes to an hour, and depends in large part on a test of "delayed word recall." Helen could have named every president from the first George W. to the latest one, but she forgot the word "meadow" and had to forget buying the coverage, too.

Most often, we associate cognitive impairment with Alzheimer's disease, which is a progressive degenerative illness that may leave the body relatively strong while the mind deteriorates. Symptoms of Alzheimer's include forgetfulness, confusion about where one is, what time it is, or even one's name. The Alzheimer's patient may experience mood swings, poor judgment, and other behavioral changes. Sometimes the signs are obvious.

Ask Me No Questions

A broker in Los Angeles tells the story of an 85-year-old applicant who was looking for long-term care insurance. When the broker called to arrange the face-to-face interview, the woman said, "I've expected your call. You wouldn't believe it. I'm now taking a bath so I should qualify for the insurance, because my neighbor told me she was turned down because she couldn't bathe herself."

Anxious for the sale, the broker thought, "Ah, at least she knows something about the triggers."

Someone would come to the house to interview her, the broker told his potential client.

"I understand from my friends that they put you through your paces," the woman said.

The broker minimized her concerns, assuring her that the interview was merely a measure of her activity and mobility. The company only wanted to know whether she used a cane or a walker and whether she could rise from her chair without help.

What a mistake!

Two days later, the broker received a call from the face-to-face interviewer. "Don't you ever send me into that type of situation again," the upset examiner began. "When I explained the details of the test to your client, she literally pushed me out the door. I had to have the building superintendent go back and get my briefcase because she was so violent." The assessor was shaken. "That woman screamed at me. She said, 'I sometimes have trouble remembering telephone numbers, and I'm not going to go through a test that can humiliate me and cause me problems.'"

Diagnosing Alzheimer's, in this instance, would probably not have been difficult if the broker had been more attentive. The applicant, as it happens, entered an Alzheimer's care facility shortly after the interview. But despite stories like these, Alzheimer's is less common than the insurance industry would like us to believe. Insurance companies use frightening statistics about the frequency of Alzheimer's disease to lure you into your insurance agent's office, but you'll be quickly rejected if their underwriters think you have even the earliest of symptoms.

What Are Your Odds?

One company statistic says that 10 percent of people over age 65 will have Alzheimer's, and the incidence increases with age. Those are certainly ominous numbers; what cognitively able, rational, oriented person, concerned about his or her own long-term safety, would not rush out to investigate long-term care options? In theory, the most oriented among us would be looking for long-term care choices by the time we're in our early 50s, long before that dreaded age 65 cutoff when our odds increase. Yet Dr. Dennis J. Selkoe, one of the world's authorities on Alzheimer's, maintains that "The vast number of people in their 70s will not have Alzheimer's disease, and that's true, too, for those in their early 80s. Thus we shouldn't think that the onset of dementia is inevitable."[4]

Is every short-term memory lapse a sign of Alzheimer's? If so, some of us exhibited our first symptoms in grade school, when we panicked at the blackboard during math class. Further, there are physical and mental conditions other than Alzheimer's that might cause temporary cognitive impairment but will also result in an automatic denial of coverage. Conseco rejects clients who have any form of aphasia, confusion, or mental and nervous conditions that have caused hospitalization within the past 24 months. A benign brain tumor that has not been operated on will disqualify an applicant. More than one company now specifically prohibits those with manic depression and imposes a six-month waiting period on anyone who has had a mild depression. Severe depression is an instant disqualifier in most cases. Appendix B includes a list of these conditions, along with others, which often result in the client's application for long-term care insurance being denied.

Forgetting the Punch Line

One man I know, a snowbird, almost missed out on long-term care insurance when he was rejected without explanation even before he was officially tested for cognitive impairment. Harry, like all part-time Floridians, had been besieged with free lunch offers in exchange for considering the purchase of the insurance, and had attended several seminars on long-term care options. He called his local insurance agent to discuss the matter. The agent loved the call. Selling Harry the policy looked like a walk-through; all he had to do was visit, pick a plan, and take the application. But after the exercise, Harry was declined.

The reason turned out to be simple. Harry's doctor, in his report, added a casual closing remark that set off a firestorm in the underwriting department of the insurance company. It seems that Harry, while physically in great shape, had admitted that he had forgotten the punch line of a joke he heard once in Florida. Harry told the doctor that this was a "Florida moment." The doctor included the casual comment in his notes on Harry's physical. No face-to-face interview for Harry, just a rejection. It took the agent some effort to arrange the face-to-face meeting, which of course Harry passed perfectly. His application was approved.

Passing the First Test

You know when you're having a physical—there is no ambiguity about the cold stethoscope or those small red hammers that bounce against your kneecaps. But sometimes you are being singled out for a cognitive impairment screening test before you realize it.

In fact, the actual screening for cognitive impairment may begin when you reveal your interest to an insurance agent or directly to an insurance company. During the first contact, which may take place when you meet your insurance agent or while you're answering a direct mail solicitation from a large insurer like TIAA CREF, you'll be asked about conditions that would automatically disqualify you as a client. These include treatment for neurological syndromes such as Parkinson's and the others listed earlier, as well as physical illnesses such as juvenile diabetes and a host of other conditions listed in Appendixes B and E and discussed in Chapters 5 and 6. A key point here is that every step of the screening process costs the insurance company money. Hence, while the company wants your business, it also wants to eliminate the cost of interviewing and evaluating customers who will obviously not qualify for the coverage.

Pass this initial cut, and you'll be asked to fill out an application for insurance that details your medical history. Your doctor will also be sent a form to fill out. So far, the routine feels similar to what you experienced when you bought life insurance; but in many ways, qualifying for life insurance is a much different matter, as Chapter 6 describes. You've been asked to indicate on the application when you will be available for a short telephone conversation with a company representative. Here enters the next step in the cognitive screening process.

Taking the Midterm on the Phone

During this 15-to-20-minute personal history interview, conducted by someone trained in screening long-term care applicants, you'll be asked for more detail about your medical conditions, medications, and activities of daily living. Look at Chapters 5 and 6 to find out how the insurance company views your physical suitability for long-term care coverage, but you should expect to be queried on the phone about your health during the past five years. Although all this sounds straightforward, the fact is that throughout the conversation the interviewer is evaluating your cognitive ability and your memory. The examiner listens for slurred speech, an indicator for stroke or the presence of medication. He or she will note unusual pauses and hesitations, rambling or inappropriate responses to questions, an inability to concentrate, confusion about health history and prescription information, which he or she may link to other neurological deficits.

One of my clients, John, should have breezed through the personal history interview that was administered by a trained examiner from one large insurance company. John arranged to have the examiner call him in his law office at 8:30 in the morning, reasoning that he would have some privacy to answer questions about his blood pressure, his golf game, and his reluctance to have knee surgery. John was sure that he would have at least 15 minutes to complete the personal history interview.

Unfortunately, the night before the interview, John's case before the federal district court was moved forward. Suddenly, he had to be ready for trial in hours, not weeks. John was swamped, but his wife was pushing to complete the insurance application. The dutiful husband went ahead with the phone conference. This was not a good decision. While he was talking to the interviewer, John was also sorting through his case notes, arranging the depositions, and motioning his associates to sit down in the conference room. His secretary buzzed him several times, and his e-mail was flooded.

John had tried cases before in the federal court, but this minor phone qualifying test nearly sank his application. The interviewer picked up what the company considers "some difficulty with memory, understanding, or reasoning." He mistook John's fatigue for the presence of medications. Besides, John was so worried about the upcoming trial that he seemed almost disoriented to the interviewer; he knew the date of their talk but not what day of the week it was.

Taking the Final: No Retakes, No Phone Calls to a Wise Lifeline

John was only 60, but because he fumbled the phone interview he had to have a face-to-face interview. John could recite the batting average of every New York Yankee and got a kick out of day trading his portfolio. He had no signs of cognitive impairment and should have been easily approved. That's the usual case for applicants under 65, who move directly from the personal history phone interview to signing forms and sending premium payments. Typically the face-to-face interview is not mandatory unless the applicant is at least 75, although such large insurers as UnumProvident test those over 70. Had John paid more attention during the personal history interview, his passing grade would have been virtually certain because of his age.

The likelihood of having a face-to-face interview varies to some degree by gender, perhaps because women live longer than men. One examiner has told me that 80 percent of the customers she interviews are women, usually widowed or divorced. Their quest for long-term care insurance is often driven by the concerns of their children, "who are encouraging them and guiding them."[5] These women may complain about the cost of long-term care and of the insurance policy they are considering, but they tend to trust the judgment of their sales agents and to acknowledge the concerns of their children.

In one case, however, a woman balked. The son of a longtime client of mine called me from Los Angeles where he was employed as the chief financial officer of a very successful dot-com company that had survived the Wall Street bloodbath. This man had married a girl from the Boston area and was concerned that her widowed mother, now age 66 and working part-time, did not have long-term care insurance.

His major worry was that if the mother became disabled, she would burden his wife and interfere with both their careers. His wife was, after all, a successful vice president of human resources who could not be expected to suspend her career to handle household tasks for her mother on the East Coast. He asked me to determine whether the mother was eligible for long-term care; if so, he was willing to pay the premium, which would probably cost $2,500 a year. To stay out of the family crossfire, I asked the young man to prepare his mother-in-law by asking her to call me if she was interested in long-term care planning.

Two days later, when we met, the mother-in-law looked me straight in the eye and said very sternly: "You're wasting your time."

She continued: "My children think they can throw money at a problem and solve it. I am not going to take long-term care insurance; they are not going to pay for it. If I become sick or disabled, my daughter is going to come here and take care of me. I took care of my mother for many years, and she took care of *her* mother. That's the way this family was established. Those are the values we believe in. My daughter will not pass off her responsibility to some insurance company." No ambiguity or fuzzy thinking in this case!

Face-to-face interviews are very expensive for the insurance companies, so the criterion for requiring a face-to-face test is essentially your age and for those cases where the medical records reflect a short-term memory concern. Yet insurance companies, since 1993, have been using this brief interview, which may be as short as 30 minutes, to pass a hasty and sometimes faulty judgment about the applicant's ability to reason and remember. The insurance company's objective is to focus on—and reject—high-risk applicants who might incur early and costly claims. For the applicant, there is even more at stake. Even if he passes the face-to-face cognitive impairment test, one of his answers to other questions asked in another part of the face-to-face interview might fuel a potential rejection of his application by a home office underwriter.

The cognitive test is administered not only to determine if there is any short-term memory loss problem present but also to double-check the information supplied on the policy application that includes questions pertaining to past or present illnesses, medications prescribed, and physicians consulted.

If, in the course of the interview, details that are in conflict with the answers previously furnished to the insurer surface, a further investigation could uncover heretofore-undisclosed information that will have a direct bearing on whether an insurer will issue you a policy.

It should also be noted that even though an individual might successfully pass a cognitive impairment test, comments in an attending physician's statement from the insured's doctor could cause concern that there might be a potential memory loss problem that could influence an underwriting decision.

Doing Your Homework: What the Exam Is Like

Passing a test means studying for it, and even the insurance companies suggest that their agents prepare clients for the face-to-face interview. Had the California broker whose client exhibited clear early signs of Alzheimer's told the woman what to expect, she would have been spared the painful experience, and the broker would not have been scolded by the examiner. At the least, the agent should explain what questions to expect and what documents and lists to have handy.

What's the interview like? Let's look, first, at the setting. A face-to-face interview always take place in the applicant's home at a time of his or her choosing. How long it takes is a direct function of the applicant's presenting conditions. One examiner told me that for "someone who works every day, and they're out playing golf," the meeting may last 30 minutes. But "someone with a lot of medical background or medical problems" requires that the examiner spend as long as 45 minutes to "get details." A longer interview means more cost to the insurance company and a greater likelihood of rejection at the conclusion of the process.

No Buddy System

When the face-to-face interview assessment forms were first developed, the customer was not allowed to have a companion during the meeting. This rule against a witness was strictly enforced, mostly for the insurance company's benefit. The insurers reasoned that without a witness, the examiner's word could not be questioned. No lifelines were allowed in this test—only the final answers.

Nor is there any written or recorded transcription of the face-to-face interview. An examiner I spoke with says there is no need, and no client has ever asked for a copy of the test, either before taking it or after the answers were filled in. Examiners are also trained to duck the question of how the client did on the test; the one I spoke with simply says to applicants, "You'll hear from your agent." The examiner also says that she has never had to return to a customer after completing an exam, although she always leaves her card "just in case they want to add something." She admits that most of these postexam calls are made to report additional medical information, primarily because the client fears being thought a cheat without an impeccably detailed medical history.

Insurance companies eased up on the prohibition against having a companion in the room when it satisfied their own needs. For example, the examiner explained that in some cases, having a caregiver present makes the testing situation less loaded. More important, the caregiver may help to keep a tight situation from getting out of hand. One applicant became agitated when she reached the delayed word recall section. In that case, the examiner was herself able to calm the client's fears, and the applicant went on to complete the recall successfully. Having a companion present might have served the same end. But if the companion had spoken during the exam, the examiner would have been required to note the event on the last page of the assessment document.

Oddly, having a companion present during the face-to-face process may indirectly benefit the client. Most companies prefer applicants who have spouses and families nearby, reasoning that these are "positive indicators" for social involvement. Nearby children are able to carefully monitor their parents, in the long term saving money for the insurance company by stepping in before a crisis arises.

Typically, though, it is just too bad if Grandma can't pronounce the names of the medications she takes, even though none would disqualify her application for long-term care. Too bad if she gets flustered and can't remember exactly when she takes them. Even the insurance examiner acknowledges that Grandma's daughter, Sis, could speed up the interview process by explaining the medications and their timing. No matter; the insurance company wants to hear how Grandma answers the questions, not how Sis does.

Two for the Price of One

The "no company" rule is also bent when both spouses are applying for long-term care policies. Of course, for the second interview the examiner changes the words used in the delayed word recall test, much to the disappointment of one couple shopping for coverage with whom I talked.

Barbara and John, successful lawyers in their mid-70s, were used to competing. Graduates of the same class at Yale Law School, partners in the same Wall Street firm, they loved to challenge each other in crossword puzzle competitions, legal trivia, and gin rummy. They viewed the delayed word recall test as one more competition, and insisted on "playing the game" together. No test was fun unless one spouse could take on the other. The examiner refused. Facing a situation they could not control, these two powerful lawyers put their application for the coverage on hold. No challenge, no prize.

Who Is the Judge?

All in all, then, your grade on the cognitive impairment portion of the interview along with your performance in the entire face-to-face interview process, are determined subjectively by the examiner and objectively by your score on a five-minute mini-exam.

The examiner is expressly prohibited from giving pass/fail feedback to the applicant; and the test form itself specifies, "Under no circumstances should any conclusion be drawn by the medical interviewer or an opinion expressed to the applicant as to the results of any portion of this survey." One examiner says she tells every applicant that she is "there only to assess them and observe them," not to make any decisions. Officially, the decision makers are always in the insurance company's underwriting department.

But don't believe it. The minute the examiner's pen hits the page, he or she is actively evaluating the status of your cognitive awareness and not so subtly influencing whether you will qualify for long-term care insurance.

The Study Questions

Briefly, the sections of the exam are these. The examiner:

1. Gathers basic identifying data, including name, address, and other information.
2. Moves to a medical history.
3. Introduces the words for the delayed word recall test.
4. Asks about assistive devices.
5. Surveys the applicant's ability to do the basic activities of daily living (ADLs), including bathing, showering, dressing, toileting, climbing stairs, eating and drinking, and getting in and out of bed and chair.
6. Asks about the instrumental activities of daily living—taking medicine, cooking, housework, and driving, and the applicant's typical daily routine.
7. Asks about tobacco and alcohol usage.
8. Evaluates mobility.
9. Takes physical measurements.
10. Tests for delayed word recall.
11. Evaluates orientation, which the test defines as "feeling and thinking," and which may be declined; questions include the date and year, the location of the interview, counting backward by threes, and solving a simple analogy.
12. Tests for construction, which requires drawing a circle (to represent a clock face without numbers), and then setting it for three o'clock, or copying a figure without lifting the pencil from the page.
13. Finally, asks the special questions requested by the insurance company.

Throughout this interview, the examiner is making his or her own observations of the client's demeanor, grooming, living environment, and untested irregularities such as unanswered questions.

Every question in the face-to-face exam has two answers, one explicit and one implicit. The insurance company wants to know your name, your activities, and whether you can recall words a few minutes after you hear them. However, more than that, it wants to gauge your short-term memory, your orientation to your environment, and the way you feel and think, considering these quick hits sufficient evidence of your cognitive abilities.

Identifying Information

What could be difficult about giving your name, address, Social Security number, and other familiar bits of information that identify you to institutions and people? Yet some of these questions reveal a great deal about your risk factors for long-term care insurance. Phil, for example, did not know his Social Security number and had forgotten to find the card before the examiner arrived. After all, Phil rarely gave out his Social Security number. He no longer included it on his checks or on his doctor's information sheet. He knew from the newspapers that identity thieves sometimes needed a Social Security number to apply for multiple credit cards. Phil even used a randomly generated number for his driver's license. But when he couldn't come up with the nine digits immediately, the examiner noted the hesitation on the last page of her sheet. Did Phil have long-term memory loss?

What about your address? The insurance company is interested as much in *how* you live. Are you in an assisted living community? Do you live with your spouse or your children? Have you moved to an apartment to avoid the demands of landscaping and snowblowing? These choices reflect your ability to live independently and thereby avoid long-term care. You'll save the insurance company's money.

Why do you have to show your driver's license? Because maintaining your license means you are mobile, a significant measure in American society. If you're still driving, but you have had a series of tickets or accidents, or if your license has conditions, the insurance company investigator will be able to find out.

You will be asked, "Who will care for you in the event of an emergency or prolonged illness?" You may be buying the insurance to avoid that very question, but the company wants to measure its chances of avoiding paying for a nursing home. If a friend or relative is ready to step in during a crisis, the company hopes you will need to use only the home care coverage. This way, the insurance company can save the dollars it would have spent on far more expensive nursing home care.

No one would suggest that you fudge this identifying information. Refusing to answer would be an immediate disqualifier, anyway. The questions behind the questions, nevertheless, will indicate how the company is likely to evaluate you.

Medical History

You've already told them and told them, and now they want to hear it all again. But the repetition is one reason the face-to-face interview includes a medical history. Besides, remember snowbird Harry's missed punch line? Typically, the examiner does not have a copy of the medical history you've already filled out, so his or her findings are an unbiased collaboration or possibly a refutation of that information. The insurance company reasons that the face-to-face medical history will uncover any disqualifying conditions somehow omitted in the doctor's report or your earlier documents.

There's much more to the medical history. The examiner explains that questions about previous medical conditions, doctors, and medications are significant because the ability to supply this information is a marker of unimpaired cognition. According to the examiner, an applicant who can't answer questions about a hearing loss, disabling headache, or angina is showing that he or she is not a good risk; indeed, "That's the whole point."

In this section, you will be asked to list any medications, prescribed or over-the-counter, that have not been previously mentioned. The absence of certain drugs affirms your insurability, but the examiner is also looking at your affect and behavior, judging whether you have omitted medications you actually take. According to one examiner, the best strategy is to gather your prescription bottles before the interview begins. The interview will go faster, and what better proof of orientation is there than managing this complex information so efficiently?

Playing Concentration: The Delayed Word Recall

This is the section of the interview that most concerns applicants, but there are some strategies that make remembering those words manageable. The first one is to understand how the recall test works.

In Delayed Word Recall—Part I the examiner reads aloud a word and simultaneously shows it to the applicant on a flash card. (There are 10 words in all.) The applicant is told that he or she will be asked "later" to recall the word. The applicant is asked to verbalize a sentence containing the word he or she has seen. The sentence may be as short or long as the applicant wishes. The examiner does not write any responses on this sheet.

In Delayed Word Recall—Part II, this process is repeated using the same 10 words. This time, as the examiner repeats the words and shows the flash cards, the customer is asked to use them in sentences, either the previous sentences or new ones. In this case, the examiner records the number of words the applicant was incapable of using in a sentence. He also writes down the exact time, because a maximum of 10 minutes may elapse before returning to this test.

Now the examiner continues the test, keeping an eye on the time. After at least five minutes have been consumed with other parts of the interview, the applicant is asked to "recall as many of the words as you can remember." While the applicant struggles with this task, the examiner also notes the customer's "responsiveness, alertness, awareness, and overall cognizance—or lack thereof—in recalling the words." The elapsed time between presentation of the list and its recall is carefully noted.

How does this test measure cognitive impairment? It tests short-term memory, which the companies have decided is their best measure of the client's "overall cognizance." Naturally, the task is complicated by the questions that occur between presentation of the words and their recall. When asking the applicant, who is doubtless rehearsing the words, about use of assistive devices, smoking patterns, or activities of basic living, the examiner is using what psychologists call an interpolated activity as a distraction device. The whole point is to prevent any rehearsal of the words. If the customer forgets the words in five minutes, how will he or she remember to take medications or to turn left instead of right on the way home?

Why is such a test an adequate evaluator of general cognizance? Once when my wife was having a bridge game, I opened the refrigerator and found a set of keys next to a brown bag holding a carton of milk. There were other cartons of orange juice and milk, all unbagged. My interest was piqued. Bridge demands concentration and strategy; my wife and her friends were first-class players. A few months later, during another of my wife's games, I went for a snack. Not only was there once again a brown bag with a carton of milk and a set of keys in the refrigerator, there was also a plastic bag from Jake's Deli filled with cold cuts, with a set of keys next to it. Is short-term memory loss catching? When I asked, the women explained that they did not want to forget their leftover lunches, so they deduced that the best way to remember was to put their keys on top of their carryout.

Here playing bridge is an interpolated activity. If there had been no distraction between coming into the house and returning to the car, the women might not have needed this cueing trick. In this case, the trick worked, no one forgot her milk, and the women enjoyed their leftover lunches for dinner. At least in theory, no one with a cognitive impairment will be able to pass the delayed word recall test. The bridge players knew what had been bid, but would an insurance examiner have determined that putting keys in a refrigerator indicates awareness or a breakdown of short-term memory?

Most of the time, you need remember only half of the words to pass the delayed word recall test. The examiner I interviewed actually reported that as many as 90 percent of applicants pass the delayed recall portion of the test. Some use unorthodox means. One woman "put all her words into a song." When asked if she could repeat the words, the client said, "I never knew I had to tell you these words." Then she "sang the song."

There are other tricks for getting through the delayed word recall portions of the test. The first suggestion has to do with timing. Make sure your interview is scheduled for your best time, when you are most rested. A thoughtful insurance examiner such as the one I interviewed will remind you to be sure a ringing doorbell, a neighborly visit, or the telephone won't interrupt you; no need to add additional interpolations to the mix. Also, the test uses very familiar words for most of us, although others may from time to time be included. To help you remember, relax, visualize the word, and place it into the context of the room; don't rush to "pop it into a sentence."

My client Helen, the newspaper-reading Dan Rather fan, got tripped up with the delayed word recall test. Helen worked with words all the time for tournament Scrabble. She could have recalled the spelling of most words in Webster's Collegiate during a contest, but she had trouble with one of the most simple words, "meadow." Here is how she explained what happened:

As a girl, she said, she had grown up in the Mattapan section of Boston. She was very familiar with corned beef sandwiches, kosher butcher stores, and trolley cars. But she lived in a six-family tenement surrounded by three-family houses. "How can you expect me to recall the word 'meadow'?" she said. "I never saw one. I was never there, and I don't recall talking about one in school." Helen forgot other words besides "meadow," but for the examiner the noun was so common and easily remembered that Helen's failure became proof of her cognitive impairment.

Still, if you have trouble with this portion of the face-to-face interview, don't give up. While short-term memory loss may automatically disqualify some people from obtaining long-term care insurance, some companies actually allow the condition, especially if it seems to be from temporary causes. For example, if the policy is a corporate one involving more than one insured, the company might be willing to overlook a temporary memory loss in order to make the sale, in a practice called a "business exception." In the same way, a new company anxious to get as much business as possible in its new marketplace may be willing to accept risks that it would later reject.

Insurers anxious to get business will provide certain amounts of coverage on a guaranteed-issue basis for corporations where several policies are involved. This means that the company merely requires that the employee be actively at work, and will not ask health questions. In most cases, however, your coverage will be put on hold until you can provide the underwriter with a letter from your doctor attesting that you have fully recovered from any surgery or injury and require no assistance in your daily activities, including the use of canes or walkers.

Assistive Devices

When you are asked if you need help "in order to get around" during the assistive device portion of the interview, the company is evaluating your level of independence. Let's say you use a cane mostly for "bumpy sidewalks," or because it makes you "feel secure." The examiner I interviewed says that this is a familiar answer, but is reluctant to estimate how frequently using a single-footed cane might prompt a rejection. Still, the list of devices is clearly hierarchical, since it begins with depending on a friend's arm to climb the stairs and ends with depending on a wheelchair to get across the room. It seems obvious that if your movement is already significantly impaired, your long-term insurance application is in jeopardy.

Basic Activities of Daily Living

In addition to cognitive impairment, the activities of daily living, discussed in Chapter 1, are the legal triggers for every long-term care policy. They include bathing, dressing, toileting, continence, eating, and transferring from bed to chair. During this part of the interview, you will need to specify whether you can perform the activities without help, with adaptive or assistive help, or only with physical assistance and supervision. If you become unable to perform any two of them and you have a tax-qualified plan, your benefits will begin. The number of necessary triggers varies for non-tax-qualified plans, but you may only need to be disabled in one of the ADLs to trigger benefit payments.

The point, then, is clear: If you indicate limitations in an ADL, you'll probably be rejected for insurance. What if, like one of my clients, you have had your hip replaced and expect to be fully and independently ambulatory in a few months? Granted you need your spouse's arm to walk from the front step out into the yard, but once you're in your garden, the pain magically disappears. The examiner must ask you about your difficulty, inquire who performs the task for you, and why you need such support. You will have difficulty convincing the underwriters that you'll be a good risk.

Instrumental Activities of Daily Living

The activities of daily living list is a legal guideline, set by the federal government to determine Medicaid coverage and is part of the definition of a tax-qualified plan. The instrumental activities of daily living are not legal triggers; the insurance company is not legally obligated to pay you benefits when you are unable to take medicine independently, to telephone, cook, do housework and laundry, buy food, pay bills, and generally handle money. Why ask, then? The examiner is trying to determine in this section whether the applicant can take care of himself or herself. Each instrumental activity is a measure of independence and, to some extent, of cognizance. As one company manual puts it: "Living in and maintaining one's own home is a positive indicator." The insurance company also considers them indicators of a client's future cognitive good health.

One question addresses the use of a power of attorney. The question is not innocuous, since such an exercise would indicate that at some point the client was or expected to be at least temporarily incapacitated. Remember that Ronald Reagan, even after he was shot, did not officially relinquish his presidential power. Although the president later was diagnosed with Alzheimer's, no insurance company could have caught him on the power of attorney question.

Perhaps no activity is more important to a senior than the ability to drive. This section, like the one on identifying information, questions that ability, asking about accidents, handicap plates, and other obvious limitations. The company wants to insure "risks" who won't need the benefits, so wisely giving up a license may be a red flag for insurance underwriters who associate driving with social life. To some, the inability to get out of the house and to maintain social contacts could be a precursor to depression and functional decline, converting the once active senior citizen into a long-term care client.

Taking a Tobacco or Alcohol Break

Your examiner will ask about your tobacco and alcohol use, but answering yes to either question is not an automatic disqualification. If, however, your doctor has warned you against either substance and includes that in his or her report, you may be a less attractive applicant.

Taking a Walk

If your examiner sees you moving naturally around the room, he or she may forgo asking you to demonstrate your mobility by walking across the room, turning around, and walking back. In any case, he or she will evaluate your ability to arise without help on the first attempt, to maintain your balance, to turn steadily, to walk without an aid, and to sit in a smooth motion. If, as the form says, you "almost fall" when turning or "plop" into your chair, the examiner may well conclude that you have a movement disorder or some other condition limiting your ability to ambulate.

Measurements

The physical exam includes height and weight measurements, with the examiner providing the scale. There are strict "build" guidelines for long-term care insurance, but the examiner I spoke to said that "nobody ever questions" her scale. Insurance companies are particularly interested in weight because obesity puts pressure on the knees, in addition to making the applicant vulnerable to physical ailments. If your blood pressure is above 140/90, the examiner will repeat the test twice to combat the "doctor's office effect." Our examiner says that she routinely tells the applicant his or her blood pressure, although she is not required to do so. If your blood pressure is elevated despite your medications, you may be at risk for a refusal.

There are no portable bone density scanners yet, but once these exist, insurance companies will send them along on face-to-face interviews. Osteoporosis can present a problem in obtaining coverage, and the examiner I spoke with says that most women volunteer the results of their bone scans.

Orientation

The orientation section of the test is less difficult than the delayed word recall, but also more subtle. The examiner asks, "May I ask you some questions about how you feel and think?" and the applicant may actually refuse to answer. One part of the test requires counting backward by threes, starting with the number 20. This test is not as difficult as those which demand counting back from 100, but difficult enough even for applicants used to balancing their checkbooks without calculators. The temptation to refuse is powerful here, but the behavior will result in a subjective note on the examiner's last page.

Keep Your Eye on the Clock

If the examiner uses the construction section of the evaluation, you'll be asked to draw a circle representing the face of a clock, then to draw the hands at three o'clock. If you have trouble, you get two additional attempts at the task. But if you fail, the examiner must note that on the test. The second part tests both dexterity and strategy, since it requires copying a figure without lifting the pen off the page. You'll get three tries on this one, too, and a failure will indicate to the examiner that you may have difficulty with cognition.

Beware the Bonus Questions

Sometimes you're answering a question that you don't realize has been asked. The underwriter or the agent may alert the examiner to a condition that might make the applicant a poor risk—for example, a stroke. In this case, the examiner looks closely for signs of a stroke, which may manifest with residual memory problems or breakdowns of language.

Does It Come Down to How Much the Teacher Likes You?

Ultimately, the examiner potentially has significant input into the success of the applicant. He or she evaluates the client's personal demeanor, grooming, and living environment. It is best, then, to put the cat out and empty the garbage before the face-to-face interview.

If you've declined to take the orientation section or you've allowed an observer to participate, the examiner will write that on the last page. Nor will you find out how you did immediately after the test. The examiner is prohibited from giving feedback to the customer, and our examiner says that even though she might have a situation in which the customer will obviously not qualify for insurance, she always finishes the exam.

What If You're Still Suffering from Test Anxiety?

If you're still apprehensive at this point, here are a few last-minute tips:

- You might search for a company that does not conduct a phone interview or impose a cognitive impairment test. There could always be one out there—perhaps one not represented by an agent, a broker, or a planner. If you locate one that suits you, contact a representative and apply for long-term care insurance coverage. This company will satisfy one of the criteria you've developed for your long-term care plan.

- If you are preoccupied with a personal or business matter, defer scheduling the test to a time when your head is clear. You have lived all your life without long-term care insurance. A few more weeks without it shouldn't make a difference.

- Have available writing instruments that you are familiar with, including sharpened pencils and pens with adequate supplies of ink.

- If you need eyeglasses for reading, make sure that you have them on your person.

- Have available a detailed list of your medications, including dosages, and the names, addresses, and telephone numbers of any physicians or facilities where you have obtained treatment during the past five years.

- Don't memorize any list of 10 words supplied to you by an insurance agent or broker to help you prepare for the test. You run the risk of being confused. Examiners frequently change the recall words and the sequence used for testing purposes.

- Not all the various long-term care insurers use the same tests; some have their own. Others go along with those used by the outsourced examining organizations. In many respects the tests are essentially the same, and the variations tend to be minor.

- You don't have to be a trivia expert or a qualifier for the *Who Wants to Be a Millionaire?* TV show to pass the test. Don't expect to be asked for the name of the postmaster general in Herbert Hoover's administration, but you could be asked the names of a few recent presidents who immediately preceded President George W. Bush.

- Stay calm during the interview. If a question seems unclear, don't hesitate to ask the examiner to repeat it. The examiner appreciates that it may be 50 or more years since your last oral examination.

- Disconnect your cell phone, and make sure you don't expect to receive any important phone calls to your home during the scheduled time period for your examination.

- If you live alone, make sure that your residence is neat and clean and there is not a stack of dirty dishes in the kitchen.

- Don't be depressed in the event you fail to pass the test. You can always request a repeat one or seek out another insurance company. Keep in mind that billion-dollar insurance companies are capable of making mistakes.

- After your policy is issued—not before—it is recommended that you discuss any concerns you might have about your short-term memory with your physician.

Endnotes

1. Selkoe, Dr. Dennis. "Alzheimer's Fears Appear Overblown." Insurance column, *Boston Globe*, April 8, 1997.
2. *Conseco Underwriting Guide to Long-Term Care Insurance*. Conseco Insurance Company. p. 2.
3. *The Shopper's Guide to Long-Term Care Insurance*. National Association of Insurance Commissioners. Glossary.
4. Selkoe. "Alzheimer's Fears Appear Overblown."
5. Interview with June Saltzberg, BodiMedex, May 14, 2001.

CHAPTER 8

Leveling the Playing Field: How to Distinguish between Fact and Fiction during the Sales Pitch

Choosing care options for your very old age is central to any prudent financial plan; and for some people, long-term care insurance is an important option. That's why I have written this book. Further, the vast majority of insurance representatives are honest, thoughtful salespeople, guided by the National Association of Insurance Commissioners' Code of Conduct for marketing long-term care products. Most insurance agents see their task as educational, to inform consumers about the exposure and actual expenses they might face in their very old age and then to suggest reasonable solutions. The insurance industry knows that, in the last analysis, the ability of companies to survive and bring in business depends at least in part on the honesty and integrity of their agents. Without the public trust, no amount of careful underwriting or actuarial calculation will strengthen the bottom line on company balance sheets.

Unfortunately, however, some long-term care salespeople use scare tactics and sales gimmickry as part of their pitch. These insurance representatives, sometimes encouraged by their companies, forget that the public is well aware of the potential need for expensive long-term care. Worse, the playing field is not level; the uneducated insurance customer is at a handicap when sitting across the table from the well-trained sales agent programmed to handle any and all objections and concerns. The less reputable agent, armed with dooms-day scenarios and smooth talk, pushes prospective policyholders toward a fast close and toward a product that might not suit their needs. The customers, with little knowledge about the long-term care product they are considering and too much knowledge about their own limited financial resources, sit aghast at the exaggerated statistics and predictions.

The purpose of this chapter is to inoculate you against the deliberately frightening warnings and the implicit threats you may hear from a less rep-utable insurance representative. We are going to demystify the hype and help you make an informed decision about the plan that most suits your needs and fulfills the goal of your old age: the maintenance of your independence and your dignity.

Paying for long-term care is going to be the "financial issue of our times," says one important industry executive, a managing general agent for more than nine companies who does business with more than one thousand inde-pendent insurance brokers.[1] This executive trains her agents on all aspects of long-term care products, provides comparisons between policies, and supports sales. Her business practice is a model for fair market conduct.

As a "wholesaler" of long-term insurance, the executive has a global view of the long-term care marketplace. Our population is aging, she explains, but the average buyer of long-term coverage is actually getting younger. Many of her customers are under 60 years old, just now free of their "dependency years," which is industry talk for those years of supporting their kids and paying off their mortgages. Often these clients are planning their retirement. A large percentage of her clients have policies paid for by their employers; the others reach into their own pockets, recognizing the value of spending a portion of their assets now to protect their precious independence later, during their very old age.

Let's translate this thoughtful executive's careful, rational explanation of the long-term care marketplace into long-term care sales-speak as it would be delivered by a less reputable insurance representative:

"Hey, Mr. and Mrs. America, we are living older but sicker! Beware: Fifty percent of us will be in nursing homes! Worse: Eighty percent of our nursing home neighbors will be our lady friends. Save your money, ladies, since you'll be a nursing home resident at least 150 percent longer than your husband will—after all, you'll be prematurely worn out by taking care of him until he dies. Four out of five couples will have a spouse requiring nursing home care. Wives, it will be you! And don't assume the kids will be thrilled to quit their jobs to manage your daily needs, either. They've got their own lives!"

How does a rational overview of the field of long-term care insurance become translated into such scare tactics, deliberately filled with emotionally charged statistics and terrifying warnings, all taken out of context? Why, in the guise of educating consumers, do some insurance companies encourage their agents to scare customers into hasty decisions by glossing over the fine print and refusing to take no for an answer?

Look at this example of promotional language in a long-term care insurance brochure: "Two out of every five Americans may need nursing home care some-time in their lives."

Think about this purported "statistic." What can it mean? How many months or years will this need last? The brochure doesn't say. And why does it say "may need"? The company might as well have proclaimed that five out of every five Americans, in other words every last one of us, *may need* nursing home care sometime in their lives. After all, who really knows?

Such brochures often warn, "The current cost of nursing home care ranges from an average of $50,000 to over $100,000 a year in some areas of the country." Those are scary numbers, but why the big spread in the dollar estimates? Besides, asks the thoughtful customer, must we all plan to spend our final days in a nursing home bed? What about these options? Some of us, after all, can expect to enjoy other forms of long-term care.

Surely most of us want a less costly alternative. We want our dollars to help us to stay at home.

Why the Insurance Industry Wants You to Buy Long-Term Care Coverage

The insurance industry has figured out exactly why it wants to sell you a long-term care policy: to make money. Above all, insurance companies are huge businesses. If the insurer is a stock company, it has a responsibility to make a profit for its shareholders. If it is a mutual company, it must make money for its policyholders. Our parents and our grandparents would never have dreamed that the very symbols of American business, Metropolitan Life, Prudential, and John Hancock—the companies from whom they purchased their initial $1,000 policies—would demutualize. Now these companies are listed on the New York Stock Exchange, and they are run by bean counters whose primary concern is to pump up stock prices with greater earnings.

Stock company or mutual company, profit comes first, and the consumer second.

Profit is the number one priority in some industry marketing guides, the sales manuals that are provided by companies to their brokers. These instructional guides stress the size of the target market and the rapidly aging population. One independent sales manual proclaims to the agent reading it: The market is untapped, simply poised for huge growth.[2] What about the poor risks out there in the market? What about the possibility that any insurance company that sells to this risky market may be unable to pay later, when these poor risks come calling? No matter; the message is clear. There is "gold in them thar hills."

There is a different message in the long-term care advertising brochures your agent hands you. These brochures state unequivocally that you need to buy long-term care coverage because it is good for you. To some extent, I agree with this prescription. I know many people will benefit from long-term care coverage—that's why I have written this book. I've also never heard of anyone returning a benefit check because it wasn't enough; they only complained that the benefit they bought wasn't larger.

GE Capital's long-term care plans will "create safeguards for yourself and your family" in the event you are unable to care for yourself.[3] TIAA CREF worries about the "rising costs of long-term care services" that might "jeopardize your financial security."[4] Yet many of these sales brochures suggest they will maintain your "independence," without promising to keep you out of a nursing home. Nursing homes, as we have seen, prefer that their residents be covered by private insurance whose rate is often 30 percent higher than Medicaid residents' pay.

In short, the insurance industry knows exactly to whom it is selling and can define precisely what makes an ideal customer. This person pays his premiums, lives a very long time, and dies without ever making a claim. Any agent who offers you a policy without asking for appropriate medical documentation is not to be trusted. You can figure that a company with a poor underwriting policy may not be in the business long enough to pay your claim when you're ready.

Stable insurance companies want to sell policies to only the very best customers, those with the least risk. And why not? To stay in business, the insurer needs to balance income and expense, risk against payout. To some extent, the actuaries who make these statistical calculations are legal bookies. When they accept your premium dollar, they're betting that you won't ever need significant benefits. You may be surprised by how this "bet" works in practice.

Fred, for instance, waited five years after his cancer to buy long-term care insurance. He figured he should now qualify for coverage, since most companies would require this five-year wait after surgery for his unique type of cancer. Now he was in excellent health. But after checking his pathology reports and chemotherapy records, two companies refused to sell Fred a policy.

A third company was happy to write Fred's long-term care insurance. The underwriters reasoned that if Fred's particular kind of cancer was to recur, he would most likely live only six months. They figured in the three-month waiting period built into his coverage, and knew that Fred would likely be claiming only three months of benefits. He was a great risk! Ghoulish, perhaps, but true.

Fred's case of course is not typical. Companies rush to write long-term care policies for preretirement adults, even those as young as 40. These individuals are especially good risks, tending to remain healthy and independent for many years. Besides, insurers know that some conditions that may require long-term care, such as Parkinson's or Alzheimer's, are actuarially likely to happen later in life, making the younger policyholder even more attractive.

Don't think, however, that the 40-year-old buyer of long-term care insurance is being taken advantage of by the big old insurance industry. This is just how the insurance business works. The company spreads out its risk by enrolling these healthy policyholders and then using their premium payments for its investments. The income from these investments pays the claims of current beneficiaries, often the parents or grandparents of the young adult buyers. Younger consumers benefit when they buy policies at a lower price; they have the option to buy policies at a lower premium geared to their reduced risk of morbidity. They also know that if they become suddenly uninsurable, or if a catastrophe should make them need the long-term care benefits, they've won the financial bet if not the physical one.

What the Insurance Industry Thinks of Its Customers

Salespeople always talk about target markets and qualified clients. That's why teen magazines don't advertise 401(k) plans and automobile magazines don't sell cosmetics. Sellers of long-term care coverage know exactly how old you are (preretirement or retirement age), how much money you have (no mortgage, $70,000 to $100,000 of liquid assets), and how healthy you are.

In addition to these qualifying attributes, the insurance industry has made several explicit assumptions about your intelligence. The central assumption, underlying the sales pitches and sales tactics, is that you know absolutely nothing about long-term care products. While you may have heard the horror stories, you don't have a clue about your options for long-term care.

The industry is correct that its customers probably know more about the cars and computers they buy than about their long-term care options. After all, the product is so new that, according to the managing general agent, these long-term care products are today where 401(k)s were 20 years ago, and where Medicare was when it first came out. This executive says that while insurance to cover us in our very old age is not yet accepted as an absolute core benefit, it will be in another five or 10 years when there will be very few people over the age of 45 who do not want long-term care insurance.[5]

The insurance industry assumes that the buyer is more than merely stupid. Because we're uneducated about long-term care coverage, we suffer from unconscious incompetence. We don't know what we don't know. Remember second grade, when you struggled with addition and didn't know that the Pythagorean theorem even existed? That's where we are with long term care coverage.

Unconscious incompetence makes for risky financial business when an insurance agent comes knocking at your door. You'll be receptive to a sales pitch because you don't have the knowledge to evaluate it; and worse, you may think you understand exactly what you're hearing. Insurance company representatives, at least those who are less than admirable, play upon this weakness in their customers; some act on the temptation to run with it. Unconscious incompetence has an obvious cure: Research before you shop—that's why you're reading this book! Look further in this chapter for some practical advice to follow when you talk to the sales agent.

Granted, the company will hand you informational material. The agent who sits at your kitchen table discussing options comes armed with glossy brochures describing the company's long-term care products. And let's say you always read any document before you sign it. None of this helps if the policy is written in official insurance language that you can't translate. The Glossary at the end of this book will help you with the big words.

You can also ask for a copy of the policy. Insurers do not always anticipate this request; and some may hope you will find it simpler to take your agent's word than to wade through the abstractions and lists of exclusions. Take the time and the plunge, or some of the policy's provisions will surprise you. Besides, the quickest way to become consciously competent is to do your homework.

Since the market is stupid, goes the insurance industry thinking, long-term care products must be *sold*—the customer does not inherently want to *buy*. To understand this assumption, consider the way you shopped for your automobile insurance. You chose a deductible you felt comfortable with and a level of collision protection based on the value of your car. You chose the limits on injury that fit with your other insurance protections. Without insurance, you couldn't register your car or get a license plate, so you went looking for an insurer; the insurer did not have to look for you. Your demand pulled the insurance through the pipeline; you wanted to buy. The insurance company didn't have to push the product or work terribly hard to sell it.

Shopping for long-term care coverage is different. The unthinking consumers, according to industry belief, have not figured out exactly how they want to spend their old age or how they are going to pay for it. Therefore, the insurance industry has an obligation to tell them what they want and need. The agent is the messenger of this news. Again, this is a fair assessment of the agent's role. The insurance representative does have an obligation to educate clients, to tell consumers why they may need long-term care in the future and what the cost of that care might be.

Too often the insurance industry translates this educational function into practice as follows: Sell fast and sell hard, present no more than two or three minimally different alternatives, and close the deal fast before the customer becomes uninsurable. Don't worry that the customer might talk to other agents, since only one in three buyers actually does so; unconscious incompetence discourages the practice, after all. Besides, the thinking goes, the salesperson is not actually pressuring the applicants but rather is educating them. It is the agent's duty to advise the customers to move fast lest they become uninsurable. Too bad that this "education" focuses on needs and not benefits, on frightening statistics instead of worthwhile product alternatives.

The growth of the Internet has created at least a measure of informational protection for long-term care buyers. Agents recognize that the careful consumer is able to comparison shop online. As a result, while agents may be tempted to accentuate the positive and eliminate the negative, they also realize that they need to give a fair representation of products or the consumer can surf the Web for more choices.

Companies also routinely advise their agents not to waste time with clients who have health or financial problems. These people are most likely to be uninsurable, anyway, and often they're merely professional shoppers, out for a little afternoon entertainment. Other clients know they cannot afford the coverage, but are too proud to admit it to the agent sitting at their table. Pitching a policy to a married couple, the agent is advised to aim his or her energies at the wife since she is supposedly most often sensitive to the pitch, less likely to be educated about the product, more easily swayed, and more likely to expect to need the coverage. The wife typically assumes that she'll be around to take care of her husband; the husband usually agrees. The wife also assumes—and fears—that no one will be around to take care of her.

Where do you, the individual consumer, stand against the mighty insurance company? You are in charge. You are the decision maker, and it's your money. Insurers want your business, and you may want their long-term care product. Armed with information, you are well able to level the playing field and to decide the details of your long-term care.

What the Insurance Salesperson Wants

Naturally, the salesperson wants to make money. But insurance sales is honorable work, and the reputable agent who contacts you is motivated by more than just the bottom line.

The Good News

Ideally, even the insurance agent who makes a cold call during your dinner hour wants to benefit you when he sells you a long-term care policy. GE Capital provides a detailed code of ethical conduct to its representatives, stressing among other items that its agents make "recommendations and present products based on an analysis of the insurable needs and financial objectives of the customer."[6] John Hancock's sales manual advises its agents that their chief job is to provide their clients with ways to manage the financial risk presented by long-term care needs.[7] Several codes of conduct developed by the insurance industry require fair comparison between products, the reasonable expectation that premium costs can be met, a determination that the coverage is appropriate and suitable, and a screening for overinsurance of long-term care needs.[8]

We all like to believe that our insurance broker has our best interest at heart, that he or she follows the NAIC code of conduct to the letter. This agent has probably been selling us insurance for years and may even be a cousin, a high school buddy, or a neighbor. It makes good financial sense for the agent to recommend the best plan, staying away from questionable companies. Successful agents know that their income is based not only on their first-year sales, but also on commissions paid for renewal premiums. Even the most aggressive of sales manuals warns against pushing clients toward companies that have frequent rate increases or are in wobbly financial shape. Renewals will disappear and, even worse, the agent will sacrifice the most valuable source of referred leads, existing clients.[9]

Insurance brokers for long-term care products, then, must put the customer's needs before their own. Looking over the privileged information on the customer's financial statement, the agent is charged by the code of ethics with making sensible suggestions for long-term care coverage. If the fit between customer and product is not appropriate, the honest agent says so. If the customer drifts toward a policy that will not benefit him or her, the honest agent says so. If the policy contains clauses that might later prove troublesome, the honest agent says so. The managing general agent I spoke with said that the biggest problem in the long-term care coverage industry is that there are not enough educated agents and brokers to sell such a difficult product.[10]

And the Bad News

Unfortunately, I can think of some additional problems with insurance agents. Just as insurance companies are primarily profit-making businesses, some agents who pitch you long-term care insurance are primarily interested in making their sales. They recognize an untapped market when they see one and are reminded repeatedly to pitch long-term care coverage to any candidate over age 35. It's no surprise that the biggest growth in long-term care sales occurs in those under 60, not even counting sales to corporations offering a policy as a fringe benefit to their key employees.

Commissions for selling long-term care coverage are also significantly higher than for other types of insurance, such as automobile policies. Insurance companies reward long-term care sales because they recognize the effort involved in writing the policy. Hence an aggressive agent can make big money.

One sales manual developed by a self-proclaimed marketing expert suggests that an agent who sells six policies a week, with an average premium of $1,300, may be paid a 40 percent commission on each sale. This productive insurance representative stands to make as much as $109,200 on long-term care insurance commissions in the first year alone. Do the math to year 10, crank in the renewals, and you will note that your friendly agent can look to a yearly income as high as $219,765 for the long-term care business.[11] And the income will keep on growing. That kind of take-home pay is certainly reasonable for a competent professional.

The agent enjoys other payoffs, too. Companies may offer "sales growth prizes"—for example, six days at a five-star Cancún resort—for the agent who writes the most business. The lucky contestants are invited to double count their premium dollars in the month the contest ends. In addition, some companies provide higher commission schedules, retirement benefits, health insurance for the family, a car, and reimbursement for other sales expenses sustained by volume producers.

Why should we object when our sales agent wins a prize for selling us insurance? Everyone loves a winner. Here's why: When the company offers a prize for sales, it is tacitly encouraging its representatives to put their own best interests before their clients' interests. Even an agent who adheres to the NAIC guidelines might be sorely tempted to spend March in Cancún, given the opportunity. The temptation is reinforced when the insurance company tells its agents that they are its "most valued customers." I always thought the person buying the policy was the company's most important customer, not the fellow selling it.

What do agents have to do in order to make the sale, earn the commission, and win the trip? One possibility is to pass themselves off as experts in the complicated provisions of long-term care products. We should be reassured that reputable agents are concerned about the NAIC code of ethics. Their company sales manuals advise them to meet the licensing standards of their state and pay attention to the changes in long-term care insurance options.

But watch out for the agent who seems to know all about long-term care choices, although he or she has no documentation to prove it. The agent may be both consciously and unconsciously incompetent. Many sales manuals advise the long-term care salesperson to become an "expert" in the product by calling a few nursing homes in the area for price comparisons. Then the agent can confidently announce his expertise when sitting down at the table to chat, figuring he won't be discovered, and reassured by company-supplied data that tells him the potential customer won't shop around.

How do you know if your broker is an expert in long-term care products? Ask some of the questions I've included in Chapter 13, "Questions and Answers." The most revealing ones will be about commissions, experience in the insurance business, experience in long-term care products, and knowledge about rate increases. If your agent is also your nephew, avoid the awkward questions by saying, "I want to learn more about long-term care insurance and maybe buy a policy, and I know that some insurance representatives specialize in the product. Could you bring in a colleague you respect, one who really knows the long-term care insurance possibilities? You could work jointly. I'd learn something, and you would, too."

What the Agent Says

If you flinch when your phone rings at dinner, you're doubtless inundated with cold calls. These calls are legal, they are legitimate sales tools, and they are sanctioned if not encouraged by insurance companies. Although many insurance companies and sales strategists prefer to use direct mail solicitations, sales motivators continue to suggest that agents spend their spare time making cold calls. If you have an old-fashioned name, you may get more than your share of these calls, since several motivators suggest that insurance salespeople pick out these names from the phone book. This is an interesting strategy for the new millennium, where children are commonly named Max, Noah, Samuel, or Rebecca.

No matter where agents find their phone lists, they are limited in what they can say to you on the phone, at least insofar as the National Association of Insurance Commissioners is concerned. Cold lead advertising is prohibited when it "fails to disclose in a conspicuous manner that the purpose of marketing is the solicitation of insurance and that an agent will contact the individual."[12] In other words, the callers have to admit to you that they are selling insurance. You should ask what the individual is selling in your first 10 phone seconds and then decide if you want to hear the pitch. Don't be surprised if the same agent calls you several times. One insurance representative who specializes in cold calling told me that she makes up to 500 calls a week, tracking the responses so that she can recontact people who said they might be interested in the future.

Finally, beware of the fast close. Some insurers have trained their agents to push for a signature at the first sales call, using a doomsday scenario so powerful that the clients feel they have no choice. If they don't buy long-term care coverage, they'll be on Medicaid or camping in their kids' basement. A few reputable agents might argue that the fast close actually works in favor of clients, since the longer they delay the more likely they are to become uninsurable. But even cold callers expect to take three visits to close the deal.

Consumers at the very least should spend as much time exploring long-term care options as they do exploring the purchase of a video cassette recorder. How can a consumer decide on a policy worth several hundred thousand dollars in the hour it would take to buy a $90 VCR? The independence of our very old age is worth vastly more than a taped copy of *Seinfeld*, and VCRs are disposable while long-term care insurance must last years. Unlike the advice you got when you took a multiple-choice test, your first impulse—to buy or not to buy—may not be the correct one. The information in this book should prove to you that buying into the fast close is a recipe for disaster.

How to Talk to Your Agent

There is no question that planning for our very old age is important. If it weren't, you wouldn't be reading this book. Yet even the most prudent consumers might become flustered when they listen to emotional sales pitches from less than reputable agents. The consumer has an inherent disadvantage, as we've seen. The agent knows the product and the sales pitch; the consumer knows very little. Agents have been trained by experts to handle objections. Their sales manuals give them a response to every question or concern the consumer has. They are trained to manage ambivalence, handle silence, and turn to the spouses if they are more responsive. Essentially, as a consumer, you are up against company training courses, industry motivational tapes the agent plays in the car on the way to your meeting, and every sales seminar he or she has attended.

You deserve to buy the policy you want. This book will arm you with responses to an unscrupulous agent's claims and predictions. Whether you are a first-time shopper in the long-term care marketplace or an experienced buyer looking to change policies, read on for ways to deflect an insurance representative's threats and to redirect him or her to the information that you really need and want.

Handling the Mealtime Phone Call

You're familiar with the experience. The soup's hot, the kids are finally at the table, and the phone rings. When you pick up the receiver, the agent starts the presentation. What do you do?

THE FAST TALKER

Agent: "I am calling from the Paragon Advisory Group to let you know that we understand you might be interested in the information that we have available to help seniors and their families."

Even though the insurance agent's code of ethics requires that the caller admit he or she has a product to sell you, the fast-talking phone representative may not give you a chance to get a word in.

Your rebuttal: "Are you trying to sell me something?"

Agent: "I'm calling to offer you very valuable informational material that has helped many seniors and their families."

Your rebuttal: "You still haven't answered my question. Are you trying to sell me something?"

Agent: "Our agency specializes in the marketing of long-term care insurance, but we take pride in the fact that after educating our prospects they will either recommend us to others or they will see the light and initiate a sale through our company."

Your rebuttal: "I don't understand just why you hide behind all these subtleties. Selling is an honorable profession. My son is a successful clothing salesman and his work has enabled him to educate his family, put a roof over his head, and provided a great quality of life. Come right out and tell your prospects who you really are."

THE ASSUMED APPOINTMENT

Agent: "Good Morning, Mrs. Benson. I understand that you are interested in learning more about long-term care insurance. I am going to be in your neighborhood next Tuesday and Wednesday. Are mornings or afternoons better for you to meet with me?"

The agent figures you'll be flustered enough to make an appointment. Besides, you must be hanging around the house all the time, anyway.

Your rebuttal: "Thank you for your interest. Please send me your material, and if I am interested and want to make an appointment with you, I will call you."

THE MISLEADING MAILER

Agent: "I'm telephoning to inform you that I have your request for a booklet on retirement income. You remember the reply card you completed in response to my company's recent mailing. We've found out that there are many other subjects and more detailed information about retirement income that individuals want to learn about. For that reason, I'd like to find out when there is a good time to drop by your home and deliver the material."

Your rebuttal: "Why don't you mail me the booklet, and if I'm interested, I'll be in further touch with you."

THE "WHAT YOU REALLY WANT TO KNOW" MAILER

Agent: "We found out that in similar situations, the information we send might not be the type of information you're looking for. Are you aware that there is very little coverage in Medicare for long-term care? Are you aware that the expenses in a nursing home would probably bankrupt you? Are you aware of the probability of your spending some time in a nursing home?"

Your rebuttal: "I thought you were advertising and offering some form of retirement information, not trying to sell me long-term care insurance."

Agent: "Long-term care is one of a number of considerations in the overall retirement planning process, and I'd like the opportunity to explain the various options to you."

Your rebuttal: "Are you going to try to sell me long-term care insurance?"

Agent: "My role is to educate you and if in the process you find that you might need long-term care insurance, I would hope you would consider me."

Your rebuttal: "Please mail me the information advertised in your mailing piece and what I indicated I wanted when I sent back your postpaid reply card."

Tools for the First-Time Buyer

If you're a first time-buyer, the agent wants to hook you in immediately so that you will attend carefully to the sales pitch. He or she does that in a variety of ways, most of them shady.

THE SCARE

Agent: "Look at these statistics showing that you and your husband have a four out of five chance to end up in a nursing home. Your children will not want to take care of you, either." The agent knows that these statistics will certainly frighten you, and hopes that you've recently spatted with your daughter as well.

Your rebuttal: "My children and even my grandchildren have assured us that we will never spend a day in a nursing home. Both of our children have large winter and summer homes with enough room to take care of us if that time ever comes. In the interim, we have the kids' old rooms to house live-in help if one of us needs ongoing care."

THE THREAT

Agent: "If you can't afford the premium, how will you afford long-term care when you need it?" Two thousand dollars a year sounds like a lot of money to most of us, even though our life insurance may cost considerably more. Besides, the agent knows that death is inevitable, even if the need for long-term care may not be.

Your rebuttal: "The insurance company takes risks. Well, I take risks in my life, too. At this stage of the game, I feel that I have complete knowledge of all the facts. I'm a grown-up and I can handle the risks."

THE PREDICTION

Agent: "You have to buy now because you'll be too sick later to qualify for the coverage and you'll need it for sure." Look around you, the agent is implying, see all your sick neighbors and friends? That twinge you have today may be the harbinger of a condition that will prevent your buying the insurance. Then you'll regret not acting.

Your rebuttal: "Mr. Agent, if you hurry down to the local convenience store before it closes, you can buy a lottery ticket and win $10 million. Better hurry or you'll regret not acting."

THE COMPARISON

Agent: "Aren't you embarrassed and don't you feel squeamish when your friends and neighbors talk about the long-term care insurance that they've purchased, which will keep them out of the poorhouse?"

The agent is playing to your 13-year-old self, when you wanted to do everything that your best friends did and have what they had.

Your rebuttal: "We don't envy our neighbors, and we don't expect to go to the poorhouse, either. We have three healthy and happy children who respect and keep in constant contact with us. Many of my friends and neighbors wish they could say the same."

THE FLUFF

Agent: "Look at these brochures, which show you that you'll have to pay about $7,000 a month just for a double room at the nursing home down the block. And how about these pictures from another nursing home over in the next town? Do you want to live like this?" Bringing out photos from the most expensive and the least appealing nursing home alternatives is intended to shock you right into bringing out your checkbook.

Your rebuttal: "The fancy nursing home brochure is pretty, but there isn't a nursing home in the United States that can provide care 24 hours a day, 7 days a week, with sensitive and caring individuals. I know that fact to be true. We witnessed the rapid turnover of help when our parents were in a nursing home, and we also observed many unskilled personnel who were insensitive. We want to stay at home, but if not, we'll look for the best alternative when the time comes."

THE APPEAL TO GUILT

Agent: "Your accountant, who referred me to you, will be disappointed if I have to tell him that I left this appointment without a signed application." You owe it to your accountant to buy a policy from me. He will think less of you if you don't act fast.

Your rebuttal: "Don't be concerned. I will help my accountant deal with that disappointment. I will also tell him about the high-pressure tactics you tried to use during our interview."

The Next Step

Once the agent has your attention, he or she may emphasize over and over why you need long-term care, instead of analyzing the benefits you should be considering.

Appeals to Your Pocketbook

I KNOW WHAT'S BEST FOR YOU

Agent: "You can afford this level of coverage and I advise it for you, even though you might want less (or more) than this policy offers."

The agent has studied your financial data, knows what you can afford, and makes the decision for you that one policy is best based on the financial data; that policy becomes the only one he or she suggests to you.

Your rebuttal: "I appreciate your interest, and the policy you recommend may be the best, but I would like to discuss it with our children and our accountant before I make a decision. Why don't you check with me in a couple of weeks?"

YOU CAN AFFORD IT

Agent: "Of course you can afford the premium. In fact, you can't afford *not* to afford the premium." The agent knows your financial data and thinks he or she can tell you how you should spend your money.

Your rebuttal: "Everything you see in this house and every asset we hold my husband earned with his bare hands. No one—but no one—is going to tell us what we can and can't afford."

JUST DROP MEDIGAP

Agent: "I know you're on a strict budget and live on a fixed income. But I have a solution. I suggest that you replace your Medigap policy with a senior HMO plan. You will have the same coverage and you'll avoid the large yearly premium increases for health care coverage. You'll have more than enough dollars left over to buy the long-term care policy I am recommending for you."

Wanting to make the sale, the agent fails to come clean with the truth about the differences between HMOs and indemnity Medigap insurance. You know better.

Your rebuttal: "If you can convince my doctor of 25 years that under the new plan he will be able to treat me as he has in the past, order any diagnostic tests, refer me to any specialists he thinks are appropriate, and not have to deal with a desk jockey who knows about insurance profit margins but not health care, I'll be happy to consider your plan."

Playing on Your Ignorance

WITHHOLDING THE INFORMATION

Agent: "I won't bother you with the small details that will only confuse you. What you need to understand clearly is that your long-term care needs will be managed well by this policy."

The agent recognizes that you know nothing about your long-term care choices except what he decides to tell you. He'll withhold whatever might jeopardize the sale even though what you don't know might hurt you.

Your rebuttal: "Sometimes small details can be important. I had a few narrow escapes with my health insurance, but the director of human resources at my plant was able to step in and prevent the company from denying the claim because of a questionable interpretation of the policy. I intend to get a second opinion and I will get back to you."

Here's another answer: "You've misjudged me. I am a stickler for details. I'm an engineer [or a teacher or a mother] and details are very important to me. I'm going to get a second opinion, and if I'm interested, I'll get back to you."

TELLING TOO MUCH

Agent: "Don't worry about your diabetes, especially since it's adult onset and you use only oral medication, not insulin injections. Besides, I'm sure you know Arthur, the deacon at our church. Several years ago after much difficulty, I secured coverage for him. He is a diabetic on insulin and there was a question as to whether the tingling in his toes was due to his diabetes."

The agent correctly understands that you will probably be able to pass the medical examination for long-term care insurance. But she talks too much. She'll tell you anything to make the sale.

Your rebuttal: "This interview is terminated. I would have hoped that any agent with whom I discussed the possibility of buying a policy would respect my privacy and confidential information. If you tell me stories about other clients, I know you'll use me as example in the future."

NOT TELLING ENOUGH

Agent: "So several years ago you had difficulty getting life insurance because of your ongoing therapy sessions? I know you needed to talk about job-related stress then and that you might have to in the future. But don't worry. The underwriting of long-term care insurance is different from the underwriting for life insurance. We don't have to mention the problem on the application."

The agent is correct that underwriters look differently at long-term care applicants than they do at those buying life insurance. He is incorrect to suggest to you that you withhold information of this type on your application, however, since the company may have the right to contest a claim within the first two years.

Your rebuttal: "I thought you were here to sell me a policy, not a worthless piece of paper. Make sure you close the door on the way out."

FORCED CHOICE ALTERNATIVES

Agent: "I want you to have a choice, so here are your two best options. Which one would you like?"

The agent knows that consumers like to think they are acting rationally. As a result, she provides the appearance of a choice, what the marketer calls a forked alternative—when the two options are basically the same.

Your rebuttal: "I appreciate that you have given me more than one company to choose from. Are there any others? I understand from a friend that his broker presented him with a spreadsheet that included six different companies. Perhaps I should check with him if you can't give me more than two companies."

The Homework Phase

Sales manuals advise agents not to leave their client's kitchen without a signature on the application. These sales consultants know that clients frequently have second thoughts, since a delay in selling long-term care often means no sale, or perhaps a physical disqualification later. Hence the agent may believe that speed is important to avoid this buyer remorse. To facilitate the sale, therefore, the agent hands the company's glossy sales brochure to the prospect.

READING TO YOURSELF

Agent: "I've set aside the whole afternoon for you, so please, take your time right now to read this brochure, which explains everything you want to know about the policy."

Remember how uncomfortable you felt in second grade when you sat in a circle to read? Most of us still feel awkward reading while someone watches us. The agent counts on the fact that you will skim the manual and ask few questions.

Your rebuttal: "I would like to read the material in a calm atmosphere and to reread it several times in case I miss something. Why don't you leave the brochure with me, and I'll get back to you when I've finalized my list of questions?"

READING OUT LOUD

Agent: "I can see you're a prudent buyer, and I'm going to leave this brochure with you. It will explain everything you need to know about the policy."

At least in this case you have the opportunity to read the information without being stared at. The agent feels comfortable leaving the brochure with you because it contains only very general statements about the long-term care options he is offering. If he leaves a more comprehensive document, on the other hand, it is likely to be unclear, abstract, and formal in its word choice. He's reasonably confident that you won't understand it.

Your rebuttal: "Can you send me literature from other companies, and would you be good enough to highlight the areas in your brochure that I should check out against the brochures of other companies? I want to know what goodies are in the other company's policies and not in mine."

TOO MUCH READING

Agent: "I can see that you are not in a position to make a decision this evening. I appreciate that, since to make a commitment for an indeterminate number of years for someone living on a fixed income in exchange for the peace of mind provided by long-term care insurance is a very difficult decision. Many of my clients were in your shoes, but they realized how important it was for them to buy coverage.

"I'm going to help you make your decision by leaving this leather-bound book full of testimonials from clients I've helped who have now accessed their benefits. There are also letters from applicants who neglected to protect themselves. I take this book on every interview, and my prospects read every single word on every page. Read the book. I'll come back on Tuesday afternoon to pick it up and answer further questions."

The agent knows you'll feel obligated to return her fancy book, and perhaps even be moved by the contents. She's figured out a way to return to your living room, whether you are interested in doing business with her or not.

Your rebuttal: "I appreciate your offer, but I certainly don't want to deprive you of the opportunity to share this material with others. Perhaps if you can mail me a copy and if I have further interest, I'll call you on the phone."

Tools for the Experienced Buyer

What about the experienced buyer, who already owns a long-term care policy? The insurance representative is happy to speak to you, too, because you are a qualified buyer. But beware the bait and switch.

YOU CAN AFFORD BETTER THAN THIS

Agent: "Well, Mr. Smith, when you bought this policy, it was probably a good deal for you. But today we have expanded home care coverage for meal preparation and you can afford the additional premium to have the additional benefit."

The agent has seen your financial data and knows you can cover an increased premium. He offers you an "improved" policy that includes relatively cheap enhancements at a relatively expensive price.

Your rebuttal: "Why don't you leave the data with me? I'm going to check it out with the agent who sold me my original policy. Isn't that the proper thing to do?"

WHAT IF YOU DROP OUT OF THE GROUP?

Agent: "Your trade association long-term care policy is nice, but it is still a group plan. Will it be available if you stop paying your dues to the organization? Don't you want to think about replacing it with an individual policy?"

You expect to be a member of the American Manufacturers Association for at least another 10 years, and you're only 45, anyway. The agent knows that your premium is very low and your probability of needing long-term care before age 60 is small. Still she is urging you to make the move now.

Your rebuttal: "What you say makes a lot of sense but I'd like to check this out with the director of the association and get his input on this very important subject."

MY GROUP POLICY WILL SAVE YOU MONEY

Agent: "Your individual policy is way too expensive. I can save you $200 on your premium yearly if you buy the one we offer all the members of the American Manufacturers Association."

The agent does indeed have a relatively inexpensive group policy available. But if you select it, you will be getting significantly fewer benefits for your money. You have saved $200 a year, but your benefits are worth thousands less, should you need to claim them.

Your rebuttal: "I understand that most group policies are not under the jurisdiction of state insurance departments and that the association members are paid royalties from the insurance premiums. I also understand that my policy will terminate if I don't pay my dues to the organization, but what I like about my individual policy is that I'm in charge of it. I decide whether I will cancel it."

The Subtext of the Sales Pitch

Throughout the sales call, remember that the agent is using the tricks of the trade to make the deal. Reputable brokers, mindful of their code of ethics, focus on the needs of their clients above all else. But insurance representatives, like salespeople in other industries, are trained to qualify their clients in the guise of doing a "needs analysis." They know that if you choose not to buy long-term care insurance, you may well be a candidate for another product, either annuities or life insurance. They recognize that they must keep you on a "yes" track by carefully shaping their questions, and that the most successful salespeople treat silence as assent and push toward a signature.

While it is important that you come to the sales visit ready to respond to the high-pressure tactics of the insurance broker, you do, after all, want the information the broker has to offer. The needs analysis is a useful way to figure out your long-term care goals. It will force you to consider your alternatives and to calculate the funds you will have available should you need long-term care. The needs analysis may even prompt a frank discussion within your family on what you are expecting in your very old age.

You and the Insurance Industry Are in This Together

Finally, then, the point is that buying long-term care insurance is a 10- or 20- or even 30-year commitment. Your relationship with your insurer may be one of the longest-lasting ones you have. Just as you distinguished infatuation from love, you need to step back from the sales pitch and consider what you want with great care.

If you are a healthy (and wealthy) adult under 60, you may have a wide array of choices when you shop for long-term care insurance. Assuming you're not taking prohibited medications and that you have annual checkups, the insurer may even send your policy by return mail—the company won't even write your doctor. If you're over 60, the process is much more time-sensitive. You can change your automobile insurer every year if you want, but the terms of your long-term care insurance policy are finely adjusted to your age and your health. Make a change and you'll alter this delicate balance.

Look past the hype, ignore the scare tactics, avoid insensitive industry representatives, and seek out a broker you trust to give you a complete set of alternatives. Take your time deciding what you want for your long-term care, remembering that you are making both a financial and an emotional decision. If you work rationally, you'll be thrice rewarded. You'll be comfortable with the long-term plan you have devised for yourself, you'll feel consciously competent, and you won't have second thoughts every time a cold caller rings your phone.

Endnotes

1. Interview with Lisa McAree, managing general agent, May 23, 2001.
2. Randall, Mark M. *LTC: 30 Days to Successful Selling.* Park Rapids, MN: ECI—Educational Concepts. 1998.
3. GE Capital. *Long-Term Care Choice (Massachusetts).* 1999.
4. TIAA CREF. *Long-Term Fact Sheet.* May 2001.
5. McAree interview.
6. GE Capital. *Guide to Ethical Marketing Conduct.* GE Financial Assurance. October 2000.
7. John Hancock. *Long-Term Care Marketing Guide.* December 1994.
8. National Association of Insurance Commissioners (NAIC) model marketing and suitability standards for long-term care insurance.
9. Randall. *LTC.*
10. McAree interview.
11. Randall. *LTC.*
12. NAIC, standard 5.

CHAPTER 9

Who Can Help You Choose the Right Policy?: Finding a Seller You Can Trust

When you go shopping for long-term care insurance, there are many professionals eager to give you a nudge in the "right" direction. Agents, brokers, lawyers, stockbrokers, financial consultants, human resources managers, and your favorite affinity group all want to tell you everything they think you need to know to select the long-term care plan you want.

The challenge for you, the premium-paying consumer, is to determine whom to trust. The information in this book will arm you with the concepts and the vocabulary to make sense of your long-term care options. As a shopper, you can bring to the table a knowledge of the benefits you prefer and the approximate amount of money you're willing to pay for them. Your grasp of concepts and vocabulary is in place. Now it's time to consider what skills and abilities your insurance representative brings to the table.

First, though, here's how the insurance company categorizes its product and its sales force:

- A long-term care insurance policy may be either an individual or a group policy.

- Individual policies are sold to you, the individual, through any of several channels, including an agent, broker, banker, or your affinity group's marketing team. Just because a group is marketing your long-term care insurance, the insurance may not be a group policy. You're getting a discount on an individual policy by buying it through your affinity group, club, union, or church.

- A group policy, such as the one marketed by AARP, is part of a "group trust." In this case, AARP has made a deal with MetLife to cover a large number of people under one umbrella and at a somewhat discounted rate.

- An employer-sponsored long-term care policy may be either an individual or a group policy. As we will see, the distinctions will be important to you.

- Long-term care insurance, like books, furniture, and virtually every other product or service, is now for sale on the Internet.

- Whether yours is a group or an individual policy, you need to approach both the salesperson and the product with cautious consideration, ensuring that its provisions and costs fit your needs.

All these choices! How should you respond when the long-term solicitations drop through your mail slot? What about that dinnertime cold call? Or the offer of a free lunch? The invitation to a seminar? What about the sales banner that floats across your computer screen when you're surfing the Net? Just who are all these people wanting to sell you long-term care coverage?

Agents

In the insurance industry, some agents are called captive since they typically sell for only one company. Their obligation is to present their company's product in each situation; in exchange, the company may pay their health care insurance, retirement benefits, and office expenses, or compensate them with increasing percentages as they sell additional policies. These agents compete for prizes and company trips, further rewards for selling their long-term care policies.

There are advantages to buying from captive agents. They know the details of their companies' long-term care products, and are able to make informed guesses about the features that would suit your needs. They can also predict your risk of declination.

Perhaps more important, this captive agent probably knows you very well, too. I am always puzzled when I hear that someone has bought a long-term care policy from a cold caller instead of consulting the insurance agent he or she has been dealing with for years. While these cold callers may pass themselves off as experts in this complex product, the agent who handles your life insurance or your automobile coverage is probably the first one you should call. Remember how your father and grandfather had a life insurance agent and a property and casualty agent. If they had a fender bender on Main Street, they called Fran; if they needed to change a life insurance beneficiary, they called Chris. Their agents knew about the milestones in their customers' lives, and probably also knew each other. Everyone was reassured by the familiarity.

Why, then, would you prefer an insurance salesperson who buys your name from a list or calls you during the six o'clock news? If you have a trusted business relationship with an insurance agent, perhaps one that has lasted 20 or 30 years, why listen to an anonymous voice on the phone? Long-term care insurance is a complicated product, and buyers tend to depend most on the advice of the seller. An industry study found that "the agent's recommendation and the insurer's reputation are the reasons most often cited for the purchase of a particular company's policy."[1]

Should you worry that your life or casualty agent won't understand the product? Some agents may not, especially those who have bought the company line about the risks in indemnity coverage or the stinginess of the reimbursement policy. While I wouldn't fault agents who genuinely believe what their marketing departments tell them, I would distrust one who will not bring in other models for you to consider. And I'd look twice at any agent who seems especially motivated by company incentives such as a trip.

I would also expect my agent to bring himself or herself up to speed on the nuances of long-term care. Those who work for major life insurers such as John Hancock, MetLife, Northwestern Mutual, MassMutual, and New York Life are actively educated in the product. And no agent who values his or her credibility with you will risk it by making an uneducated presentation. At the least, the agent should bring along a salesperson more familiar with long-term care products, so you can both learn something. If you decide to buy, you'll have the security of knowing that your long-time agent stands behind your decision.

But there are drawbacks to using captive agents, who are expected to offer their business to the companies with whom they have contracts. The agent has a strong financial incentive to keep the business in-house. For one thing, he or she is assured of commissions from the renewal premiums. But what if the agent's company doesn't want the long-term care business because of the client's medical history? The agent is usually able to offer the business to other insurers, acting in this case as a broker.

Independent Brokers

In the strictest sense, the independent broker represents the client and not the insurance company. His fiduciary obligation is to work in the client's best interest, shopping for a policy that suits the client rather than forcing the client to accept a specific model or plan.

Why not simply call a broker? UnumProvident, for one, uses only this type of sales representative. If you call a broker, you know that he or she will be familiar with the plans of more than one insurance company. You can assume that your best interests match his; you want to buy the most appropriate policy, and he wants to sell it to you. In fact, data says that consumers are used to comparison shopping, so that "a high proportion of one company's nonbuyers turn out to be another company's buyers."[2]

Working with the wrong broker, however, may have disadvantages for the insurer and indirectly raise its costs—and therefore yours. The broker who sends your application to a company not likely to accept you for medical reasons is adding underwriting costs to the acquisition expenses and losing credibility for himself or herself. Multiple applications cost multiple dollars, and the increased cost of doing business becomes translated into higher premium prices. Besides, unless the broker does an especially good job of explaining the alternatives, you may find yourself befuddled before your choices and unable to commit.

Industry sources maintain that independent agents, brokers, and captive agents accounted for most of the long-term care policies sold in 2000. This isn't surprising, since long-term care policies are good business. Compared to property and casualty policies, long-term care policies tend to require lower levels of service and offer terrific opportunities for cross-selling. It should be no surprise that the number of solicitations you're receiving for long-term care coverage is increasing.

Other Sellers of Individual Long-Term Care Policies

If you haven't gone insurance shopping recently, you may be surprised who is sitting at the table when you draw up your will, evaluate your portfolio, or replace your certificate of deposit. Planning for the possible need for long-term care is central to retirement planning, and selling long-term care policies is good—and big—business.

Lawyers

Perhaps there was an insurance agent sitting next to your estate planning lawyer at your last appointment. A good estate planner knows that long-term care costs can eat up an inheritance; similarly, elder law attorneys are trained to look beyond Medicaid for long-term care funding. After all, these professionals recognize that the clients sitting before them are concerned with preserving their assets and ensuring the independence and well-being of their old age. Why else would the consumers have made the appointment?

Financial Planners

Frequently, the first suggestion of long-term care insurance comes from your financial planner. The question you should ask is whether the planner is being paid a commission for selling you a policy.

Not that there's anything wrong with that. After all, we accept without question that our insurance agent makes a commission on our automobile policy or on our life insurance premium. What's wrong with a financial planner working for that money, too?

And even if you compensate your planner only for his or her time, not for any product you might buy, the planner still may be profiting indirectly. The planner might have a networking relationship with several brokers, to whom he or she routinely refers clients appropriate for long-term care. These brokers return the favor by making referrals to the planner.

The worst-case scenario, in my opinion, is when the planner doesn't even bring up the need to plan for long-term care, insurance or not. Some insurance agents would respond, "Okay, Mr. Planner, and I'll tell your clients to send you the bills for their long-term care." Financial planners, at the least, should follow industry suitability standards and advise clients with assets between $500,000 and $1 million that they might find themselves spending down their assets to pay for their own long-term care, and that's not considering inflation costs or the potential for catastrophic need.

Financial Planning Organizations

When you visit a financial planning organization, there is at least no ambiguity about who is networking with whom. These firms typically feature most financial services under one roof. In many instances, you will have access to a broker, a planner, and a C.P.A. who will share your information and make informed recommendations.

There is an appeal to filling out one set of financial and medical information for all your advisers, assuming that you have complete confidence in their privacy policy. Of course, you'll probably also get a call from the organization's stockbroker and bond seller.

Bankers

Just as your banker has gotten into the life insurance business, he or she may also be offering long-term care coverage. If you're young and healthy, you might as well look over the marketing material; if you have a troublesome pre-existing medical condition, you might as well leave the brochure on the counter. Many times, you may make just as good a deal with a broker or an agent, who has more than one plan to offer you.

The marketing strategies of these banks depend mostly on their countertop brochures, statement stuffers, and lobby signs. But that will likely change in the near future. A number of banks are starting to realize that a more professional and sophisticated marketing approach for long-term care insurance is warranted. As a result, banks are buying or making strategic alliances with the better financial services firms that offer a full range of insurance and financial products. In the process, they are allying with a staff of well-trained and experienced agents and brokers.

Protections

You may be reassured to know that you're not on your own entirely when you shop for an agent. Agents and brokers must be licensed in their states, but in some instances they do not always need to show any skill beyond signing their names. State divisions of insurance will often track complaints against agents, brokers, and other sellers, but they won't always reveal those complaints to you.

Do degrees and initials after someone's name impress you? Here is what they mean: Someone with a CLU is a chartered life underwriter. A ChFC is a chartered financial consultant. A CLTC is someone with training in long-term care insurance. Just how valuable are these degrees? They may mean that your salesperson knows how to take a course and study for a test, not that he or she is really adept at the details of long-term care planning. But these certifications do signal that the bearer has been exposed to courses in insurance and financial topics; some might have even taken statewide licensing tests.

Keep on doing your homework. And make your tax dollars work for you by getting educated in what you're buying. Eighteen states have allocated resources to public education about long-term care risk, exposure, and the availability of insurance for long-term care.

The best protection you may have lies in the actions you take:

- Get the agent's name, address, and telephone number—home and office— in writing.

- Read your policy when it arrives. Don't assume it matches exactly what you were sold.

- Tell another person about the policy's details and location. You may not be able to tell them about it when you need to claim benefits.

- Pay by check. Never ever pay by cash. How else can you prove you paid at all?

- Always write your check to the insurance company and not to the agent or broker who sold you the policy. That way, you'll know who will be able to cash it.

TIAA CREF: Buying by Mail

Industry sources indicate that approximately 10 percent of long-term care policies are sold in other than face-to-face interviews.

The insurance industry classifies TIAA CREF as a home-office seller. If you have had any dealings with this giant financial institution, you know that it has eliminated agent and broker commissions. However, the TIAA CREF has membership rules, eliminating some potential customers from buying its policies.

Buying by mail doesn't let you avoid underwriting procedures, either. TIAA CREF requires a detailed application and a doctor's statement, although you won't need a cognitive interview and won't have to reveal whether another insurer has turned down your application for long-term care coverage.

Affinity Groups

These groups include the clubs, professional associations, and trade groups to which you belong. In this case, the group provides an endorsement through an insurance company that makes available a discount on an individual policy. Again, you're buying an individual policy through a group membership.

Saving money is attractive, so why not reach for one of these affinity group policies? Maybe you should. But check out the offering very carefully.

Ask these questions:

- What happens if I quit the group? Can I keep the policy?
- If I quit the group and can keep the policy, do I also get to keep enjoying the discount?
- What happens if the group quits the insurer? Does the policy allow any return of premium?
- What long-term care policies are available to me through an agent or a broker? In other words, can I do better on my own?
- Can I negotiate individually within this offering, or am I stuck with a "one size fits all" policy?
- What about my preexisting conditions? Will the insurer listen to the details before rejecting me? If the company accepts me, will it pay off at claim time?
- Can I have confidence in the company writing the insurance policy? Will it still be around at claim time in 20 years?

Group Policies

A group may offer an individual policy, as we have seen, or it may offer a group policy. Similarly, the long-term care policy offered by your employer may be either an individual or a group policy. More on employer-sponsored long-term care insurance later.

Don't feel confused.

Group sales are big, big business. Ask MetLife, which is the company behind the AARP offerings. A study by the life insurance management research association (LIMRA) estimates that such group sales now account for 6 percent of all long-term care sales, up from 4 percent in 1999.[3]

Organizations that offer long-term care policies, either group or individual, are doing a valuable educational service. Their mailings have been important in raising public awareness of the potential for long-term care costs, news that may be reaching consumers who don't sit down on a regular basis with an insurance broker or a financial planner. These consumers pay a storefront office $75 to do their income tax forms, and they count on their certificates of deposit for income. Why else would AARP and MetLife choose the "Peanuts" characters to illustrate their long-term care insurance product?

The problem is that the sales tactics used by some of the organizations can be unnecessarily alarming and self-serving. The AARP brochures warn that "one in two Americans over age 65 will receive care in a long-term facility."[4] A quick look at earlier chapters should show you the flaw in this statistic; most of these people will not stay in long-term care long enough to qualify for benefits. While the brochures correctly warn that many people will not qualify for Medicaid coverage, their estimates for the cost of care do not consider geography or family contributions.

AARP's advertising seems to be working, since their 1999 fact-finding brochure claims MetLife has sold over 65,000 long-term care policies to AARP members.[5] But the company doesn't tell us how many mailings it shipped to sell to those 65,000 policyholders, nor how many applicants were rejected on medical grounds.

What the mailings do tell us is that many people prefer to shop for long-term care insurance by mail. Insurance agents and brokers must scrutinize their interviewing skills (and also read Chapter 8 on sales tactics) to figure out why so many consumers are turned off by face-to-face insurance pitches.

But my sense is that buying this type of policy by mail is in the long run a poor idea. Each applicant, especially AARP's market of preretirement and retirement members, presents different underwriting issues. While the brochures are strong on risks and benefit coverage, they are very short on underwriting exclusions. The issue of prescription medications is barely mentioned.

Furthermore, you must read the small print very carefully to figure out what AARP gets out of its affiliation with MetLife. In fact, the AARP trust retains income from the investment of monies on deposit in trust accounts. "MetLife pays approximately three percent of member contributions to AARP and its affiliates for use of the AARP trademark and other services. Amounts are paid for the general purpose of AARP and its members"[6] Well, good, you say. You want AARP to have the money it needs to advocate in behalf of seniors. Remember, however, that you may therefore be paying several percentage points more than you need to in premium costs, to help out AARP in this indirect fashion.

At the least, the treatment of price is unnecessarily misleading. The giant insurer, MetLife, seems to be talking out of both sides of its mouth. In a memo to New England Financial Management, a wholly owned affiliate whose agents sell MetLife's individual long-term care insurance, the company says it has "never had a rate increase."[7] Yet an AARP brochure sent to all prospects for AARP-sponsored MetLife group long-term care insurance plans spells out this warning in bold print: "Hurry," because "this kind of rate won't last forever."

Purchasing a group policy doesn't allow for effective comparison shopping. The limited plan choices and benefits that were in place when the product was first offered still remain in some group contracts; older, healthy buyers may get a better price in a more comprehensive policy by shopping on their own. You won't be able to shop for comparable policies by calling an AARP toll-free number, either. In the long run, dealing with an agent or a broker in a face-to-face setting is the best way to find out about policy options from several companies.

Nor are group policies regulated by each state. While these policies may carry protections equivalent to individual policies, they are not required to do so. The AARP brochure alerts consumers that their state probably offers free counseling. But don't go looking for any more detailed information.

And what of your privacy? Many seniors already buy their Medigap coverage through AARP. When you call AARP, the organization places you in its computerized filing system. Will the company be able to cross-reference callers' health? Privacy laws apply only if the consumer has submitted an application. Who can feel comfortable about private medical information when such huge companies as Eli Lilly admitted in July 2001 that it had mistakenly released the e-mail addresses of 600 patients taking Prozac?

When I investigated the AARP offering, I reached an anonymous information gatherer who requested details of my medical history. I was refused an underwriting guide that would have answered my questions without revealing my secrets. When I called, for example, I was told not to worry about privacy. I wanted to know what would happen if a potential client, not an existing applicant, had a preexisting condition. Could the person on the other end of the phone do a prescreening process without my identification? An independent agent or broker could provide this service.

Nevertheless, were it not for membership loyalty and educational messages, sometimes self-serving as contained in advertising brochures, thousands of members who have purchased AARP long-term care insurance would not have otherwise purchased that coverage from any other source.

Employer-Sponsored Long-Term Care Insurance

One of the fastest-growing markets in long-term care insurance is the corporate or business market, as large and small employers recognize that the benefit is central to employee retention and productivity. This benefit is also fueled by tax considerations; look at Chapter 4 on tax treatment of long-term care premiums and benefits for more details.

Despite these practical and financial incentives, only 7 percent or fewer of all full-time employees in 2000 were actually offered this benefit.[8] Most of these were employees of very large corporations. Seventy-two percent of covered employees paid the total cost of the premium, unlike life or health care insurance to which employers typically contribute at least in part. This type of bulk buying allows for reduced cost, and the employer does tend to make the premiums easier to manage by allowing payroll deductions. At the least, employers frequently offer information about long-term care as part of employee retirement planning, encouraged perhaps by the Long-Term Care Security Act of 2000, which allowed the federal Office of Personnel Management to negotiate discounted rates for federal workers.

Get the Details

You may think that an employer-sponsored long-term care policy is a first-class fringe benefit, but there are still some important questions to ask before you sign on.

ARE YOU BUYING A GROUP OR AN INDIVIDUAL PLAN?

If your plan is an individual one, is it portable? In other words, can you take it with you if you change jobs? Will the discounted rate continue to apply? Are other family members eligible for coverage? Will they receive the discounted rate?

If your plan is a group plan, ask the same questions.

WILL YOUR EMPLOYER CHIP IN?

Obviously it would be preferable to have long-term care insurance be part of your fringe benefit package, with the boss paying at least some of the cost; but don't count on it. And don't let the boss's reluctance (or inability) to contribute be the deal-breaking factor. You may still be getting a very good buy.

IS THERE ANY ROOM TO NEGOTIATE BENEFITS?

If yours is a group plan, you may not have many choices. But if your employer is large enough, you may have more choices than you expect. Still, don't count on an extensive menu of options. For that, you may have to default to an individual policy bought from an individual seller.

WHAT ARE THE UNDERWRITING STANDARDS?

If your employer is offering a long-term care insurance, is it guaranteed issue? In other words, do you need to pass medical underwriting or are you automatically eligible, as long as you are actively at work for the company? You may need only to state that you have no disabilities in the activities of daily living to be covered for the insurance. If you are an employee with a troublesome pre-existing condition, a guaranteed policy may present a valuable opportunity to plan for long-term care costs.

DOES THE POLICY TERMINATE AT A SPECIFIED AGE?

Employer-sponsored group life insurance usually provides a conversion option when an employee retires. What about your long-term care employer paid plan? Underwriters are aware that many employees who are guaranteed the opportunity to convert from their employer's policy to a permanent policy might take the conversion because otherwise they would have trouble passing a new physical impairments screening. They are now retirement age, after all, and have probably developed one or more conditions that might jeopardize their chances of buying a new long-term care policy. As a result, the retiring employee could find any premium for a conversion policy higher than the going rate for the employee's attained age at the time.

Also, since the employee covered by his or her company's long-term care policy has not shopped for the coverage, he or she is often only vaguely aware of the details of the insurance policy. Upon retirement, however, these workers are bombarded with offers from other insurers. The path of least resistance, often, is to sign with the existing company and skip the free lunches, early evening seminars, and mealtime phone calls. The last thing the retiree wants to think about is jousting with an eager insurance agent.

In the process, however, the consumer finds himself or herself tied to one company that might not offer the broadest of benefits. He may have a reimbursement policy when he would have preferred an indemnity plan, had he only known. The benefit amount may be too small; he may not have inflation protection.

The retiree should not cancel the plan he owns, but he should take the time to see what his options are in the wider long-term care market. If he is in the kind of good health many 65-year-olds are today, he may be more than pleasantly surprised when he sees what new and better benefits he can buy with his long-term care insurance dollars.

Why Look a Gift Horse in the Mouth?

If you have a medical condition that would otherwise threaten to make you uninsurable, say thank you to the boss and sign up for the policy. You are not likely to have another alternative or opportunity to cover your potential long-term care costs.

If you are healthy, and if your employer isn't paying a part of the premium, you might shop around for comparison's sake. Still, when any employee, even a key one, scrutinizes this benefit, he or she risks appearing ungrateful at best, and distrustful of management's judgment and generosity at worst.

The curious employee, then, is in something of a bind. Inquiring about the master long-term care policy that stands behind the certificate handed to you by your human resources manager may brand you a troublemaker, a clubhouse lawyer, or someone with an undisclosed, potentially costly, preexisting condition. The policy itself may be too dense for someone outside the insurance industry to comprehend, anyway.

After all, you have accepted the job because you have confidence in your employer. You assume that the people in charge of such benefits found a reputable, knowledgeable agent and selected a trustworthy insurance company. The human resources people should be able to get all the information you're looking for and answer your questions clearly. They want you to focus on your job and trust them to do theirs.

Shopping Online

Now that we're accustomed to buying anything from books to prescription drugs online, it is no surprise that the Internet provides several tools for long-term care investigation, as well as purchase. You can scan alternative benefits, you can comparison shop, and you can buy a long-term care policy with the flick of your mouse.

But do you really want to buy a benefit package worth as much as $200,000 for you and your spouse the same way you buy a $19.95 novel or a discounted airline ticket?

One problem with online shopping is that anyone can post a web site and make promises; you don't know from whom you're buying. Slick marketers can say almost anything on their web sites and consumers will think they are reading truth. Also, some Internet sites charge the insurance company an up-front fee for the privilege of selling its product online. When you surf, then, you may not be looking at all your options.

Besides, if you're reluctant to tell your medical history to an 800 operator, why would you give personal and financial information to a screen name? Despite the privacy promises, the fact is that you don't know who is on the receiving end of your data.

Also, while that best-seller will be the same book whether you've picked it up at the corner store or ordered it online, the subtleties of long-term care coverage may make this type of shopping much more troublesome. If you didn't want to buy your couch online or distrusted the clothing maker's online catalog because you couldn't try on the sweater, it seems foolish to choose a long-term care policy without expert, face-to-face advice.

Take a look at Quotesmith.com, an online insurance site that is now offering long-term care insurance quotes. The complexities of the policy and the comprehensive underwriting involved will be obvious the first time you log on. Question number 5, the one that asks about your medical history, is a perfect example. In tiny font, you are presented with a dense list of exclusions, conditions, and elimination periods that will turn off anyone without a wall-size computer screen or 15/15 vision. You'll receive an array of "offers" from companies whose names are familiar and unfamiliar.

Many major insurers such as UnumProvident do not yet participate in this marketing channel, preferring a "professional insurance advisor" who uses "face-to-face" contact to explain the complexities of the coverage.[9] Prudential Insurance also believes that long-term care sales are best done face-to-face so that the policy can be customized and the benefits and payments explained.[10]

Most insurance companies have web sites to explain their products. The sites can be useful educational tools, but they also generate leads for the insurer. If you're actually interested in long-term care insurance, however, the follow-up phone calls may be just what you want.

There are software packages available to allow you to wade through your choices. One company, StrateCision of Needham, Massachusetts, run by CEO Ted Pass, offers software products that compare features and benefits of more than 42 insurers that sell 106 policies. The agent or broker marketing long-term care insurance to you may hand over a StrateCision printout to demonstrate the relative merits of the policies you are considering. You can also purchase comparison printouts directly from the company.

The difficulty with all these sources of information, in the long run, is that insurers sometimes play their cards close to the vest. When I queried them about lapse ratios, for instance, I bumped up against the wall of proprietary information. There are simply some pieces of information that the companies do not want you to know—and that's why in Chapter 13 I've included a list of "Questions the Insurance Company Hopes You Never Ask." You're the customer. You have a right to ask.

Replacing Your Policy

The fast answer about whether to replace your policy is this: If you want to replace one long-term care policy with another, do so with the utmost care; better yet, don't do it at all.

Admittedly, there sometimes will be no choice. You've dropped out of the group that sponsors your original long-term care coverage so you don't have a policy anymore. Your benefits are so limited that they won't do you much good on judgment day, when you make a claim. Your company has gone out of business. (Sometimes, you're actually in luck when the company goes out of business. Read the next chapter to see why.)

Most companies require that when you replace one long-term care policy with another, you read, understand, and sign the replacement form. This notice requires that you acknowledge several significant changes in your coverage when you replace your old long-term care policy with a new one. With some companies, you'll begin a new waiting period for preexisting conditions, even though you might have satisfied these conditions in your earlier policy. You also enter a new contestability period.

The replacement information also suggests that you speak to your present agent or insurer before making the shift to a new policy. The new insurer has an obligation to notify the existing carrier that negotiations are under way to replace their contract. This gives the existing company's agent an opportunity to talk to the client, making sure that he or she has all the facts.

Unfortunately, many companies, through either benign neglect or paperwork glitches, do not make this notification to the existing company. By the time the news has traveled through one company's bureaucracy to another, it is too late for the heart-to-heart talk to make much difference.

Most of the time, replacing a policy simply means giving a new agent a beefed-up first-year commission, without much benefit for you. Less than reputable sellers have an incentive to replace your policy with another one. Perhaps they'll entice you to make the switch by offering a new benefit package. Look carefully. Often these new "benefits" aren't worth the money the new policy costs.

Besides, your entire medical picture may increase your premiums without buying you a significant increase in benefits. You'll need to go through the underwriting process again if you change companies and even if the policy is for a reduced amount. You will be older and could have to pay higher premiums.

If you must replace your policy, don't cancel the old one until the new one is approved. Watch your timing. If you switch during the middle of your old policy's term, you may not get a refund on the premiums you've paid, plus, if applicable, you'll have to start a new elimination period for preexisting conditions.

How Much Time Should Your Shopping Take?

Some insurance sellers believe in the fast close sale, either for the sake of their commissions or for the well-being of their clients. An agent might argue that any delay in the purchase of a long-term care plan often means not buying, because the client becomes uninsurable while making up one's mind. This is an unselfish motive for the agent to push a quick close. The seller also benefits from the first year's commission and cuts off the likelihood of buyer's remorse. Look at Chapter 8 on sales tactics for more details on this type of selling.

In fact, the decision to buy long-term care insurance is best made in three stages. The alternatives are too complex and the decisions involved are too emotionally loaded to be done quickly.

Stage One: Information Gathering

You're in stage one right now, by reading this book. You are information gathering, considering what you want for your long-term care, who might provide it, and how you might fund it. You're asking significant life questions about your very old age, perhaps talking to your spouse and your children.

Who initiates this conversation? Studies show that your spouse most often will. Other times, long-term care considerations are prompted by suggestions from your children, a financial adviser, your lawyer, or your accountant. Whoever starts the conversation is doing you a favor by alerting you to the risks of long-term care costs and by advising you to incorporate this planning into the big picture of your old age.

Stage Two: Financial Planning

Next is the financial planning stage. The long-term care insurance seller will come to see you with a suitability form. He or she should help you carefully analyze what levels of care you prefer when (and if) you should need long-term care. There will be a range of suggestions for how you might pay for it. Your insurance representative may start at either end of the buying equation. He or she will ask what benefits you want and then find policies to provide them, or may ask how much you can afford to spend for the insurance and show you what you can buy for those dollars.

In this stage, you should talk to as many brokers as you require to feel comfortable. If it takes one for you to feel okay, that's enough. But you need not stop with the first agent who visits. Your choice of an agent is crucial to the decision-making process, since data shows that your policy choice is most often influenced by the agent adept at explaining the insurance and the available coverage options.[11]

Stage Three: Committing to Your Choice

You've thought about your future needs, analyzed your choices, and now it's time to make the purchase. The underwriting process takes some time, of course; Sandy DeMartino, registered nurse and MetLife's individual long-term care underwriting manager, says her company prefers to wait two weeks from the receipt of the application to begin phone interviewing, simply to make sure all the paperwork is in place.[12] An experienced agent or broker will tell you when you can expect the underwriting to be complete and the policy to be in place.

Some Final Rules of Thumb

Whether you buy your policy from an agent or a broker, through an affinity group or a group trust, remember to ask these questions:

- How much experience does the seller have in long-term care?
- How much training does the seller have?
- How long has the seller been in the insurance business? Will he or she be around in 10 or 20 years when you may need to make a claim?
- Do they have backup in place in the event they are unavailable for policyholder service?
- Are you comfortable with the seller's information, patience, and ability to educate you in the policy?
- Have you been presented with a choice of policies? Are you comfortable with the benefits? Premium? Regulatory protection? Portability? Rate history?
- Are you likely to qualify physically and cognitively for the policy your insurance seller is offering to you?
- Has he or she used suitability guidelines? State regulators discourage sellers from targeting those with incomes under $20,000. Have you answered

questions about income and assets? Are you sure you won't qualify for a government-paid long-term care benefit?

- Do you trust your seller? Can you talk frankly with him or her? Do you think he or she will keep your confidences?

All in all, taking three months to shop for a $200,000 purchase isn't very long. Keep reading this book; surf the Internet; go to free lunches; collect mailings; talk to your friends, your kids, your neighbors, your insurance agent, and the fellow in the aisle at the grocery store. Your time is well spent.

After all, this purchase may be the determining factor in the independence of your old age. It may let your kids help you as much as they can, without sacrificing their own well-being in the process. It may give you dollars to stay at home.

Endnotes

1. LifePlans,Inc. *Who Buys Long-Term Care Insurance in 2000: A Decade of Study of Buyers and Non-Buyers.* Prepared for the Health Insurance Association of America, October 2000. p. 3.
2. Ibid. p. 32.
3. Life Insurance Management Research Association (LIMRA). 2000 Individual Long-Term Care Sales by Distribution Channel.
4. AARP. "The AARP Long-Term Care Plan Fact-Finder." 1999. p. 14.
5. Ibid.
6. Ibid.
7. MetLife. *Why MetLife? Long-Term Care Talking Points.* Prepared for New England Financial Management. p. 22.
8. Report, Findings, and Recommendations of the Working Group on Long-Term Care. United States Department of Labor, Advisory Council on Employee Welfare and Pension Benefits, November 14, 2000.
9. UnumProvident memo.
10. LifePlans, Inc. *Who Buys.* p. 32.
11. Ibid.
12. DeMartino, Sandy. *Long-term Care Insurance Underwriting.* MetLife training video, February 7, 2000.

CHAPTER 10

Choosing a Company: Ensuring That the Company Will Be There When You Need It

When you buy a long-term care insurance policy, you and the insurer are exchanging vows. Perhaps you're not promising fidelity until "death do you part," but close enough. Think about it. You and your insurer could be exchanging money and legal documents for the next 20 or 30 years, maybe longer as our life expectancy increases.

Given this extremely long time frame, it makes sense to check out the financial well-being of your insurance company. Interestingly, consumers are likely to buy automobile coverage or even life insurance, another long-term arrangement, without carefully scrutinizing the stability of the insurance company underwriting the policy. But smart consumers think more than once about the company underwriting their long-term care insurance coverage. They recognize that they are making a $200,000 or more purchase, and they are insuring the independence and dignity of their old age. These smart consumers want to give careful consideration to their choice of insurance companies—perhaps not as much as they gave to choosing a spouse, but certainly a lot more time than it took to test-drive a new car or pull that VCR off the electronics store's shelf.

At least 41 percent of long-term care buyers consider the company's reputation as central to their choice, and 33 percent of buyers look primarily at the financial ratings of the insurance.[1] And there are lots of choices. According to Weiss Ratings, there are at least 118 companies offering long-term care policies.[2]

Even the best computer dating service probably did not present you with such good choices.

In the long run, choosing the right insurer may turn out to be as important as choosing the right benefits. We have only to remember the junk bond debacle of the late 1980s to understand the risk of doing business with financially unstable companies. That experience taught us that you may have selected and paid for the most comprehensive home or nursing care coverage, but if the insurer isn't around in 20 years to pay off, you've got nothing.

Assuming you're affiliating with your insurer for the long haul—and why wouldn't you be?—how are you to choose the company to write your long-term care policy?

There are several ways of approaching this selection:

- Compare price to benefits, just like when you shopped for your VCR or your car. Remember, however, that you're into big bucks and long-term commitment. Your VCR may be disposable after two years and your car may last eight years, but your long-term care insurance will go on and on and on. There is vastly more to think about when you're affiliating with an insurance company.

- How old is the company? Has this insurer been around long enough to make accurate predictions about its future costs? If it is primarily a life or property and casualty insurer, does it make sense to buy long-term care coverage from it?

- Ask about claims service. In some ways, scrutinizing service first is akin to buying a car because you like the look of the technician scurrying around in the repair bay. But long-term care insurance service is vitally important. That's why major insurance offers care managers; they don't want you to be stranded by the roadside when you go to make a claim.

- Look at lapse ratios. Try to analyze why consumers have not maintained their long-term care policies over the long haul. Was there something amiss about the policy or the benefits? Or were these lapsed policyholders simply unqualified customers?

- What about claims denial? If the company you are considering seems to have a tendency to say no at claims time, ask why. The answer may surprise you.

- Evaluate, on your own, the company's financial stability. Do they have the reserves to pay the claims that may come due in 20 or 30 years?

- Finally, the most familiar way to assess the strength of a company is to see what the major ratings services, A.M. Best, Moody's Investment Service, Fitch, and Weiss have to say about the company you're considering.

Here is how each of these evaluative techniques can contribute to your decision making.

Comparing Price and Benefits

No one wants to pay more than they need to for any product or service, let alone one as expensive as long-term care insurance. You're reading this book to figure out exactly what features and benefits you want in a long-term care policy and to learn ways to deflect high-pressure sales pitches designed to push glitz and not substance.

How much do premiums vary among similar policies offered by major insurance companies? If you looked at Internet offerings, you might think there was a lot of difference. But several insurance experts I interviewed argued that, generally, policies that have similar benefits have similar price tags. You are not likely to spend hundreds and hundreds of extra dollars for one company's insurance policy as compared to another.[3]

Martin D. Weiss, chairman of Weiss Ratings, Inc., an industry maverick, points out that there are complex benefit differences that result in significant price variation. Some of these differences are a result of geography, the policyholders' anticipation of long-term care costs determined by where they live. But others, especially those premium differences resulting from indemnity versus reimbursement models and from the calculation of elimination periods, are avoidable; they are also too complicated for most long-term care shoppers to grasp.

If you find a long-term care policy that costs 25 percent more than another, is it a poor buy? You may be getting what you pay for. That $200 VCR may have features that the $150 one does not. If Company A's premium is high, perhaps Company A knows something about long-term care actuarial risks that Company B does not. Company A is collecting enough money to be sure it will be around to pay your claim in the long-term.

And the low-ball premium? Most experts would tell you to watch out: If the company is selling long-term care coverage at less than the going rate, there must be something wrong. Maybe Company B is so eager to build its business that it issues policies somewhat indiscriminately. But this conclusion is simplistic since a lower premium may reflect a more cautious underwriting policy, not a risky one. Because the company has been in the business for a while, it has the actuarial data to figure out what its future costs will be. Company B prices its policy realistically because it knows it will have the future funds to provide its share of your long-term care.

Are you so eager to affiliate with Company A that you will pay increased rates because you have a preexisting condition? Will you accept an extended waiting period? Such factors affect just what any underwriter may decide to offer you. If you don't pass muster with your initial company's underwriter because of that condition, you won't be able to exchange vows. Yet another company may be eager to invite you out.

The interactions in long-term care insurance between price and benefit, then, are too subtle to be used the way you would if you were shopping for a VCR.

Consider Longevity

In addition to the price/benefit ratio, another way to evaluate an insurer is to ask how long it has been in business. The longevity of a company is often a direct indication of its long-term health. If the insurer has been around awhile, it has claims and pricing knowledge. But how long has your potential company been in the long-term care insurance business? Do you really want to be in the first generation of its customers? If you find that thought exciting, join the DeLorean automobile fan club or read reports of first-generation software catastrophes.

Compare Service

Let's say that the major insurers are within dollars of each other, and their benefits are essentially the same. What other measures might you use to decide between policies? Here is the time to evaluate the quality of service each company provides. Unfortunately, unless you know someone who has already accessed these benefits, your investigation here may have to concentrate on what the company is willing to tell you.

Ask for a claims kit. Does the insurer maintain an 800 number, answered by a human being and not voice mail, 24 hours a day, 7 days a week? If not, how long will you have to wait for a return phone call?

How long will it take you to get your check? In other words, what's the lag between claims submission and payment receipt?

A professional care manager told me that accessing benefits is essentially a multistep process for most insurance claimants. The initial call comes to the company's care managers, who then manage the claims process. These managers arrange to have a field care manager, typically a licensed nurse or social worker, assess the client's situation. These field care managers report whether the client is disabled in one or more of the activities of daily living. This is the first of a series of regular assessments, often as frequent as every six months.

The field assessor sends the determination back to the office care managers who forward it, without judgment, to the insurer. The company then makes the final determination about payment of benefits, sometimes appointing a local care manager paid for by the insurance benefits.[4]

Clearly, this process can take some time. If your agent is around to facilitate the process, things might speed up. That, by the way, is another reason to think carefully about buying from an individual who will be around, in the flesh, to help you out. Try getting the 800 operator to drop over to fill out the claim forms for you.

Consider Lapse Ratios

A lapse ratio indicates the number of policies that have been terminated because the renewal premium was not paid. Why should this statistic matter, especially since lapse rates are declining overall? Few insurers want to tell you their lapse rates, anyway. While keeping their own lapse rates confidential, the UnumProvident spokesperson told me that the industry average for individual long-term care policies was somewhere between 4 percent and 5 percent annually; he believed the group rate to be between 10 and 12 percent annually.[5]

It might appear that an insurance company would welcome a lapsed policy. The way this thinking goes, the company gets to use the customer's premium money but never has to fork over any benefits. What a good deal. In fact, some policies now make available nonforfeiture clauses at increased premiums, which return some dollars to the consumer after he or she terminates the coverage.

Also, long-term care insurance sellers now follow suitability guidelines when they make sales calls, thus reducing the possibility that they might sell to customers who cannot afford the premium or who, in a calmer moment, will realize that they don't need the coverage.

Claims Denial

Certainly you don't want to have to fight with the company when you apply for your benefits, so a record of claims denials may appear to be a telling statistic. The problem with this number is that you probably won't be able to uncover it; but ask, anyway. And even if the company will tell you how many claims it contests, you won't know whether these were legitimate denials based on misrepresentation or the result of "post-claim underwriting."

Financial Stability

Most insurance salespeople will tell you that, after benefit and premium considerations, the most important question to ask about your long-term care insurer has to do with its financial stability. As we have seen, buyers choose an insurer because of its reputation, which may be more a reflection of its perceived financial stability than the actual state of its health.

Loss Ratios

So how do you determine statistically if your suitor is worthy? You might look at loss ratios, if you can find them. These loss ratios help measure solvency by comparing the amount of premium paid out in claims to the amount kept back for reserves, expenses, and profit. Interestingly, loss ratios for companies selling individual policies average about 60 percent, which means the company is holding back 40 percent for profit and costs and spending 60 percent to pay benefits to its policyholders. The loss ratio for group policies is different, because their premiums are discounted for the group marketplace. For group policies, 70 percent of premiums are returned in benefits.[6]

You want the insurer to make enough profit to stay in business. But does it seem greedy that the industry is using 40 cents of each dollar for its expenses and profit, while spending only 60 cents to take care of its policyholders, perhaps your grandparents and parents? The Department of Labor study suggests that lawmakers are concerned about these ratios. The retention must be reduced for "policy makers to justify further tax incentives for long-term care products." Why spend federal dollars to further enrich the fat insurers? Participants in the Long-Term Care Working Group suggest that the insurance industry needs to pay a higher percentage of its gross income on benefit payments before Uncle Sam will support the further deductibility of premiums and take the budget hit.[7]

What if you already have a policy from a wobbly insurer? You may not be completely out of luck. Many states have established "guarantee funds" which pay policyholders if their insurance company goes under. However, these funds are not like FDIC insurance on your savings account. You may not get a dollar-for-dollar premium refund or benefit payment if the insurance company nosedives. You also may have to wait for your check for as long as a year. Litigation takes time. Oddly, sometimes the best thing that can happen from a policyholder's point of view is that the wobbly company is swallowed up by the financially healthy big fish. The fish buys the company to grow its long-term care business, and it has the resources to handle claims as they come due.

Ratings Services

You've been familiar with ratings since the first time you were turned away from a PG-13 movie. You may even keep *Consumer Reports* on your bedside table. Understanding the financial health of an insurer that is selling you long-term care coverage is especially important. If the company isn't around to pay your benefits, you may encounter problems. Several well-known rating firms evaluate the financial health of insurance companies; these rating firms are familiar names—A.M. Best, Standard & Poor's (S&P), Fitch (formerly Duff & Phelps), Moody's, and Weiss Ratings.

Joseph Belth, professor emeritus of insurance at Indiana University and editor of *The Insurance Forum*, a monthly newsletter "for the unfettered exchange of ideas about insurance," has some advice for buyers of long-term care insurance who become confused and concerned when trying to determine the financial strength of an insurance company.[8]

Each year since 1991, Belth has published a special ratings issue of his newsletter "to assist consumers and those who want to provide professional advice to consumers" about the financial strength of insurance companies. The special issue is especially valuable because it offers a kind of one-stop shopping. The September 2001 special ratings issue, for example, contains a ratings list of 3,782 financial strength ratings assigned to 1,715 life-health insurance companies by the five rating firms I've listed earlier. The issue also includes a watch list of 729 companies.

What is important to understand about Belth's newsletter is that it does not itself rate the strength of insurance companies. Instead, what Belth does is explain the ratings and provide a clear chart of the ratings. Belth also provides some rules of thumb for extremely conservative, very conservative, and conservative buyers, allowing them to see at a glance which insurance companies have been highly rated by at least three of the five rating firms.

See Table 10.1 for Belth's listings of the rating categories used by the rating firms. Belth notes: "The ratings in a given rank are not necessarily equivalent to one another. . . . [The] lists do not include Best's financial performance ratings (FPRs) or S&P's public information ('pi') ratings."

What should be apparent here is that you need to forget what you learned in high school about calculating your grade point average. In the universe of rating firms, an A+ does not always signal the strongest rating. In most cases, an A+ rating means the company is one or two categories below the highest.

Imagine what your high school principal would have thought.

Further, as Belth carefully points out, each rating firm uses somewhat different criteria to establish its ratings. Depending on the rating firm, the rating may measure financial strength by using several years of financial statements and may or may not use qualitative data regarding management experience. Some rating firms include on their lists insurers that have asked that the ratings not be published; others do not. All the rating firms except Weiss charge the insurance companies "substantial annual ratings fees."

Belth also establishes a watch list based on low ratings from the rating firms, a low risk-based capital ratio, or four or more abnormal insurance regulatory information system ratios. The latter is a complex set of standards established by the National Association of Insurance Commissioners.

Using the rank numbers in the table, Belth offers rules of thumb for evaluating the financial strength of insurance companies. Again, it is important to remember that Belth himself does not study the financial data of insurers. Rather, using the ratings, Belth suggests that consumers look at companies with high ratings from at least three of the five rating firms.

"The extremely conservative consumer should select a company with high ratings from at least three of the five rating firms," says Belth, with "high ratings" defined this way:

Best: A++

Fitch: AAA, AA+

Moody's: Aaa, Aa1, Aa2

S&P: AAA, AA+

Weiss: A+, A, A–, B+

The "very conservative" consumer may be willing to look at companies with high ratings from at least three of the five major firms with "high ratings" defined this way:

TABLE 10.1 Rating Categories

Rank Number	Best	Fitch	Moody's	S&P	Weiss
1	A++	AAA	Aaa	AAA	A+
2	A+	AA+	Aa1	AA+	A
3	A	AA	Aa2	AA	A–
4	A–	AA–	Aa3	AA–	B+
5	B++	A+	A1	A+	B
6	B+	A	A2	A	B–
7	B	A–	A3	A–	C+
8	B–	BBB+	Baa1	BBB+	C
9	C++	BBB	Baa2	BBB	C–
10	C+	BBB–	Baa3	BBB–	D+
11	C	BB+	Ba1	BB+	D
12	C–	BB	Ba2	BB	D–
13	D	BB–	Ba3	BB–	E+
14	E	B+	B1	B+	E
15	F	B	B2	B	E–
16		B–	B3	B–	F
17		CCC+	Caa1	CCC	
18		CCC	Caa2	CC	
19		CCC–	Caa3	R	
20		CC/C	Ca		
21		DDD	C		
22		DD/D			

Source: Joseph Belth. *The Insurance Forum, Special Ratings Issue*, September 2001.

Best: A++, A+

Fitch: AAA, AA+, AA

Moody's: Aaa, Aa1, Aa2, Aa3

S&P: AAA, AA+, AA

Weiss: A+, A, A–, B+, B

The "conservative" consumer should consider companies with high ratings from at least three of the five rating firms with "high ratings" defined this way:

Best: A++, A+, A

Fitch: AAA, AA+, AA, AA–

Moody's: Aaa, Aa1, Aa2, Aa3, A1

S&P: AAA, AA+, AA, AA–

Weiss: A+, A, A–, B+, B, B–

If your appetite is whetted for more information on ratings, you can reach *The Insurance Forum* at P. O. Box 245, Ellettsville, Indiana 47429-0245 or find it online at www.theinsuranceforum.com. The phone number is 812-876-6502. The special ratings issue is available for $20.

Trusting the Ratings

Obviously the rating firms serve a valuable function, since no single consumer (or insurance agent) could gather the data available to these huge firms. We, as potential policyholders, need to know that we're not throwing our premium dollars down a black hole, and that the company will survive to pay us back in benefits should we qualify for them.

How trustworthy are the ratings? That's a good question. Just as forces beyond the control of an insurance company and unrelated to its financial condition can affect the stock price in either direction, these forces can play into a rating firm's evaluation. Should a company decide to downsize, change its CEO, be subjected to a legal action, or restructure its organization, it risks having its ratings downgraded. Companies have the opportunity to state their case to the rating firms, but the consumer needs to tread cautiously even when consulting the rating firms.

And don't be fooled by agents who suggest you replace your existing policy with one from a different company, just because your original company's rating has changed. The new agent will benefit from such a switch, but you might not. The seller receives higher commissions on first-year premiums. But for the consumer, replacing an existing long-term care policy is fraught with risks, including the likelihood of new underwriting problems, higher premiums, and longer waiting periods. It may be more reasonable to check into the health of your original insurer.

It is also important to remember that ratings change. For instance, as Belth notes, "Ratings are under continuous review and subject to change and/or affirmation." That is, rating firms are always studying the insurers, altering or maintaining the ratings they assign. And since these rating firms may change their ratings at any time and for a variety of reasons, the wise course is to go directly to each firm's publication or web site to find the latest information. If a yearly check on your insurer's financial health is enough, Belth offers a concise and valuable alternative.

Finally, and most troubling, the insurance companies themselves often obscure the meanings of the ratings. When some rating firms announce that a rating was reduced, you might not be concerned. If a student came home with a BBB+ average, wouldn't Mom and Dad be thrilled? But that's merely "good," according to Fitch. Talk about grade inflation!

Insurers know that these ratings aren't clear to most consumers, so they advertise them without a context. For instance, a company may say its financial strength is rated A (Excellent) by A.M. Best. True, but we've seen that A++ and A+ are actually higher ratings. While the marketing statement is technically correct, it is misleading.

Who Can You Turn To?

Any consumer, and especially a senior, must feel confused by the very data meant to help make the best decision about long-term care coverage. The best a consumer can do is check online or in the library to decipher the ratings code of the rating firms.

Don't forget, also, that your state has an insurance department whose job it is to answer your questions. Even if you are unable to get specific information about companies and ratings, you will be directed toward the information.

Shopping for the safest long-term care insurance company is in the end a matter of hard work and faith. The consumer must do his or her homework carefully to be sure that the dollars paid today will return the benefits that may be needed in the coming years. But the effort is worth the payoff, since you are spending a few hours now to have years of independence in your very old age.

Determining the future viability of an insurance company is not an exact science. Information presented in this chapter can help you assess the current financial health of various insurance companies, but factors beyond everyone's control can impact future results of insurers. These factors include world events, like the September 11, 2001, tragedy; fluctuating world global financial markets; interest rates; changes in insurance company management; acquisitions and mergers; and the most important component, claims experience.

Endnotes

1. LifePlans, Inc. *Who Buys Long-Term Care Insurance in 2000: A Decade of Study of Buyers and Non-Buyers.* Prepared for the Health Insurance Association of America, October 2000. p. 32.
2. *Long-Term Care Premiums Vary Widely: Policies Too Complex.* Weiss Ratings, Inc., June 4, 2001.
3. Interview with Marc Cohen.
4. Interview with Kathy Campbell and Pearl Prevoir, LifePlans, Inc., June 2001.
5. UnumProvident memo, Jay Menario, vice president and director of long-term care sales.
6. *Report, Findings, and Recommendations of the Working Group on Long-Term Care.* U.S. Department of Labor, Advisory Council on Employee Welfare and Pension Benefits, November 14, 2000. p. 19.
7. Ibid.
8. Belth, Joseph. *The Insurance Forum, Special Ratings Issue,* September 2001.

CHAPTER 11

Caregivers

We must find better and different ways to care for people with chronic medical problems, because not only is the patient at risk, but so is the caretaker.[1]
—Dr. Murray Feingold, WBZ TV, Boston

The average woman can expect to spend 17 years caring for a child and 18 years caring for a parent.[2] However, if you want to stay at home in your very old age, you may not be able to find a caregiver to help you.

Informal—in other words, unpaid—caregiving from family members is the backbone of the long-term care system in this country, yet most of us still feel guilty that we don't do enough when aging and ailing parents need our help.

How have these double binds happened?

For many people, the rewards of caring long-term for a disabled family member or friend far outweigh any financial, physical, or emotional cost. If Grandma comes to live in your house, your children have the advantage of her patience, wisdom, and love. You have the pleasure of returning the love and care she gave you and your siblings. By pooling your resources, both you and Grandma may be able to improve your standard of living, perhaps move to a larger house and enjoy shared comforts. All three generations have new opportunities for socialization and emotional support.

At least that's the way it used to be for informal caregivers.

Now the picture is very different. The informal caregiver is often a working mother. Already stretched too tight by the demands of the children at home and the boss at work, Mom runs by Grandma's apartment to be sure she has a microwavable dinner. She rushes out at lunch hour to drive Grandma to the doctor's and taps into her household money to pay for her mother's prescription medications.

Meanwhile, Grandma feels trapped between her desire for independence, her fear of a nursing home, and the disabilities that make it harder and harder for her to live at home on her own. Grandma may also not be her old self. Children have difficulty understanding that aging can prompt personality changes, so that an elder's depression over his or her health becomes translated into expressions of anger and blame. Thus the caregivers determined to give everything they have to their relatives, can never give enough. What remains is guilt.

More adult Americans in their 40s and 50s are now caring for their loved ones at home and can expect to need some form of long-term care themselves. In this instance, perhaps, the development of medical technology has been a mixed blessing. We are living longer, but often are not hardy enough to care for ourselves. Outpatient surgery has replaced procedures that required three recuperative hospital days, which would qualify us for a Medicare-paid stay in a skilled nursing facility. This same technology, including simpler I.V. units, feeding tubes, and improved medication schedules, have allowed patients to come home to recover, instead of going to a skilled facility at the government's expense.

At the same time, women are working in ever-increasing numbers. These women are career minded and upwardly motivated. They may live hundreds or thousands of miles from their ailing parents. If they live around the corner, they may be unable to cancel a meeting or delay a report to rush to the emergency room. Employers might understand that Mom needs to leave early enough to pick up junior at day care. But unless bosses have been there, they tend to be less understanding about the requirement that Dad exit his adult day care facility by 6:00 P.M. each day.

The apparently reduced options for long-term care often seem terrifying, too. No one wants to go to a nursing home, and many may not even have the chance since the bankruptcy of nursing homes has increased due to reduced entitlement payments and the difficulty of finding well-trained professional staff. According to a Department of Labor study, "Nearly 1,900 skilled nursing facilities that care for more than 225,000 patients are in some state of bankruptcy"—which is 11 percent of the total beds. The projected need for registered nurses, licensed practical nurses, and nurse's aides in the next 20 years is growing much faster than the schools can produce them.[3]

Assisted living communities were unheard-of when the first long-term care insurance policies were sold, but today even these facilities run the risk of catering only to the most wealthy. Most are not equipped to provide the extended, intense levels of care that the very old and frail patients may require, nor are they able to hire and pay staff skilled enough to deliver these services.

It seems, then, that the caregiving system, overwhelmingly driven by unpaid relatives and friends, will remain by default, even though our social and economic systems may make this level of home care untenable.

To respond to these difficulties, a new category of elder care specialists has developed. The professional case manager may be hired by the insurance company as part of the long-term care patient's benefit plan, or clients may hire their own independent care managers. These professionals, whether case or care managers, assess need and plan care. At best, they are planners/therapists; but at worst, they are gatekeepers in the model of HMOs.

Identifying the Caregivers

It probably comes as no surprise to you that the typical caregiver is a "married woman in her mid-forties" who provides "an average of 18 hours a week of caregiving, works full-time, lives near the care recipient, and has an annual household income of $35,000." Figure it out. If the woman is in her mid-40s, she probably has a child or two still at home. If her annual income is around $35,000 (in 1997), the family likely needs her financial contribution.[4] If her family income is higher, she may be a professional moving up in her career.

Informal caregivers are not necessarily women—many are men caring for their wives. Ninety-one percent of unpaid caregivers are family members; 41 percent of these are children, 24 percent are spouses, and 26 percent other relatives.[5] *The MetLife Study of Employed Caregivers* reports that working caregivers of people with long-term care insurance "tend to be older (average age 53) than working caregivers of those without insurance. These working caregivers for insured patients are more likely to be male, have some college, make incomes above $30,000, and be a spouse. But they are less likely to be living with the care recipient."[6]

Also not surprisingly, women are those most likely to be the unpaid caregivers, and they are also those most likely to require caregiving during their lives. Stepping out of the workforce to provide loving but unpaid care to parents, in-laws, or spouses means that these women are less likely to have their own money in place to fund their long-term care costs. Clearly, it is a double bind for women to live longer and to live poorer than men. And many women simply have no choice in the matter of living poorer.

What Types of Services Do These Unpaid Caregivers Perform?

Most informal caregivers help their loved ones with such tasks as laundry, grocery shopping, or making doctor's appointments. These are among the instrumental activities of daily living. The unpaid caregiver who lives near his elderly parent may help him to write checks, make his doctor's appointments and drive him to the physician's office, prepare his dinners, or count out his prescription pills. Having a relative nearby to support someone who needs this help is important to long-term care insurers. They know that this informal level of help means that the client is less likely to need assistance with his basic activities of daily living.

Such informal caregiving lasts much longer than most people expect it will. Caregivers anticipate spending at most two years helping their disabled patient, but in reality the care often lasts as long as 10 years. Not surprisingly, the need for more and more hours of caregiving time increases as the years pass and the condition of the patient, presumably, worsens.

Costs of Unpaid Caregiving

Where should I begin this recital of the costs of caregiving? With the expense to housing? Lost income? Falling productivity? Stress to the caregiver? As the population has aged and people have begun to live into their 90s and even to 100, the public had become more and more aware that 70-year-old Mom may need to tend to her own mother, living in a nursing home, while granddaughter helps them both.

Living Expenses

Despite the advantage of pooled resources when you take a loved one into your home, the few dollars of increased income may go back out the door in the form of additional expenses. If your patient is in a wheelchair, your house may need structural adjustments to doorways and bathrooms, not to mention staircases. There are often increased phone and utility bills, food costs related to diet restrictions, and extra miles added to the family car.

Dollar Costs

Think about this. When you or your neighbor opt to provide long-term care for a family member in your home, you are making a present to everyone on the block—indeed, everyone in the country. Each informal caregiver contributes toward an overall savings of about 18 percent of the total national health care spending, which was $1.1 trillion in 1997. In fact, the value of informal caregiving exceeds the cost of nursing home care by about 170 percent.[7]

This care isn't free to the caregiver, naturally. The National Alliance for Caregiving and the National Center for Women and Aging at Brandeis University found that over their lifetimes, caregivers sacrificed on average as much as $659,000 in lost wages, Social Security benefits, and pension benefits.[8] This lost income, in turn, contributes to the pattern of need when the caregiver herself enters the patient population.

Informal caregiving also has productivity costs of between $11 billion and $29 billion a year.[9] This loss of productivity happens, according to the *MetLife Study of Employed Caregivers*, every time the employee leaves to check on spouse or patient, passes up a promotion or a better job, or drops out of the workforce completely because Mom's demands are simply too great to leave room to juggle a job.[10]

The Nondollar Costs of Unpaid Caregiving

While caring for a relative over the long term has its own psychic rewards, the sense of returning love for love may become muted by the demands of constant care. Caregiver stress reveals itself on many levels.

Many caregivers are busy, even frantic, providing for their loved ones' instrumental needs, doing their laundry, dropping off prescription pills, seeing that they make their poker game or meet friends for coffee and a rehash of the day's news. The joy of being together is lost. Working parents obsess over spending quality time with their children, and the problem compounds proportionally for caregivers of the very old or very frail, especially when there is little hope that Mom or Dad will improve. Studies find, then, that when funds are available to provide for the instrumental needs of a patient, unpaid caregivers are freed to provide spiritual and social support. The caregiving hours remain the same, but the behaviors change toward more social and loving interactions.

Emotionally caregivers may find themselves drained and depressed by the on-call, sometimes crisis-driven nature of their sandwiched obligations. Many studies report the increased frequency of depression among long-term caregivers. This stress is obviously affected by the caregiver's work status and living arrangements. If the patient is significantly disabled, the stress is often higher as well.

Caregivers themselves run the risk of getting sick because they don't have time to tend to their own health problems, feeling obliged to work through their own illnesses. This increased stress actually translates into physical problems. Dr. Murray Feingold, medical editor for WBZ TV in Boston, talks about "caregiver syndrome," which includes symptoms of "fatigue, anxiety, depression, and feelings of withdrawal or separation from society." Dr. Feingold reports that these caregivers experiencing this stress may actually produce a decreased number of white cells, lymphocytes, thus placing them at increased risk for infection and immunological problems.[11]

Support for Caregivers

Caregiver support groups sometimes post a kind of bill of rights for their members. Generically, such a list stresses that the caregiver has certain rights:

- To take care of oneself.
- To seek help from others.

- To maintain one's own interests.
- To feel and express anger, depression, or other negative feelings from time to time.
- To reject manipulation through guilt.
- To receive gratitude and consideration.
- To feel pride in helping a loved one.
- To remain an individual.
- To demand increased institutional support for all informal caregivers.

Has society deserted the unpaid caregiver? Is she (or he) left alone and without the social and emotional supports that are necessary to keep this loving duty from becoming an onerous one?

Support from the Family

Two sisters share the care of their dad, a cheerful and pleasant 75-year-old man diagnosed with Alzheimer's. Dad lives alternately with each sister, moving between them every two weeks. His daytime, weekday "sitter" goes to both houses, and on the weekend the custodial sister handles Dad's needs. These young women decided when Dad was diagnosed that they would always live within 10 miles of each other. They knew that neither they nor their husbands could physically manage full-time care for Dad or pay someone else to do it. Together, they've gone beyond prayer and finances to keep Dad happy at home.

I share this story with you because you've probably heard mostly its flip side, in which one child bears the whole burden of a parent's care. Often that primary caretaker is the local child, and siblings contribute money and an occasional weekend off. The need to watch a patient 24 hours a day, 7 days a week is too much for even the most dedicated caregiver, paid or unpaid. If you doubt that, scan the local headlines for stories of Alzheimer's patients wandering off, or isolated and frail elderly suffering from heat exhaustion or failed oil burners.

Clearly families need to share the responsibility of caregiving, but they can't do the job alone.

Support from the Employer

Study after study has argued that the employer actually saves $3 to $5 for every dollar it spends helping employees find elder care resources.[12] Long-term care insurance for employees actively at work is of course an important first step, since at least the support is in place for employees struck down by Christopher Reeve type–accidents. In some cases, healthy parents may be eligible for the discounted coverage, too.

Today's elderly Mom probably doesn't have long-term care coverage, however. Even if she could be included in the employer's plan, she probably couldn't pass the physical underwriting. In this case, the employer may provide adult day care centers, maybe even next door to the child day care center the company subsidizes. To make business trips possible, some companies arrange for respite care, or at the least provide their employees with a list of adult care facilities in the area.

Support from the Government

It is time for the federal government to give more back to the informal caregiver, who is making a huge contribution to the national budget. There are several ways this reward could be structured.

First, via the pocketbook. The Clinton Administration flirted with an above-the-line tax deduction for long-term care premiums. That incentive won't help this generation of caregivers, but it can certainly help the next one, by making long-term care insurance a more attractive option.

Then, via the information highway. Studies indicate that caregivers want more information about funding sources, treatments, and care options. The federal government is in an ideal position to make this news accessible. How might the caregivers themselves contact legislators about important issues? The Patient's Bill of Rights, making its laborious way through Congress at this writing, may help informal caregivers by simplifying the bureaucratic maze and demystifying insurance language.

Some supports, of course, are in place. According to the AARP, Congress in October 2000 reauthorized the Older Americans Act, which includes funding for a National Family Caregiver Support Program under Title III. This program provides support and respite care to family members who are caring for their older relatives at home, and will offer training, counseling, information, and assistance. But the Act was funded with only $125 million in 2001, a measure of the limits of Congress's commitment to the program. Some states have set up similar caregiver support programs.

Support from the Insurance Industry

Those who buy long-term care insurance and the companies who sell it now seem to agree that paying uncertified workers, including family members, is a good use of long-term care benefits. Particularly in indemnity policies, but more and more frequently in reimbursement models, people may select benefits that allow their family caregivers to be paid. Many long-term care policies now include provisions for paying unskilled caregivers, including family members, for providing long-term care services.

Obviously paying Sis for managing Mom will relieve much of the financial burden she assumes when she quits or cuts back on her hours at work. Also, it allows more choice for policyholders in rural areas where certified home health care workers are less available to use their insurance benefits to pay for home care. Besides, if Sis decides to use the benefit income to fund breaks from caregiving, she may do so.

How Does Long-Term Care Insurance Fit into the Caregiver Picture?

The insurance industry has recognized that even informal caregivers need support. That's only good business, since the company has a vested interest in keeping policyholders off claim. If the informal caregiver knows how to manage the client, the insurer won't have to pay benefits quite as soon.

How then should the insurer support even those caregivers it is not paying?

- Through training: Many long-term care insurance policies offer caregiver training as part of their benefits. Most often, of course, the policyholder has paid for this training in premiums.

- Through clarifying benefits: The Gerontologist study found that claimants often wished for additional customer support, improved claims processing, and more advice about benefits.[13] Dealing with a disability is difficult enough, but wading through the claims process can be daunting.

- Through case managers who assess the patient and manage his or her care.

Case Managers Employed by the Insurance Company

If an insurance representative has pitched long-term care coverage to you, you may be familiar with the role of the case manager. These professionals, usually registered nurses or social workers, are employees of the insurance company who oversee your benefits if you qualify for long-term care insurance payments. The conflict of interest in their job is obvious. The case manager— sometimes the insurance policy calls them care coordinators or privileged care coordinators—advocates for the patient. Indirectly, the patient has paid for these care coordination services through premiums. But the case manager works for the insurance company.

The case manager's paycheck comes from the insurance company, not from the patient. The case manager must follow a set of rules and regulations established by the insurance company, or Medicare, or the hospital, or the HMO. The freedom to suggest alternative care options is always bound by these rules and limited by these regulations.

Whatever case managers believe about the best long-term care of their clients, they report also to their employer, an insurance bureaucrat. The case manager may have the client's best interests at heart, but must keep the employer in mind. What this means is that in general the case manager may become a gatekeeper as much as an advocate. There is at least the appearance of an inherent conflict of interest for the case manager, no matter how much he or she wants to serve the client's best needs.

Case Management Services

Typically, the case manager enters the client's long-term care planning process when the insurance company does. When you call to make a report that you are disabled, the insurance company notifies one of its case managers, who is typically employed in a central office. That person in turn begins the process of certifying disability by sending another professional, a field case manager, to write up an assessment of your condition. Remember, while long-term care insurance policies vary slightly, most often you will have to be certified that you are unable to independently perform two activities of daily living or be certified as cognitively impaired before you can tap into your benefits.

The assessment report goes back to the insurance company bureaucrat who either does or does not certify the disability. Often the first case manager, the one you initially called, has no input into the certification decision. Even the field case manager may be the insurance company's eyes, but not its brain. Whether you will actually qualify for your insurance benefits is decided somewhere in the bowels of the organization.

Let's say you are certified as disabled. Now a field case manager either visits you again or uses the original report to "assess your needs and along with you, your family and personal physician, develop a Plan of Care." In the GE Capital plan, the manager "helps you complete claims and paperwork," then "helps schedule care and services in the comfort of your home and community." GE Capital's brochure says that it is the job of the "Privileged Care Coordinator . . . to be on hand to help make sure you receive quality care, remain in control of your life, and maintain your independence and dignity."[14]

Obviously, the insurance company's case manager provides a valuable service. You've purchased long-term care insurance to help you manage as well as pay for your well-being in your very old age. Having a company case manager is better than having no help at all, after all, especially if your relatives are too far away to help you arrange for care or check on your well-being. Even if you are still cognitively able to make choices about the services you need and the providers you want, you'll probably need help locating them. If you are disabled, your family needs the same kinds of support.

Drawbacks to the Insurance Company's Case Manager

You've paid for the case manager's services and, to some degree, you need them. But using an employee of the insurance company to manage your care may have some real drawbacks:

- Does the insurance company, either in the policy language or informally, encourage the use of one type of facility rather than another? Will the "pool of money" policy be useful only in a nursing home, not for at-home care?

- What is to prevent the case manager from being too stingy, limiting money the patient believes he or she needs? The pool of money that is paying the case manager in a reimbursement policy controls the upper limit of daily or weekly spending; but it doesn't establish a minimum. In an indemnity policy, the patient must show one certified service daily to be entitled to the full daily indemnity payment.

- Does the case manager have to abide by specific company guidelines for facility use? If so, some patients may be placed prematurely in nursing homes when home care might be a feasible alternative.

- Is the full range of alternatives being presented? The tendency of patients is to trust that their insurance case manager has surveyed the whole field, but what if the manager is offering only a "forced choice" of two similar plans of care—a tactic reminiscent of those used to sell long-term care policies.

- What is the relationship between the case manager and the nursing home or facility? Does the case manager have the ability to negotiate levels of care? The insurance company brochures say that the case manager "works independently of the service organizations he or she recommends."[15] But what about the guidelines set by the insurance company itself?

- While you may have "freedom to choose your long-term care providers and services," can the case manager move outside insurance company lists of these providers? The TransAmerica brochure warns that "not all providers and services may be covered by your TransAmerica policy."[16]

- The case manager serves as an informal counselor, listening to patients and family members, offering support if not advice. What happens when the formal demands of the job become too demanding to allow these informal services to continue?

The Independent Care Manager

The independent care manager, a professional hired by the patient, may fulfill the same tasks as the case manager employed by the insurance company. She or he will talk to you and your family, help establish a plan of care, and select caregivers and service providers.

Nevertheless, there is a significant difference between an insurance company's case manager and the independent care manager you employ on your own. Your independent care manager has no conflict of interest. Above all, "the patient is the client," and the independent care manager is his or her advocate, according to Meredith Beit Patterson, an experienced private elder care consultant and longtime board member of the National Association of Professional Geriatric Care Managers.[17]

While the insurance company's rules and regulations limit its case manager's suggestions, only professional standards and ethics bind the independent care manager. So far, these geriatric care managers are not state licensed, but most are also social workers, nurses, or therapists who are licensed in one of those specialties. Patterson, whose practice is in Concord, Massachusetts, is directing the development of ethics and standards for the National Association of Professional Geriatric Care Managers.

Why Have a Case Manager and a Care Manager?

Is there any reason to hire an independent care manager if the insurance company has also sent a case manager to see you? Many experts say yes. The independent care manager is your most objective advocate; he or she works only in your best interest and is not diverted by any other voices, including those of the insurer, the hospital, or squabbling family members.

Here is a story that explains the way an independent care manager can change the direction of long-term care. It comes from Meredith Beit Patterson:

The independent care manager received a call about a woman whose path from hospital to nursing home seemed predetermined. The woman was a retired schoolteacher who had never married. Now she was about to be discharged from the hospital and was too weak to return to her home. The 80-year-old had lived frugally her entire life, saving her money, but she was physically unable to make alternative arrangements for long-term care and there were no family members able to make the arrangements for her. It appeared she had little choice.

Then a friend heard through the grapevine about the independent care manager. She called in a last-minute attempt to find alternatives for this alert if frail teacher. The care manager visited the schoolteacher, assessed her condition, and considered her options. She learned that the elderly woman had saved enough money to pay for 24-hours-a-day, 7-days-a-week home care. Her savings would cover assistance not only with the basic activities of daily living, but with the instrumental activities—the haircuts, the dressing and socializing—that may make life worth living.

The independent care manager arranged for the woman to return to her own home, where a team of service providers cared for her. The teacher avoided premature nursing home placement. In this instance the professional care manager was able to put in place a network of service providers that helped keep her in her home environment without being prematurely institutionalized.

Independent Care Management Services

According to Patterson, the best time for an elder care consultant or independent care manager to meet clients is before they need long-term care. The independent care manager can help the client, and the family, understand long-term care options and make plans for future possibilities.

Why should an independent care manager start this conversation? Because it is too hard for the children and because most of us don't want to talk about long-term care. We may have our wills in place, the college costs of our children and grandchildren funded, and our retirement portfolios balanced, but we look the other way when the question of long-term care options is raised.

Sometimes, the private elder care consultant is called in by the patient's children who are now worried that Mom and Dad may become unable to care for themselves. Sis calls to report that Dad has had a second stroke, and while he seems to be recovering, the children want him to meet with the care manager to consider alternatives for next time. Often, however, Dad isn't interested in this discussion. He's made his will; he takes his prescription medications. If the time comes, he'll do what he has to do. And if that delay in planning leaves Mom in the lurch, too bad. Mom doesn't have the nerve to raise long-term care issues with Dad, either.

Here is where the independent care manager's therapeutic training can be invaluable. Patterson, a licensed social worker, for example, knows how to introduce the topic of long-term care choices to resistant clients. We have seen elsewhere that when this loaded issue is raised by untrained insurance salespeople, it often features doomsday scenarios. Bringing an independent care manager into the conversation raises the level of the discourse and frees the participants from blame and rancor.

The independent care manager does everything the insurance company case manager does, and much, much more.

Advocating within the Medical System

Medicare rules require a three-day notification of discharge, but some patients are still surprised to learn that they must go home in the morning. Consider, for example, the Alzheimer's patient who was notified that he needed to leave the skilled care hospital by a letter left on his bedside table. The patient couldn't read the letter, and his family never noticed it. Now the patient needed to find a place to go in a hurry.

The independent care manager understands Medicare and the words on the patient's medical chart. She may intercede with the medical staff, asking them to look again at the patient's condition and consider that the family is looking hard for an appropriate placement for their father. The hospital may be able to justify a few more days, long enough for the family to put a plan in place. This intervention can be especially important when family members are far away or are too distraught to hear the suggestions of a hospital social worker. Rather than assuming the social worker knows best, the independent care manager evaluates all the choices and can ease the patient's transition from hospital to other types of care.

The independent care manager may also interface with the patient's primary care doctor—that is, if there is one. Patterson reports that such doctors are rarely in the picture. That's no surprise. A squad of HMO doctors today often treat patients in large, multipractice offices. If their assigned "personal care" physician isn't available, the staff simply switches them off to someone else in the practice. The specifics of medicine are so often dictated by HMO regulations that it hardly seems to matter which physician actually listens to your heart or reads your chart in the hospital. You probably won't see the same doctor more than twice, anyway.

Given the impersonality of this type of care, the independent care manager is a translator. The independent care manager knows when and how to access doctors. Not uncommonly, she may be in the hospital when the physician makes rounds. She'll play phone tag so the family doesn't have to. The independent care manager can interpret the sometimes dense reports of doctors who may be uncomfortable delivering a less than optimistic prognosis. She knows how insurers and Medicare treat physical disabilities and can anticipate whether the patient will qualify for insurance benefits or skilled rehabilitation.

Formal Counseling

Like the case manager, the independent care manager is at least partially a counselor. In this case, however, the counseling obligation is formal. The independent care manager recognizes that part of her job is to mediate between siblings and, sometimes, between children and their parents. She is an objective voice because her loyalties lie clearly with the patient.

Developing Service Alternatives

You probably called the care manager initially because you simply had no idea what to do with Mom once she was released from the hospital. Planning care alternatives is the task we most often assign to care managers. But unlike case managers paid by insurers, care managers are free to gather many options and to discuss them with the client and his or her family.

The independent care manager can be on the scene, acting as the eyes of family members who live far away. Since they live locally, these care managers can check on the patient with some regularity, so that family members aren't taken by surprise by catastrophe.

Are there drawbacks to hiring an independent care manager? You have to pay them, for one thing. Granted that you've also paid through your premiums for the insurance company's case manager, so you are buying the same service twice. But as we have seen, the service is not the same.

While we are waiting for the government to make informal caregiving easier, independent care managers can be the support that informal caregivers need to help their loved ones spend their last years with dignity and comfort. Investing in counseling and advice from a geriatric professional can have long-term rewards in stress reduction for the caregiver and a better life for the patient.

If you would like more information about the National Association of Professional Geriatric Care Managers, contact the organization at 1604 North Country Club Road, Tucson, AZ 85716-3102 (telephone 520-881-8008 or online at www.caremanager.org).

For many generations, taking care of our older family members was an honor and a gift. Families treasured the opportunity to give back love to those who had nurtured them. Even though social and economic realities are very different in the twenty-first century, the desire to honor our seniors is still real. Informal caregivers, supported by independent care managers and, in some cases, by long-term care insurance coverage, may mean the most wonderful old age.

Endnotes

1. Dr. Murray Feingold. "Medical Minute," WBZ TV, Boston, 1998.
2. *Report, Findings, and Recommendations of the Working Group on Long-Term Care*. U.S. Department of Labor, Advisory Council on Employee Welfare and Pension Benefits. November 14, 2000. p. 12.
3. Ibid. p. 26.
4. National Alliance for Caregiving and AARP. *Family Caregiving in the United States, Findings from a National Survey*. 1997.
5. Department of Labor Report, p. 12.
6. *The MetLife Study of Employed Caregivers: Does Long-Term Care Insurance Make a Difference?* March 2001. p. 3.
7. Department of Labor Report, p. 12.
8. Ibid. p. 13
9. Ibid.
10. *MetLife Study of Employed Caregivers*.
11. Feingold. "Medical Minute."
12. National Alliance for Caregiving and AARP. *Family Caregiving in the United States*. Panday, Sheel M., and Barbara Coleman. *Caregiving and Long-Term Care*. Public Policy Institute, AARP, December 2000.
13. Cohen, Marc A., Jessica Miller, and Maurice Weinrobe. "Patterns of Informal and Formal Caregiving among Elders with Private Long-Term Care Insurance." *The Gerontologist*, Vol. 41, no. 2, pp. 180–187.
14. GE Capital. *Long-Term Care Choice (Massachusetts)*. 1999.
15. TransAmerica Occidental Life Insurance Company. *Long-Term Care Insurance: Care Coordination*. Marketing brochure.
16. Ibid.
17. Interview with Meredith Beit Patterson, July 10, 2001.

CHAPTER 12

The Envelope Please: The Nominees for Best Long-Term Care Insurance Soap Opera

Spending money now to protect against future catastrophes is no one's idea of fun. But some of the things buyers do when they shop for insurance are surprisingly funny—and also sad.

Today many couples are in second marriages, children live thousands of miles from their parents, seniors receive confusing solicitations from insurance agents, and employers are just waking up to the value of this new fringe benefit—long-term care insurance. It comes as no surprise that the consideration of long-term care insurance sometimes prompts special behaviors from buyers in special circumstances.

Insurance has been my business for more than 50 years. I have learned that no other insurance product involves as much input from as many family members as does the consideration of long-term care coverage. I have witnessed valuable discussions of health and financial concerns, but there have also been moments of greed, fear, suspicion, and virtually every emotion you can name.

These stories illustrate some of the most memorable examples.

It is not the intention of the author to breach any client confidentiality or to disclose personal details of those who may have sought his advice over the years. Even though the situations that follow reflect actual real-life experi-

ences, all the names, ages, occupations, and details of medical conditions have been changed. Any similarity to actual people is purely coincidental.

Long-Term Care Insurance in First Marriages: Having and Holding

Promising to care for each other on your wedding day is dreamily romantic to the young bride and groom. Sometimes, though, health turns into sickness, and the obligations go beyond romance. Often, this happens after many years of marriage, but even these couples find themselves tested.

The Denial Syndrome

It's human nature to avoid the idea that we might need long-term care in our very old age. When avoiding that potentiality costs the spouse his or her good health, the price of denial is too high.

Bill and Sherry set up an appointment with their agent to talk about buying long-term care. Bill, who was 79 years old, showed up for the meeting in his running clothes, dripping wet. His message was clear. He wanted to let the agent know that he, at least, would never enter a discussion of nursing homes. He wouldn't even apply for coverage.

Only women went to nursing homes. Men died on their feet.

As far as the husband was concerned, he would die from a heart attack on the jogging track. Or he would die on the golf course with a smile on his face. No way was he going to spend his last months in a nursing home.

His wife, however, did fill out an application. But she had had cancer and couldn't qualify for a preferred rate. Peeved, she said, "I'm not buying long-term care coverage, either. Why should I overpay for a protection I may not even need?" Her husband's reluctance had indirectly influenced her.

Sadly, within two years, the husband needed long-term care.

The man had shortchanged his wife. She spent her last years lifting him on and off the toilet, and now had back problems. There was no one around to help lift her. The runner had died. She spent her assets keeping him at home, and now had no choice herself but a nursing home.

Denial can be a powerful disease fighter for many people, but when it costs a healthy spouse her own long-term independence, the fight isn't fair.

Don't Tell Him I Called

Sometimes one spouse, influenced by experiences with parents or friends, recognizes that long-term care insurance is a good idea. But no matter how loving the couple, the worrying spouse may not have the clout or the stamina to convince the partner to take their risks seriously.

Jennifer, for example, was very much concerned that her husband was not taking care of himself. Sometimes he skipped his blood pressure medication, he rarely paid attention to his diet, and he smoked a pack of cigarettes a day.

Now her husband was about to retire and their income would drop. Jennifer was worried that there would not be enough money to pay for any long-term care expenses that might develop. Her husband refused to spend the money for long-term care insurance.

Jennifer had a thought: Why not get a policy on her husband without his knowing about it? Naively, she had the notion that insurance policies were like sweaters you bought for Father's Day. She didn't know that her husband would have to sign the application, provide a medical history, and undergo physical underwriting. His signature would testify to the truthfulness of the application's information and would attest to his willingness to buy the coverage.

Jennifer needed her husband's active participation if he was to buy a policy. Had she tried to proceed without it, she would have been playing with fire and risking a jail sentence.

It's the Challenge, Not the Money

Jim and Betty were wealthy seniors, moving between Boca Raton and their suburban home in Cleveland. Long-term care insurance salespeople had courted them for years, but Jim always refused a meeting. The pressure tactics and harassment of dinnertime phone calls had soured him.

Betty felt differently. She was concerned about protecting their $3 million asset base, and she didn't want their two daughters to act as their caregivers if she or Jim had chronic medical problems.

The wealthy couple was at a stalemate, until their property and casualty broker dropped by for a prearranged meeting to discuss their values for the renewal of their homeowner's policy.

Jim agreed that the $10,000 diamond pendant he had given Betty on their 50th wedding anniversary should be listed separately on their jewelry schedule. He agreed that their house has increased in value and reaffirmed the worth of their oil paintings and sculptures.

Then the insurance broker with whom they had worked for 25 years brought up the subject of long-term care insurance.

The broker told them he had been reluctant to enter this field because earlier products were not as strong as they now are. He had not wanted to injure long-standing relationships with his property and casualty accounts by recommending fly-by-night companies with poor products. As a broker, he could sell them a policy from any of a number of companies, but suggested UnumProvident's indemnity policy.

When the broker explained the way an indemnity product works, Jim agreed with Betty that they should buy the insurance.

The broker knew that UnumProvident was a company with strict underwriting requirements. He asked each partner about medications and health problems, and sent them some literature and a premium quotation.

After Jim wavered yet again and broke several appointments, he finally decided to "get the application over with" by filling out the form, and gave the broker a deposit.

Four weeks later the UnumProvident underwriter called the broker to say that Jim would not qualify medically for the insurance because of the cardiac history received from his doctor.

Feeling blindsided by his long-time client, the broker asked Jim if there had been some mistake. Did he indeed have a cardiac problem?

Jim laughed. "Here we go again. I had this problem when I applied for survivorship life insurance."

Jim had Yamagochi syndrome, a cardiac condition called atypical hypertrophic cardiac myopathy. Unlike the usual hypertrophic cardiac myopathies, Jim's syndrome is a benign disorder, which the insured had had for more than 30 years. His cardiogram, abnormal because of the enlargement in his heart, had been consistent for 30 years. He had always been stable.

In fact, Jim carried a copy of the cardiogram with him, keeps backups in his and his wife's cars, and gave copies to his children. "If I'm in an accident or need treatment in an emergency ward of a hospital, the doctors will need the cardiogram or they'll think I'm in serious trouble with all kinds of heart problems."

When he was turned down by UnumProvident, Jim's desire for long-term care coverage increased. He wasn't used to being refused. After he documented his condition with a letter from his doctor, his broker went to work to find him a policy.

He called an underwriter at MetLife, a sometimes aggressive company that is proud to have occasionally beaten its rivals in difficult underwriting cases. After six weeks, MetLife agreed to write coverage for Jim, but the company wanted an extra premium and would offer only 50 percent of the home care coverage Jim applied for.

Jim was annoyed; the broker was embarrassed.

In the midst of all this, a representative from John Hancock called Jim following up on a direct mail campaign that included a long-term care insurance solicitation mailed to Jim two weeks earlier. In short order, the representative contacted Hancock's underwriters, explained Jim's condition, and arranged for standard insurance for his new client.

Jim bought long-term care insurance even though he had been resistant. The Hancock broker was thrilled with the easy sale, and Betty protected her assets.

This couple learned that underwriting can be a tricky process. Here's what happened: As a general rule UnumProvident is considered one the most stringent underwriters on the street. The company maintains that in order to preserve the integrity of its pricing policy, it must be restrictive in its underwriting. MetLife, sometimes aggressive and willing to beat UnumProvident in certain difficult cases, felt that Jim's enlarged heart could present the risk of disability. But John Hancock had the opinion that this man has functioned well, was very active, played tennis, did some part-time management consulting, and was not affected in any way by his condition.

This situation reinforces the need for consumers to make certain that the broker or agent they select to represent them has the ability and willingness to do the company shopping for them, especially when medical issues are involved. No one company is always the best one to choose to underwrite all cases.

And Don't Buy That Kind

Jim was able to buy long-term care coverage because his medical condition was not a threat to his morbidity. But sometimes one partner or the other has a significant physical problem that will prevent their buying long-term care coverage, no matter how much they want it.

Elsa, a retired teacher, age 74, was a perfect candidate for long-term care insurance. She had just completed a 20-month siege of ministering at home to her ailing husband, who eventually died. He had Alzheimer's disease, and to honor a pact between them she resisted any and all efforts to place him in a nursing home.

Fortunately for the couple, both children were successful with Wall Street firms and had low six-figure-incomes. The children were able to fund the enormous cost of round-the-clock home care in the last six months of their father's life.

Now Elsa was ready to buy coverage for herself. But before the long-term care agent was able to open his mouth, he was told in no uncertain terms, "I only want a long-term care insurance policy that covers me for home care. Even though my children and I have a loving and caring relationship, I don't want them coming here from out of town to visit me when I'm sick with the knowledge that there's a nursing home policy available that will pay the benefits for me if I qualify for nursing home care." Elsa feared that if she had a nursing home policy, she risked premature placement if her condition deteriorated.

Unfortunately, Elsa was not eligible for any type of long-term care coverage—neither nursing home nor home care. Elsa was a chain-smoker. She had developed emphysema because she completely ignored her own health while tending to her husband. In addition, she was on heavy medication for severe depression caused as she watched her husband deteriorate before her eyes.

Elsa has ignored herself, and now she was uninsurable. Her kids would have to come up with the money to help their mother, just as they had helped their father, or they would be forced to watch her spend her assets to care for herself and then end up, supported by Medicaid, in the nursing home she dreaded.

Our Last Act Together

Long-term care insurers offer premium discounts when both spouses buy coverage at the same time from the same company. These discounts, sometimes as much as 20 percent, can be a powerful buying incentive. They may even tempt couples on their last marital legs to buy the coverage, even though they recognize that divorce is on the horizon.

One long-time client, Arthur, called me with ominous news. He and his wife, Katie, in a "final act together," wanted to buy long-term care insurance.

But they looked so healthy when they walked into my office that I said, "You look extremely healthy and happy. I just don't understand how you can say the purchase of long-term care insurance is your last act together."

"We have filed for divorce," Arthur explained. It will be official in about three months. Do you think we can get long-term care insurance issued by that time?"

They were after the spousal discount.

They told me the truth; I told them the truth.

Once a policy is issued with a spousal discount, the insurer rarely takes the discount away. Even if one spouse dies, the remaining spouse will continue with the spousal discount. If one spouse decides to drop his or her policy because of financial considerations or a competitive offering, the remaining spouse gets to keep the discount as long as the premiums are paid. If a couple ultimately gets divorced, the company would typically honor a good-faith request to maintain the discount.

In this instance, however, it could be argued that there was an attempt to defraud the insurer. Since the divorce was in progress, the insurer might use the existence of the legal documents to claim fraud.

Long-Term Care Insurance in a Second Marriage: Sickness or Health?

Second marriages may sometimes present complicated choices for the bride and groom and their adult children. Unlike the spouse you grew up with, whose health and well-being were familiar concerns for you, the new girlfriend or boyfriend may not be as forthcoming about the state of their health. Sometimes it takes only the threat of a physical exam to put the brakes on the marriage vows.

Share and Share Alike

Many couples who enter second marriages plan very carefully so that each pays for his or her share of the costs. However, even the most careful planners may discover that they have overlooked important areas that will prevent them from splitting all those costs right down the middle.

John, age 66, and Helen, age 52, each entered their second marriage 10 years ago. They set up a careful prenuptial agreement, spelling out all the contingencies that could occur if one died or the couple divorced. They also agreed to an allocation of household and personal expenses.

Their health insurance costs were part of this elaborate plan. They would divide these costs equally, with the understanding that so long as Helen was employed, her health insurance would be covered by her employer. When she reached age 65, Medicare and Medigap supplemental insurance would, like John, cover her. Each would have the same coverage.

But 10 years ago, when Helen was 42 and John 56, neither thought about the possibility of needing long-term care insurance. Now, at 52 and 66, the cost of this insurance would be very different for each of them.

How might they now maintain their commitment to an equal distribution of expenses?

They went over several different scenarios including one that had Helen purchase a policy with 5 percent compound interest inflation factor and have John take a higher amount without any inflation but for a shorter benefit period than Helen. But they realized that if they bought the coverage and one or the other required benefits, there could be irritation that could rupture their union.

They finally resolved that since they currently had enough money to buy the policies, John would, this once, have to extend himself financially. He would not be a burden for Helen or force her to interrupt her upward career path to care for him, since she had several years of advancement ahead of her before retirement.

You Show Me Yours, but I Won't Show You Mine

Some second marriages get derailed before they happen, especially if one person has a medical secret he or she is unwilling to share.

Carol and Oscar had a terrific time at their 52d wedding anniversary party, but that night Carol suffered a stroke. Their three daughters, concerned for their mother and their father, kicked in to help.

The daily caretaking fell to Geraldine, who had never married. She had promised Carol that she would keep her at home as long as she could, so Geraldine moved in to help Oscar with her care. The second daughter, Dorothy, lived 800 miles away; and the third, Amy, lived around the corner with her husband and young children.

After a year of loving care, Carol died. During a family gathering to help their father distribute his wife's clothes and keepsakes, the girls surprised him with a ticket for a weekend Caribbean cruise. Reluctantly, Oscar accepted the ticket, sad about letting his daughters pay for the trip and lonely for his wife.

But as these trips go, Oscar was seated at a table with Mary, a lovely lady from the same suburb. She had just lost her husband after a five-year battle with Alzheimer's.

It was love at first sight for both, as they shared the tales of their spouses' long illnesses. After a six-month courtship, Oscar and Mary decided to get married. They made a prenuptial agreement with no problem.

But Mary had another requirement. She wouldn't marry Oscar until he could produce a long-term care insurance policy. If they had to delay the marriage, she was willing.

Oscar's daughters, initially thrilled by their father's newfound love and happiness, had second thoughts about Mary.

The girls knew that Oscar had spent down his assets keeping Carol at home, even though Geraldine did most of the caregiving. Oscar had needed to buy medical equipment and supplies, and Carol sometimes required the unreimbursed care of a skilled nurse. They understood that long-term caregiving could be very expensive, even for the patient who stays at home. While no one admitted it, they felt that the insurance benefits would relieve them of a responsibility and allow Geraldine to go back to work, let Amy spend more time with her family, and free Dorothy of the guilt she felt when she couldn't help take care of her mother.

They agreed to chip in to cover the cost of the long-term care insurance premium—with one provision:

The girls said, "Dad, we're willing to pay for your long-term care insurance and we know you will qualify and get a policy because you're in good health and take good care of yourself. But we have one stipulation. We want you to tell Mary that we will pay for your insurance provided she produces a policy covering her own long-term care costs. If she's not willing to take care of you if you have an illness or disability, why should you be willing to take care of her?"

When Oscar told Mary of his daughters' requirements, his new love was aghast. She simply would have no part of it. Mary said, "I'm a lady of means. I have more than adequate funds to pay for all the long-term care expenses that I might have."

Why wouldn't Mary go along? Geraldine, a nurse with a sixth sense for physical ailments, had an idea that Dad's fiancée had a condition she was afraid to disclose. She urged her father to press the issue.

This time, Oscar told his girlfriend that the daughters would even pay for her policy. Mary's response: "I have never been so insulted, and I think that we weren't meant for each other." That was the end of any marriage plans.

What happened? Nine months later, when Geraldine was staff nurse at the local emergency room, Mary was admitted with congestive heart failure.

"Come Pick Up Your Father"

Sometimes a couple enjoys their second marriage until a health crisis occurs. Then everyone—adult children, the second spouse, even the grandchildren—can get into the act.

"Come pick up your father." That was the message Gloria, who lived in suburban Westchester, New York, found on her answering machine when she came home from her weekly mah-jongg game. She was so terrified by the words that she could hardly dial the number of her father's home in Philadelphia.

Alfred, age 84, had been married for eight years to a Philadelphia widow he met after Gloria's mother died. The couple met in Atlantic City, courted at the gambling tables, married in Philadelphia, spent winters at Ruth's condo in Boca Raton, Florida, and summered at Ruth's apartment in Philadelphia. The arrangement was perfect for the couple and all the adult children.

Now Dad was sick. And Gloria, just beginning her own second marriage, did not have the time or the emotional stamina to be at her father's beck and call. Ruth's children did not have the inclination to look after their mother.

Everything had been fine while the seniors were healthy, able to drive their cars, shop in the supermarket, and get to their doctor's appointments on time. Trouble began to develop when Alfred showed early signs of Alzheimer's disease. Initially Ruth was able to take care of him, but now she was calling upon her own children, living nearby, more and more often. Her own health was deteriorating.

Besides, her children were incurring expenses for Alfred's care that they were not anxious to pay.

Finally, despite Ruth's intense love for her second husband, her children would no longer let her be Alfred's caregiver, nor would they assume that responsibility either physically or financially. They did not want their mother or themselves to be caregivers or to pay the freight for anyone else to look after Alfred.

That's when they called Gloria. They told her that if she didn't come to get Alfred within 48 hours, they would put him on a plane home.

Alfred lasted three months in Gloria's house, and then her own new husband paid her dad's bills at a local nursing home. The son-in-law was willing to pay the cash but not the emotional toll of caring for the Alzheimer's patient. The old man died at the nursing home a year later.

Sadly, Alfred was deprived of his wife's love and comfort during the last year of his life. And she really wanted to be with him at the end. Both had been reasonably healthy on their wedding day and could have qualified for long-term care insurance. But they thought the premium was disproportionate to their spendable income, so they decided against it. For better or worse, they had to live with that decision.

Uncovering the Hidden Agenda

Most of the time, a couple enjoying a second marriage buys long-term care insurance for the same reason anyone does, to ensure the independence and dignity of their old age. But sometimes, there is an ulterior motive underlying the application process, even for partners who each appear to be healthy.

After jousting with their insurance agent for more than a year, Nancy and Bert agreed to have a thorough discussion with the agent about long-term care insurance.

The couple's marriage, the second for each, was going well. Both had children, but all the kids lived out of town; there was concern on both parts that if either one became sick or disabled, the spouse might not be physically suited to be a caregiver. They agreed they could afford the premiums; but while Nancy was anxious to apply for the coverage, Bert was dragging his feet.

The ulterior motive began to be revealed during the agent's visit with the couple. The very conscientious agent, who always did a bit of preunderwriting during the interview process, found that Bert and Nancy had different doctors in different hospitals. Both were on medications, but there appeared to be no medical issues to alarm the underwriters.

The agent explained the application process to Bert and Nancy, describing the underwriting procedure, which required a completed application, a medical records check, and, for Bert because of his age, a cognitive impairment test.

A deafening silence developed. Abruptly, it seemed, Bert had changed his mind, refusing to pursue the insurance that day. He told the agent to leave, and that he and his wife would need time to discuss the matter.

The next day Nancy called the agent. She said, "You indicated that on some occasions, subject to the applicant's authorization, you could get the appropriate medical records. If we give that authorization, before you go to any insurance company, can you provide me with a copy of my records and those of my husband, Bert?"

The agent quite properly said, "Bert's medical history is a private and confidential matter. I can't give you any data without his permission."

Nancy replied, "I can understand now why my husband is reluctant to pursue the matter any further."

Nancy's real reason for pursuing long-term care insurance was to resolve some doubts she had about her second husband's medical history. She had the feeling that he never told her about conditions that might surface and cause problems at a later date.

Nancy hoped to use the underwriting process as a vehicle to flush out information she should have determined before she said "I do."

What a Body

A senior citizen, like any other person, may be blinded by love. No matter how much passion he (or she) feels, however, it is often a good idea to keep one's eyes wide open.

One day I received a call from a very disturbed gentleman seeking my advice. Although I wasn't his insurance agent, the caller said, he had read my insurance columns in the *Boston Globe* and heard me speak. He was facing what he thought was a unique problem and wanted some guidance.

He and his wife, both in their second marriages, had long-term care insurance; when they bought the policies two years earlier, he was 77 and his wife was 74.

Now the wife had been diagnosed with Alzheimer's.

At the same time, her son from her first marriage called the man with another troubling piece of news.

"We appreciate everything you've done for Mom," the son told his stepfather, "and we know that you have long-term care insurance policies. But rather than face a scandal, we have the means to pay for Mom's home care or nursing home care from our own pockets. We want to protect our family's name."

Scandal? What scandal?

It seems that the wife, to whom my caller had been married for more than 20 years, had lied about her age all that time. She was actually seven years older than she had said, and four years older than her husband was.

Now what should he do? If he made full disclosure to the company, he was afraid of a fraud charge. But the company also might never find out the truth. He could also simply let the policy lapse.

I explained to the caller that with life insurance, it is actually not uncommon for the certified death certificate to reflect a birth date different from the one in the policy. In the case of life insurance, the company takes the annual premium and determines how much of a reduction in coverage there would be at a higher premium for an increased age. Then it pays the claim.

Long-term care insurance handles these circumstances differently.

For one thing, there are volumes of records that would reflect the wife's actual age, including Medicare and hospital records. If the insurance company never sold a long-term care policy to someone over 80, too, they would refund the premiums and refuse to pay benefits.

Besides, if the wife were actually 81 instead of 74 when she applied for the insurance, she would have been asked to take a cognitive impairment test. That test, in turn, might have shown the early signs of Alzheimer's and she would have been denied the long-term care insurance.

"How were you fooled?" I then asked him.

"What a body!" the husband replied.

I left my concerned caller to plan his next moves, but if I had to guess, I'd say that he let the policy lapse and let his wife's grown son pay her home care and nursing home care costs.

Had she told the truth back in the days when they were courting, her longtime husband wouldn't have been faced with this unpleasant choice, and she might have been relieved of keeping a secret for 20 years.

Employer-Sponsored Long-Term Care Coverage: What Is the Bottom Line?

Long-term care insurance as a fringe benefit of employment is still rare. But more and more employers appreciate the attractiveness of this benefit, and lawmakers encourage its use through tax deductions. While employer-sponsored long-term care insurance comes in several different packages, it generally makes good sense to accept the coverage. But there are times when you might do better shopping on your own. Consider these examples.

If You Don't Qualify for the Company Benefit

Many adults under 40 have little experience with insurance physicals. Since we graduated from our pediatrician's practice, we have only had checkups every two or three years. We're young and healthy, and never expect surprises. So when our company offers long-term care coverage that requires medical screening, we think little of it.

Tim, age 35, was employed for eight years as a computer programmer at an electronics manufacturing company. He was satisfied that he had job security and was in line to become a home office executive in the next few years.

Tim was already well insured. His company provided him with fully paid HMO health insurance, short- and long-term disability, dental insurance, and group life insurance that provided two times his annual salary. Ten years ago a college roommate had convinced him to avoid future uninsurability by buying a $500,000 20-year term life insurance policy at less than $1,000 in annual premiums. This life insurance policy was issued on a preferred basis.

Now the human resources department notified all employees that they could now buy individual long-term care policies available to employees of the company and their spouses on a discounted basis. The employer was taking advantage of the "list billing discount" offered by a number of long-term carriers. In this discount, the employees and spouses can be covered, and one bill is sent every month to the employer. The employer handles the bookkeeping and deducts the premiums from the employee's weekly paychecks. This simplified billing system allows the employees to enjoy a 5 to 10 percent discount.

In turn, the employees and their spouses had to go through the typical underwriting process. They could select their benefits packages, but they had to use the insurance company designated by the employer.

Between the time Tim bought life insurance and this latest offer, he developed colitis. He had been hospitalized several times and was now on heavy doses of steroids to control the problem. Still, he assumed that he would qualify for the long-term care benefits just like he had for his other company-paid coverages.

Much to his surprise, he was contacted by the company's insurance agent, who told him that he had a personal matter to discuss. Tim was flabbergasted when he was told that because of his colitis history and steroid regimen the company (which normally would decline him for long-term care insurance) had made an offer to write him a 25 percent additional premium. His total premium was relatively low because of his young age.

Tim felt like a second-class citizen. Why was he singled out? He told the agent that he would like to get a second opinion.

Of course, that was Tim's prerogative. The agent offered to check out other companies or let Tim contact his own agent. Grateful for the agent's understanding, Tim asked him to search the market.

It turned out that the company plan actually meant the best deal for Tim. Because his employer had many potential policyholders, the company's clout actually saved Tim money. In fact, other insurers wouldn't even sell a policy to him. Besides, if in the next few years his condition stabilized, there were no flare-ups, and the steroid prescription was reduced, he could request a reconsideration. And his individual premium could not be raised, even if his condition worsened.

In the long run, Tim was able to buy an individual long-term care policy at a reasonable price because his employer was large. Had he shopped on his own, Tim might have paid more or been rejected. Although the company did not pick up the bill for Tim or any of his colleagues, it made valuable coverage possible at a fair price.

When a Fringe Benefit Becomes As Important As Salary

A corporation may buy a group long-term care policy because the CEO or other top-ranking employees have medical profiles that would disqualify them for individual coverage. Even if these key people could buy individual policies, they might have to pay additional premiums because of preexisting impairments.

The employer arranges for group long-term care coverage because it is guaranteed, as long as the employer has enough workers to meet the guidelines of the underwriters. In turn, this benefit may be the one to make a valuable employee stay on the job.

Jack was 39 years old when his company instituted a group long-term care insurance policy that didn't require any premium payment at all from Jack. The amount of premium his employer spent for him was negligible considering his age and the benefit provided.

However, Jack was a very methodical fellow who liked to have a yearly consultation with his financial planner. Together, Jack and the planner outlined Jack's assets, reviewed his retirement savings, and discussed his insurance policies.

Jack didn't think much about this free benefit until he developed a potentially disabling condition, chronic lymphatic leukemia (CLL). As frightening as it sounds (and CLL can be very serious for some people), patients with this illness have been known to live for more than 30 years.

Underwriters like to wait about two years before considering this type of condition. Some will want to charge extra premiums at that time; others will prefer to wait to see how an individual responds to medication and just what medication has been prescribed.

Jack needed to satisfy his peace of mind. He was now worried about the details of his long-term care policy. He discreetly reviewed his book of benefits and the company's master long-term care policy to see if he could take his insurance with him if he left the company voluntarily or if the company went bankrupt.

What had seemed like a casual benefit now was central in Jack's job plans. And, ironically, this benefit made him loyal to his company and caused him to forego plans to look for a promotion elsewhere in the industry.

When the Fringe Benefit Becomes a Trap

Jack, who might now have difficulty qualifying for long-term care coverage, was grateful to his employer for providing the benefit to him. He valued his job and was even more committed to the company's financial well-being.

For older employees considering retirement options, the age might come when they can't afford to move on because it would mean giving up affordable long-term care coverage.

Bert, a 48-year-old treasurer of a payroll processing firm, was surprised to learn that because the CEO had medical problems that precluded obtaining individual long-term care insurance, the company was buying a group of individual policies for 10 members of the firm and their spouses.

Under the insurance company guidelines, only the actual employees of the firm could be included for guaranteed-issue underwriting. This meant that for a modest amount of coverage, these employees would not have to have any physical exams, answer any medical questions, or take any cognitive tests. The spouses, however, would require underwriting. The employer, because it was a C corporation, could deduct the premium for employee and spouse as a fringe benefit.

Bert's policy would be paid up in 10 years. The total monthly premium for his policy and his wife's was $650. He was the recipient of a $7,800 long-term care premium paid for by the company, which took a deduction. And Bert did not have to pay any income tax on the $7,800.

Bert appreciated the benefit but realized that he was virtually locked into that job. If he had to come up with $7,800 after taxes to pay for the policy on his own, he would need a gross income of $12,000. That was too much for him at age 48. Besides, every year he worked on the job the more expensive any replacement coverage would become so if he wanted long-term care he would have to keep the existing contract and pay it on his own if he were no longer a member of that firm.

Unlike Jack, Bert had no significant medical problems that might make underwriting-difficult, but he valued the long-term care insurance benefit too much to lose it by changing jobs.

What Are You Really Buying with Your Premium Dollars?: The Smart Shopper

Perhaps more than any other insurance product, long-term care coverage is loaded with emotional choices. It is tempting for many consumers to put on a metaphorical blindfold and pin the tail on a policy or insurance company without actually checking out the details. This blind faith can lead to open-eyed disappointment down the line, if the consumer needs to make a claim.

If It Was Good Enough for My Dad

Once in a while someone chooses an insurance company because their parents bought from the same place. In the following example, that reason may in the long run be sufficient. But imagine if you were still shopping for Oldsmobiles because your father drove one in 1958.

Sarah told me exactly why she had bought long-term care insurance from GE Capital. She said that General Electric had made her first refrigerator, the one she and her husband purchased 40 years ago when they first married.

And that refrigerator still works! It is in their summer cottage on the Maine coast.

Besides, they believe the GE Capital long-term care commercials they see on *Meet the Press*.

What better reason could there be for choosing GE?

Don't Press Me for Details

Seniors especially may have bought long-term care insurance after their spouse died, but without adequately thinking about what they were purchasing. Asking them about the policy, however, will only make them uncomfortable.

Sadie, a widow of seven years, bought a long-term care insurance policy five years ago while she was in Florida. She was paying $1,200 a year, with $100 taken automatically from her checking account each month.

That's a good deal for someone her age, but the problem was that Sadie didn't know exactly what benefits she had. She just knew that she was "covered." Home care? Nursing home coverage? Benefit length? Who knew?

She encouraged all her friends to buy the policy.

Long-Term Care Is Not Chore Care

If you think you're covered for certain kinds of services, you are likely to be very disappointed when you learn you're not. This scenario happens most often when policyholders compare their benefits with those of relatives.

Edith was stunned when she received a call from her and her husband's insurance agent saying that their long-term care insurance company, currently paying the bills for her husband's home care, had rejected a $100-a-month bill submitted by their gardener. After all, Edith said, "My brother-in-law has been disabled and at home for two years. His insurance company pays the gardening bills."

In this case it appeared that the insurance company indirectly paid for her brother-in-law's gardening. Edith's sister and brother-in-law opted for the indemnity plan of insurance that was paying them $200 a day as long as the policyholder was disabled. Because her brother-in-law's actual expenses ranged between $100 and $125 a day, he had money left over to pay the gardener.

Edith's husband had a reimbursement policy that paid for actual expenses incurred in connection with his care and treatment. It didn't cover the gardener. Some home care policies are better than others and extend to various chore services, including minor repairs, changing storm windows, and snow shoveling, but to pay for one's hobby of gardening is a real stretch.

Edith, here, was also reacting to the good news and the bad about the policy. She listened to her brother-in-law exaggerate the great treatment he was receiving from his company, but never figured out the reasons why. She would have been just as vocal if the company had refused to pay legitimate expenses; but at least in that case her complaints might have been justified.

Don't Go Looking for a Free Lunch

Some people have heard about long-term care coverage but don't understand just what the insurance involves. They associate it with Medicare benefits supplied by the government. What a disappointment when these consumers find out they are not eligible for coverage.

One insurance agent received a call from a neighbor asking about the purchase of long-term care insurance. The agent asked the caller how old he and his wife were.

The caller said, "Oh, the insurance isn't for me. I'm very healthy. I don't need the coverage. I'll buy it when I need it. But my wife just came home from the hospital after suffering a stroke. I don't think Medicare and her Medigap insurance will be enough to cover the caregivers that I have to hire."

The caller didn't understand that insurance companies are not like the federal government, which makes Medicare available for everybody at age 65, at the same premium regardless of their health. Besides, he bought his Medigap insurance during an open enrollment period when it was a guaranteed issue, with the same premium for everyone.

Insurance companies are not charities. They have the right to pick and choose which risks to insure. They won't write fire insurance for a burning building, after all.

I'll Trade You My Indemnity Medigap Policy for Your HMO

The consumer should fire any agent who suggests you trade your indemnity Medigap insurance policy for an HMO, then use the premium difference to pay for your long-term care coverage. Too often, consumers find that they have lost the care of the doctors and specialists they depend on. Even long-term care insurance isn't worth that trade-off.

His insurance agent, for instance, assured Bob that changing from his indemnity Medigap policy wouldn't have any consequences on his health care. He could still go to the city's biggest teaching hospitals in case of a crisis. And he could use the money he saved to buy a long-term care policy.

The agent, in this case, was doing a bit of cross selling. He could increase his income with the commissions on Bob's first-year long-term care premium, and while he already had the client's life insurance business, he didn't have anything to do with his health care coverage.

But when Bob looked further into switching Medigap coverage, he was dismayed to learn that the family practitioner he and his wife went to was not in the proposed plan. Worse, he would have to find a new ophthalmologist and chiropractor, since neither would be paid by the proposed HMO. Bob was still interested in long-term care insurance coverage, but he knew he had to find a different way to pay for it.

It wouldn't have been a good idea for Bob to cash in his life insurance coverage, either. While the pool of money paid by long-term care insurers may be bigger in dollars, say $300,000 compared to Bob's $200,000 life insurance policy, he would see the cash only if he actually needed long-term care.

His beneficiaries would receive the $200,000 life insurance policy for sure, as long as Bob paid the premiums until his death.

Take What You Can Get

Unfortunately, a detail in one's medical history may complicate the purchase of long-term care insurance. In these cases, policyholders may understand just what they are buying with their premium dollars. They have no choice but to take what they can get.

Justin, newly retired, was planning a 30-day Mediterranean cruise with his wife Elaine. With their two children grown and happy, they had savings for retirement and expected to enjoy the good life.

But there was one cloud. When Justin retired, he lost his group life insurance coverage, which was three times his salary. As his salary increased so did his group life coverage. It had been issued on a guaranteed basis, so Justin had never had to submit to a medical examination or answer any health questions on a medical form.

Justin could convert this group policy to an individual one, but the premium cost was very high. The insurance company figured that the only employees who would select this option probably had no choice. Their medical histories would have prevented them from buying from another company.

This was true for Justin, and he was a healthy man. He and his wife had undergone couples therapy for specific situational issues—ones which most underwriters would overlook. But Justin had once taken medication to help him through a temporary depression. He was too private to allow a paper trail about that prescription, so he decided to skip the life insurance conversion. His family would have to do without that protection.

Now Justin's wife was concerned about having no life insurance. If he were to die before she did she figured she could manage without any payoff, but what really scared her was that they might have long-term care needs that would use up all their savings. What would they do then?

For peace of mind, they reluctantly settled for a $100-a-day benefit for a three-year period without inflation. They knew this coverage was inadequate, but it gave them, particularly Justin's wife, a temporary Band-Aid and a token bit of peace of mind.

Heading for Court

When you agree to the terms of your long-term care insurance, you've made an agreement to pay a set amount of money for a set of benefits. But what happens if you're disabled between the time you pay a deposit and when you receive the insurance? That depends on the company you're dealing with.

Six weeks after Martha applied for long-term care insurance, gave her broker a $500 check payable to the company, and was issued a binder, she was diagnosed with Alzheimer's disease. According to Martha and her family, the first time she mentioned any memory problem to her doctor was six months earlier when jokingly she said she had a senior moment when she tried to remember the punch line of a joke. Something must have surfaced during her subsequent routine six-month checkup with her internist that prompted him to send her to a neurologist, who brought forth the diagnosis of Alzheimer's.

She told her broker.

Her broker told her not to worry. She had paid her $500 and the meter stopped. There could be no question about future insurability because of changes to her health from then on.

Besides, Martha's doctor told her it would be a while before she would qualify for benefits under her long-term care policy. She was still highly functional and was not a danger to herself or third parties for the foreseeable future.

Martha called her lawyer. The lawyer said, "You don't need to tell the insurance company. They can investigate you at great length and detail your medical background for the first two years. If they find any misrepresentation at all they can rescind the policy."

So long as Martha's Alzheimer's does not qualify her for benefits under her long-term care insurance, there will be no problem. But binders vary by company. Some insurers would have offered her very limited coverage, perhaps a lump sum payment. Others will assume all responsibility. Still others say, "Even though you have paid a deposit, you will not be issued a policy. Here is your money back."

The Assisted Living Myth

It is strange but true that some buyers of long-term care insurance have the mistaken notion that if, 10 years after the policy is issued, they decide to move out of their home into an assisted living facility, they simply have to let their insurance representative know.

If you have a car accident, you may only need to call your insurance agent to start the reimbursement process, but long-term health care coverage is different. Even if assisted living is covered in a plan, the policyholder has to qualify for the care by being certified as being unable to independently perform two of the activities of daily living or being cognitively impaired.

Elsie called her insurance broker to say she was planning to move from her house into the local assisted living community. Elsie was physically lucky that her only real difficulty was managing her bath. She handled all the other activities of daily living very well. Her policy included reimbursement for assisted living, but Elsie didn't yet qualify.

Indeed, if Elsie had been significantly impaired, she might not have been able to move into an assisted living community, anyway. Often this level of care doesn't provide enough support for patients who have more than two disabilities. Elsie may have ended up in a nursing home instead. If Elsie's more significant disabilities had developed while she was in the local assisted living community, she could have been notified that she needed to move elsewhere.

Who Is the Client?: When the Patient Isn't the Purchaser

Experienced salespeople know that the "buyer" may not be the real decision maker in a transaction. The sales meeting becomes especially interesting when the decision makers come to the table with hidden agendas.

The Kids Won't Grow Up

Seniors may feel very loved when their children offer to fund their long-term care insurance policies. But sometimes the agent who arranges a meeting to discuss the policy comes in for some nasty surprises. He or she may find himself in the role of family therapist, as the kids work through their childhood issues.

The agent went to a meeting to determine the best type of policy the kids could arrange for their 75-year-old mother, now living alone. The father had died five years earlier, and his oldest son, Harold, was running the family's three men's stores.

Harold's opening question was, "Who is going to pay for this premium?"

That was it. The "kids" talked about every financial issue except long-term care insurance.

In unison both daughters argued that Harold must pay; after all, he got the family business and they were left out in the cold. Doris, whose husband was an auto parts salesman, was struggling. Her sister, Gracie, lived 500 miles away.

The way the kids saw it, Dad favored Harold, and Mom favored Doris. Gracie, bitter and neglected, felt like the outsider. Why should Doris have allowed their mother to subsidize her salesman-husband's gambling junkets?

"You might not think that we didn't know what was going on. We knew that when your husband was allegedly in California on business trips, he was actually at the tables in Las Vegas. Our mother on many occasions had to come up with the rent money because of your husband's uncontrollable gambling habit."

Doris was furious. She blurted, "You didn't even know that Mother had a stock windfall several years ago. The bank stock that Dad never talked about had accumulated, and when the bank was taken over Mom made a mint." The family secrets were all exposed.

By now, the agent had learned more than he wanted to know. When Harold turned to him to suggest that he deal directly with their mother, the agent politely refused. Working with the children without their parent's consent to the meeting had been a mistake. They would have to find a different representative to start fresh with Mom.

Even that windfall stock profit didn't reassure the kids. As the agent left, he heard Gracie challenging her siblings about the consequences of Mom's running out of money. Who would care for her then?

Playing Columbo

The medical criteria for long-term care coverage are different than for life insurance, a fact that confuses some consumers. Besides, many of us like to keep the details of our health history to ourselves. Parents don't always tell their children every time they have a questionable result during a physical.

An attorney friend asked me to visit his dad, who was stonewalling other long-term care agents trying to sell him a policy. Dad lived alone, and there was no caregiver available to take care of him if his health declined.

Dad's objection seemed simple. He thought a long-term care policy should be issued just the same way he got Medicare coverage. He could go down to the

Social Security office, answer a few simple questions, and be automatically covered. No one wrote to his doctors; no one came into his house for a face-to-face cognitive test. This was the way he preferred to buy long-term care insurance.

I told him that under the rules of the game, the only way he could get insurance was to allow the agent to complete an application; he would answer questions about his health history, provide details about any medications he used, and then give the names of all the doctors or specialists he had seen within the past five years.

No chance of that, said Dad.

The son was my friend, so I said, "Okay. No sense in talking about insurance, either. Let's talk about the Red Sox or the Patriots."

Dad was flustered that I didn't want to pursue long-term care coverage. He said, "Why don't you just leave, then?"

On the way out the door I turned to him à la Lieutenant Columbo and said, "By the way, how old did you say you were—72? Would you tell me one thing— can you sleep the entire night without having to get up to urinate?"

"Are you crazy?" he answered. "I get up at least once if not twice a night."

"Would you kindly tell me the diuretic you are on for your blood pressure?"

How did I know? It was obvious.

Dad hadn't told his son about his elevated blood pressure that was now controlled with medication. Since he had been unable to buy life insurance 35 years earlier, he thought he would be turned down for long-term care coverage.

I assured him that times and medical technology have changed. Barring other health problems, he would have little trouble buying long-term care insurance.

Then both he and his son would feel much better.

Thanks but No Thanks

An insurance agent is of course delighted to receive an unsolicited call from a prospective buyer eager for a visit. The contact may lead directly to a sale, especially if the call is the result of a referral from another happy customer. But other times, there can be a big surprise.

One night at home I received a call that every agent or broker selling long-term care insurance would salivate for.

"Mr. Lipson, I've surveyed the market, and I'm ready to buy long-term care insurance. May I come to see you in your office as soon as you can see me?"

Nancy walked into my office for our meeting with a briefcase loaded with material about long-term care insurance. It was as though she was selling *me* the policy.

She was not worried about money; she was the recipient of a significant inheritance. But she wanted always to feel independent, and that's why she wanted a long-term care policy that would provide generous benefits for home care, assisted living, and a nursing home if required.

She told me in extended detail how she was turned down by two companies and offered insurance from a third, but at a 50 percent increase in premium.

Nancy's folder contained one of the most detailed medical histories I'd seen in a long time. She had office notes of her visits with her primary care physician, the results of her mammograms, bone density test, laboratory reports, copies of cardiograms, and statements from her gynecologist, cardiologist, psychiatrist, and rheumatologist.

Either an underwriter had been overwhelmed with such detail and figured that where there's smoke, there must be fire or Nancy suffered from the one plus one equals three syndrome. All those conditions, in themselves not troubling enough to cause declination, might combine to make problems.

For example, if a client has controlled blood pressure, an underwriter will either look the other way or issue standard long-term care insurance. If an insured is a few pounds overweight, but all other factors are normal, the underwriter could extend the prescribed weight limit and offer standard insurance.

But add controlled hypertension to slight overweight, and the alarms go off.

Nancy's bone density was borderline and she was diagnosed with osteopenia. She took 20 mg of Zocor a day for her elevated cholesterol. Because of a pain in her side that bothered her when she got out of bed, her doctor sent her to a rheumatoid specialist. Despite trying every diet imaginable, Nancy was still five pounds overweight.

Nancy allowed me to talk informally with an underwriter. By now she had no medical secrets, anyway. Within 24 hours, I called her to say that, subject to completing the application and verifying the data, I could provide a long-term care policy for her.

But she didn't want the policy. She was grateful for my efforts, which had confirmed her confidence in my ability. But that wasn't really the point.

"Now that a multibillion-dollar insurance company is willing to take my risk, I'm convinced I don't need the coverage. They wouldn't want to take my premium unless they thought that it was a good bet for them. I'd rather see my money in my bank account than in the coffers of a multibillion-dollar insurer. I'll pay for my possible long-term care expenses on my own."

Am I a Collector?

Few of us would think of an insurance agent's sales pitch as a highlight of our social calendar, but some consumers actually enjoy the process of talking to long-term care sellers. It doesn't matter that these consumers aren't actually in the market to buy.

Gertrude took great joy in telling her friends at the senior center that every Tuesday afternoon she had a private long-term care seminar at her home. She served refreshments in exchange for information.

She would call a different agent from a different company to visit her on Tuesday afternoon. Unfortunately she did not have the means to buy insurance, but she enjoyed the different sales presentations. It took the sixth agent to figure out what was going on.

Shirley, a very savvy sales representative, became annoyed when Gertrude kept saying, "Metropolitan does that differently," "GE Capital has a better home care plan," or "UnumProvident's indemnity plan makes a lot of sense."

Shirley said to Gertrude, "How do you know so much?"

"Wait a minute," Gertrude replied. She went to her den and brought back two bundles that represented the data from five insurance companies. There were five sample policies, several different proposals for various benefit plans with each company, multiple copies of state regulations, and other guides for long-term care insurance.

Exasperated, Shirley then said to Gertrude, "Are you a collector?"

"That's right, my dear, and you're the only one who figured me out. If I had the means to buy, I would buy from you."

Crisis Calls

When a caller says, "Come right over—I want to buy long-term care insurance," there has usually been a long-term care crisis in the family. Often, these are emotionally laden.

Ed called me about his good friend, Melvin. It seems that for the previous year Melvin's wife Evelyn had been battling and eventually lost a battle with esophageal cancer.

During the time that Evelyn was in and out of hospitals and rehabilitation facilities, the couple's children avoided the problem. They left the care of their mother to Melvin, whose severe arthritis had forced him to take early retirement from his job as a chief financial officer of a medical equipment company.

Like Ed, many of Melvin's friends were eager to help during that difficult year. Sometimes the two sons visited, but both had separate agendas. One was fast-tracked at a prestigious law firm where he put in 12-hour days. The other had just lost his young wife to cancer after a two-year battle; he could barely stand to go into the hospital to visit his mother. The boys would have to deal with their behavior for the rest of their lives.

But now, Ed wanted me to talk to Melvin about caring for himself if something went wrong. He was not likely to be able to count on his children.

I indicated that on the surface it was highly unlikely that Melvin could get insurance. His arthritis was very bad, and only if he was not disabled, did not use a cane or walker to move around, could drive a car, and was on acceptable medication would an insurer even consider him.

The real issue was that Melvin had to start the inquiry himself. His friends couldn't do it for him, no matter how loving their motives. If I called Melvin to say that his friends believed the two sons, prides of his life, had let him down, Melvin would despair. If I delivered the message that the two sons would not help their father in his old age, he might grow frailer on the spot.

Ed would lose his friend Melvin, and Melvin would lose his most valuable support system, his friend Ed.

CHAPTER 13

Questions and Answers

Questions Most Insurance Companies Hope You Never Ask

When you go shopping for long-term care insurance, you don't have to have all the answers. You just need to know how to ask the right questions.

Will asking these questions make the insurer pause? So what? You're spending significant dollars to buy significant potential coverage. You have a right to look closely into the details of your purchase. In some cases, you will be asking about basic policy features the insurer has already included; in others, you will be addressing more problematic areas. In all cases, the most consumer-friendly insurance companies understand that long-term care coverage is a new product for most people. They will welcome your questions.

Here are some you should ask:

- **If your policy excludes claims resulting from treatment for alcoholism or drug addiction, will it pay for a dependency that results from physician-prescribed medications?**
  While you may have agreed that you will not qualify for long-term care benefits if your disability is caused by an addiction to drugs or alcohol, an addiction to a physician-prescribed painkiller may be a shared responsibility. Look at your policy to see how your insurer would treat this eventuality.

- **Do you automatically provide waiver of premium for both home care and nursing home coverage without an additional premium if the feature is not included in the basic policy?**
  Some insurers treat home care differently from nursing home care when it comes to waiving benefits. Do you want to be subjected to a special waiting period before your premiums are waived because you choose to be cared for at home and not in a nursing home?

- **When on a claim do the provisions of your inflation rider still apply, or does the maximum daily benefit in effect at the start of any claim remain constant?**
  When you bought your policy, you selected a benefit that would pay you for several years, often three, four, or five. You may also have bought an inflation rider, to protect yourself in the very long-term against rising costs. Now you need the long-term benefits, but have discovered that each year the cost for your care is increasing by 3 percent to 5 percent or more. Will the inflation option rider you purchased continue to be operative while you are on claim?

- **What range of bone density levels are in your underwriting guidelines to determine whether an applicant can receive preferred, standard, rated, or no coverage at all?**
  Unfortunately, osteoporosis becomes a fact of life for many of us as we grow older. Each insurer's underwriters have their own guidelines for acceptable bone density levels. It may pay you to shop around for a company that doesn't penalize you if your bone density is not ideal.

- **Who in your company will have access to my medical data contained on my policy application and information obtained from my doctors?**
  Your medical data is your own business. It's private. Your agent has a legal obligation to respect your privacy, but what about the company's paper handlers? Does the insurer have a privacy protection policy in place that prevents unauthorized employees from having access to your records?

- **What percent of policies result in a claim for restoration of benefits?**
  Restoration of benefits is actually a phantom benefit, since it says that your maximum policy benefit will be restored if you are able to go a set number of days without treatment for a condition. Unfortunately, if you take one pill for this condition during those days, you can be disqualified.

- **How many hours of training do you provide for your new agents?**
  Long-term care insurance is a new and somewhat complicated product. The agent needs to know what he or she is talking about to serve you well. Is the training ongoing and reflective of all current changes in policy forms?

- **What percentages of applicants are reviewed by someone in the company with a medical degree?**

  Medical underwriting for long-term care insurance policies deals with morbidity rather than mortality. If an underwriter understands physical conditions, he or she is much more able to evaluate the applicant's insurability. If the underwriter uses a check sheet of conditions, the marginally suitable consumer may be out of luck.

- **Do you have any plans to market your long-term care product on the Internet?**

  Internet marketing raises questions about privacy. Besides, long-term care policies are often too complicated to be clearly explained online. But don't confuse an insurer's web site information with online marketing. The insurance company's explanation of its product on the company web site should be as clear, straightforward, and reliable as you would expect to get in a face-to-face meeting with an agent or broker.

- **What has your lapse ratio been for the past three years?**

  If the insurance company has a high lapse ratio, that means that the company is selling long-term care policies to unqualified buyers. These consumers have trouble paying the premium in year two or year three, and allow the policy to lapse. A high lapse ratio may also reflect the fact that the policyholder was a victim of high-pressure sales tactics that may be condoned by the insurer.

- **Who is your major competitor?**

  And what does that company have that you don't have? If you know the benefits offered by the competitor, you'll be in a better position to decide which ones you want (and don't want) in the original insurer's plan.

- **What is the average number of days it takes for a claim to be approved?**

  Granted that your long-term care coverage will have a waiting period, usually 100 days, before the benefits start paying. If you're a senior, Medicare may kick in for some of that cost. Still, you've bought long-term care insurance so you won't have to pay your whole bill out of pocket. Do you want to wait extra days while the company determines whether you are certified as disabled? Or for the company's care coordinator to help you arrange your care?

- **Do you have any plans to make an indemnity rider available under your policies?**

  If your insurer now swears by the reimbursement model of long-term care insurance, why is the company considering the indemnity model? Which one is actually best for you in your situation?

- **Will you pay for the cost of a private care coordinator?**
  If your insurer already provides, as part of your benefits, a professional care coordinator, it may not want to complicate matters by adding another advocate. But the private care coordinator has only one boss, the patient, thus helping to eliminate a conflict of interest in this very important service.

- **What type of complaints, including those to your state's insurance office, have been filed against the insurance company?**
  Long-term care insurance doesn't come with a lemon-law sticker on the window. How will you know what to watch out for in long-term care insurance if you don't know where the coverage pitfalls are or which unprofessional sales tactics to be on the lookout for?

- **During the past two years, has the company had any discussion, direct or indirect, with any other insurer or investment banker about the possible sale of the company or its long-term care book of business?**
  You've checked the company's ratings, but not those of its every suitor. If a larger, healthier company is about to gobble up your insurer, you may be fortunate. But what if the suitor is less attractive? You may find shopping for a new policy is an equally unattractive alternative: You'll be older and perhaps less healthy. Besides, why does the insurer want to sell its long-term care business? Does it anticipate being unable to pay benefits down the line?

- **How many times have rates been increased since the company started to write long-term care insurance?**
  The company keeps saying that your premiums cannot be increased, but it really means that you can't be singled out for an increase. How often has your class of policyholders had its premium raised?

- **When does your waiver of premium become operable: simultaneously with the payment of benefits or 90 days after benefits have been paid?**
  Insurers typically waive your long-term care premium if you become disabled, but some companies include a special waiting period after your benefits begin before your premium stops. Others limit the waiver of premium to clients in a nursing home; if you receive home or community care, you'll have to continue sending premium checks.

- **During the past three years what enhancements provided in new policy series were made available with and without insurability and with and without extra premiums for in-force policyholders?**
  Does your long-term care insurance company care enough about you to give you legitimate enhancements at no additional cost and no additional underwriting scrutiny?

- **Will you put in writing, signed by an officer of the company, your current claim practice in respect to alternative care and whether this practice will be followed in the event I have a claim under my policy in your company?**
  Don't take your agent's word for any benefits. Get it in writing. And get it from a company officer whose word is a legal contract.

- **Do you conduct postclaim underwriting?**
  The underwriters, theoretically, approved your coverage when you bought your policy. It is illegal in many states for them to scrutinize your health history again when you make a claim. And if you're disabled, you won't be in good condition for that kind of legal battle.

- **Will I be covered by a group or an individual policy when I buy from an association like AARP?**
  The differences between group and individual policies can be very significant in terms of portability and coverage options. Saving a few dollars through a group plan may not be the best option for a healthy applicant.

- **If I am to be covered under a group policy, will the insurer provide me with a copy of the master policy? Will the certificate I may receive be derivative of that master policy?**
  Long-term care insurance policies are complicated and detailed. You need to see exactly what benefits you're buying and what conditions will trigger them.

- **What fees are being paid to those who manage the group plan?**
  Your group discount may not be as good a deal as it appears. If the insurer has enough of a margin to give up to 3 percent in fees to the group, you may be able to find another policy in the individual market that has better benefits for almost the same premium.

- **If I have bought from a group trust, what fees are being paid to sponsors or directors?**
  Did the sponsor or director shop in your best interest or their own? Was the bidding rigged to favor an insider?

- **Is my call to the group insurer being recorded? What information is going into the computer? Can I get a copy of the notes they've taken of our conversation?**
  Your agent has an obligation to keep your personal information private. But does the intake person on the telephone have the same obligation?

- **Do you allow the agent who wrote my policy to be involved in any claim that I might have?**
  Your agent wants to keep your business, and an experienced agent knows how to talk to the company bureaucrats. You trusted the agent enough to give him or her your business and may want him or her to advocate for you in the event of a claim.

- Under the terms of your binder, am I fully covered for the benefit plan I selected from the moment I signed the application and gave the agent a check?

  I've given you my money in good faith. What if your underwriting process is so poky that I have a stroke between now and when the policy is issued? The other company I considered told me they would evaluate my application in only two weeks, but I waited for you.

- Have any rating firms downgraded your financial ratings during the past year?

  Long-term care is a long-term bet. The consumer needs to know that the company will be around to pay the benefits at claim time. While ratings may be downgraded for a variety of nonfinancial reasons, the consumer has a right to be alerted to the change.

- How many different policy series has the company written since it began writing long-term care insurance?

  If your company introduces a new policy series, it may mean that the existing policy is not properly priced. Long-term care insurers are reluctant to raise premiums for fear of losing market share. Instead, they prefer to eat their losses on the old series, but roll out a new contract and justify higher premiums by adding enhancements and bells and whistles.

- What is the ratio of your actual claims versus anticipated claims?

  If the actual claim exceeds the anticipated claim, the insurer has several options: increase the premiums, tighten underwriting, resist questionable claims, and reduce service capabilities.

- What percentage of your in-force business contains a nonforfeiture benefit?

  A low percentage would indicate the cost is too expensive and the extra premium would be better spent to increase existing benefits.

- Will you pay for any expenses that are payable under my Medicare coverage?

  Some forms of indemnity coverage will pay the full daily benefit regardless of what Medicare pays for.

- How many claims have you had under your temporary insurance benefit?

  Temporary insurance receipts, sometimes called binders, can be unclear. You need to know just what is covered and what your limits are.

Questions and Answers for Consumers

About Benefits

Q: My policy was issued several years ago. I neglected to include **inflation coverage** and because of a change in my financial circumstances, I'm anxious to add that coverage now. Can I add it to my existing policy, or do I have to take out a new policy?

A: Anytime after a policy is issued, you can increase your benefits. However, insurers will require medical evidence just like they did when your policy was issued. In addition, if you do qualify, you will have to pay the premium at your now attained age rather than the premium rate that was in effect when the policy was issued and you were younger. As a general rule, you'll be best served by going back to your original company to increase the coverage rather than starting fresh somewhere else.

Q: What happens if there is a **dramatic change in my health** after I sign an insurance application but **before a policy** is issued?

A: Read the binder. Some companies say, "We stop the clock; we are on the hook for any changes in your insurability." However, the company might not issue the policy after determining just what's in your record. Therefore, the fine print in most binders will focus on that point. To avoid any problems, the insurer may simply say, "We will bind you for $10,000, no matter what happens, until we make a determination about accepting or rejecting you."

If you conceal this change in your health, your binder is unclear, and the policy is issued, you could have some uneasy moments during the first two years of your coverage—the contestability period.

Q: If a three-year **benefit period** policy is purchased and there have been no claims at the end of three years, what happens to my policy?

A: Buyers often ask this question. The benefit period means that the company will pay benefits for that amount of time or until the pool of money is drained. Your long-term care policy will be in force as long as you pay the renewal premiums when they come due. That can be three years, 30 years, or even longer.

Q: Should I choose an insurance company that will make available **discounts at a home health care agency** in the event I have to access benefits under a long-term care insurance policy?

A: If an insurer directly or indirectly controls which home health agency you use, you may be buying into a form of managed care. After all, the insurer wouldn't recommend the agency unless it was satisfied that the care provided was cost-efficient for the insurance company.

Q: Once I buy a policy, do I have the option of **increasing or decreasing the coverage**?

A: You can reduce your coverage and reduce your premium at any time, and without any penalty. However, if you decide to increase your coverage by increasing the daily benefit or period of years or by adding an inflation feature, you will have to go through the entire underwriting process just as you did when you originally bought the policy. In addition, your premiums will be based on your then attained age and could be subject to the policy series that might be available at that time.

Q: Will my policy cover me if I retire to a **foreign country** and require benefits there?

A: Currently there are a few companies that will cover you beyond the confines of the United States. If retiring to a foreign country is a real possibility, you should ask your agent to make available to you quotations from those companies that provide that benefit.

Q: What is the difference between **homemaker services** and **chore services**?

A: Different insurers tend to use different definitions for these types of services. As a general rule, homemaker services include meal preparation, doing laundry, shopping and household paperwork, and performing incidental chores.

Chore services at times involve heavy lifting, such as household repairs, taking out trash barrels, and the type of services usual to the maintenance of a residence that do not require services of a trained aide.

Q: What is the **ideal waiting period** to be selected in a long-term care insurance policy?

A: For those over 65, Medicare provides some coverage for up to 100 days. Therefore, it is prudent to buy a 100-day deductible. Some insurers provide a 90-day deductible. Those under 65 should consider a zero- or 30-day deductible, because they do not qualify for Medicare and the extra premium charge to reduce the deductible from 100 days to zero or 30 days is very small because of the applicant's age.

Q: When should a **lifetime benefit** be considered?

A: If a corporation seeking tax deduction pays the premium, a lifetime benefit may make sense. Otherwise buying a benefit period of five years and including inflation coverage should take the sting out of most conditions that could develop.

Q: Do I need to buy the same **daily benefit for home care and nursing home care**?

A: No. You can buy as low as 50 percent of your nursing home benefit for home care, but because of the small price differential, I would strongly urge you to consider a home care benefit equal to the nursing home daily benefit.

Q: Is **restoration of benefits** a good buy?

A: Some companies include this benefit as part of their basic policy form; others make it available for an additional premium; and some don't offer it at all. If you purchase this option and you use benefits from your policy, and then recover and don't need benefits for 180 days, your policy benefit limit will be reinstated to the full value prior to your initial disability. But if you have a condition serious enough to require benefits, do you think it is likely that you will go without any treatment, including a prescription medication, for six months?

About Underwriting

Q: A year ago I was declined for life insurance because of **elevated blood chemistries** that developed during my insurance physical examination. Does this mean I will be automatically disqualified for long-term care insurance?

A: That depends on what the elevated blood chemistries indicated. Was it a temporary situation or a life-threatening condition? If repeat blood tests are normal and whatever occurred was temporary in nature, you could find an underwriter willing to consider your application along with a complete medical workup.

Q: How much should my **therapist** tell the insurance company if the company communicates with him in connection with my application for long-term care insurance?

A: He has an obligation to answer questions presented to him by the insurance company. If he believes a clarification of any sensitive issue is in order, he may provide supplementary information in the form of a letter to the insurance company. Keep in mind that all documentation should be presented to the underwriter before a final decision is made. Once the underwriter has made up his or her mind, it can be hard to change.

Q: Is there any possibility of my obtaining long-term care insurance with the history of a **stroke** in my medical records?

A: Some insurance companies will not consider any stroke history at any time. However, there are some major insurers that will look at best-case strokes after periods of stability that can range from 3 to 10 years.

Q: Does a history of **cancer** automatically disqualify me from coverage?

A: No. Many cancers will be considered two years from the date of termination of treatment. This means that if you had a surgery and no radiation or chemotherapy, you start counting from the date of surgery. If further treatment was required, the two-year point starts from the date of your last treatment. Some companies have been known to accept cancers less than two years after treatment. When you meet with your agent to discuss long-term care insurance, bring a copy of your pathology report and ask the agent to check your coverage possibilities out in an informal basis with one of the underwriters.

Q: Does use of **steroids** automatically disqualify me from obtaining coverage?

A: Steroids can cause a problem, and certain underwriters will not consider applicants whose dosage is above a certain level. It is best to learn ahead of time what the underwriter's attitude will be toward your steroid use.

Q: What happens if **I forget** to tell the insurance company about a **past medical condition** before my policy is issued?

A: Insurers don't punish those who have a memory lapse about an ancient condition, now past. Underwriters are concerned with deliberate attempts to hide medical issues. For your peace of mind and to ensure the validity of your contract, advise your agent of any information that you may have omitted or not discussed during the application process.

Q: My doctor tells me that I'm 30 pounds **overweight**, yet I have never been on any medication, I work out with a trainer two days a week, and I am actively at work at age 68. My agent tells me that according to the height and weight chart of the long-term care insurance company he does business with, I am off the charts and uninsurable. I don't understand insurance company underwriting.

A: Tell your agent to go to another company, or fire your agent and get another one. The height and weight of GE Capital takes into consideration individuals with your medical profile. GE Capital has a maximum weight table it uses in combination with any present medical conditions. It also has a more liberal table for those who are overweight but have no medical conditions. You might be able to qualify for GE Capital's underwriting.

Q: Why do some companies offer coverage for individuals over the **age of 85** where the rates are so high and the average medical condition at that age are often poor? Don't these clients just generate a lot of applications and expense, but no coverage?

A: Companies that offer insurance to applicants over the age of 85 realize these applicants are not new cars right out of the showroom. Their underwriting criteria are based on what can be expected for those over 85. There are different criteria for blood pressure, cholesterol, and bone density. Elderly applicants also realize that they may need coverage, because they see what's happened to their friends. They want peace of mind at any price and are reconciled to the notion that they could have saved thousands of dollars in premiums had they bought policies when they were younger.

About Alternatives

Q: Under what conditions will **Medicare** pay for home health care?

A: There are several conditions, and all must be met. You must be confined to your home, and the care you require must be skilled nursing care, physical therapy, occupational therapy, or speech therapy. Your physician will have to determine your need for home health care and prescribe a home health plan or treatment, and that treatment must be provided by a certified home health agency participating in Medicare.

About Premiums

Q: What options do I have if my premium for long-term care insurance **increases**?

A: You have three. You can cancel the policy, pay the increase, or pay the same premium and receive reduced benefits. Keep in mind that the first increase may not be your only increase. There will probably be others.

Q: Should I **pay** my premium **yearly**?

A: Insurance companies would like you to pay a single annual premium the first year because that eliminates any ambivalence, buyer's remorse, or the chance that a competitor will knock at the door. However, premiums can be paid semiannually or quarterly. If you're conscientious, you might use monthly premiums, but the insurance companies have found these to be cumbersome, causing late premium notices. Most companies prefer the monthly check-o-matic arrangement that allows your bank to pay your insurance company without involving you in any of the paperwork.

Q: Why does my agent care about whether I pay my premium through an **automatic withdrawal system** at my bank?

A: Several companies give agents bonuses in commission if they convince the consumer to use an automatic withdrawal system. This system ensures continuity, it is painless to the insured, and it is a pattern that fosters good lapse ratios for the insurance companies. The risk is that the insured may change banks but forget to notify the insurance company.

Q: What is the **10-pay** system?

A: The 10-pay system is aimed at younger applicants, who choose to pay their lifetime premiums in 10 large premium checks. The advantage to the insured is that he or she pays the cost of the long-term care premiums while at one's highest salary level. But the insurance company is taking a statistical risk, trusting that their underwriters have made a good bet about this young person's long-term morbidity prospects. If the underwriters guess wrong too often, the company won't have the dollars to pay benefits years later.

Q: What are the advantages of **both spouses** buying a policy at the same time?

A: There can be premium savings of 10 to 20 percent, depending on the company. In the event one spouse buys now and does not receive the spousal credit, it will be available for both spouses whenever the second spouse applies for coverage.

Q: In the event of a claim, should I consider paying for my own **private care manager**?

A: If a claim is imminent, you will be well served by interviewing a few geriatric care managers and learning from them what they have to offer and how they can guide you through the maze of decisions that you could be forced to make when a member of the family requires long-term care.

Q: I pay extra for my life insurance because I am a **cigarette smoker**. Will I have to pay extra for any long-term care insurance I might purchase?

A: Many long-term care insurers provide preferred health discounts so long as you can answer a number of questions in the negative. One of the questions is whether you have had any tobacco use within a period of time, usually two to three years. You will not qualify for this preferred discount, which could be as much as 10 to 20 percent off the premium. Not getting the preferred discount is a way the insurer is telling you that you will pay more for your insurance because you smoke cigarettes.

About Shopping

Q: Does it make sense to hedge my bets and buy **two long-term care policies** that provide my total benefit?

A: No. The major insurance companies can provide you with one policy that has adequate limits to meet your needs. If you have two policies in force, when you have a claim you could be involved with two care coordinators and have more paperwork when submitting bills for payment.

Q: How credible is the long-term care information that is available on the **Internet**?

A: If a major long-term care insurer provides the information, you can rely on the fact that the information is credible. In addition, these companies will usually provide an 800 number and help you find an agent who can meet with you to clarify any questions you may have.

Unfortunately, just about anyone can obtain a web site to make available self-serving long-term care information calculated to generate leads from consumers who might ultimately become buyers.

Q: Should I rush into buying a policy because of an impending change due to my **forthcoming birthday**?

A: This argument is a long-time ploy of unscrupulous agents. Take all the time you need to make an informed, rational decision. Most companies will allow you to backdate a policy up to six months to save the increased premium your age may require. Some will allow you to backdate only 30 days. What this means is you will have a policy that will be effective prior to your approval, and your first renewal premium will reflect less than a year's coverage, so that you will continually be billed at your current age before your impending birthday.

Q: Once I decide to buy a policy, **what information should I have ready** when an agent comes to take my application?

A: You should have the names, addresses, and telephone numbers of all the doctors and specialists you've consulted within the past five years. You should have available the medications you take, the dosages, and the reasons the medications were prescribed. Also decide to whom you wish the insurance company to send a late premium notice in the event you are out of the country or incapacitated when a premium is due. This can be anyone you designate, including a relative, friend, or personal adviser.

Q: How can I **expedite the issuance** of my policy?

A: Alert your doctor's office to the fact that you've just applied for long-term care insurance and that the insurance company will either write for or send a representative to pick up your medical records. Ask if they would be kind enough to promptly respond to that request. If a cognitive impairment test is required, take it at your convenience but in a timely manner.

Q: Is it a good idea to buy long-term care insurance from a **bank**?

A: In recent years, a number of banks throughout the country have entered the financial services arena. They have done so either independently or in partnership with established financial services agencies. Banks in general are very vigilant in guarding their reputations for stability and security and can be counted on to give careful consideration to any partnership or marketing of long-term care products. In the future, there will be more and more cross marketing of financial services. If the bank can satisfy you that the individuals who respresent them in the sale of long-term care insurance have credible experience, you should have no problem making the purchase from the bank.

Q: Thanks to **Internet shopping**, I just purchased a 20-year guaranteed annual premium term life insurance policy and saved myself $400 a year over what my agent wanted to charge me. Should I shop for long-term care insurance the same way?

A: Long-term care insurance is a very different product. Not all insurers provide their rating schedules to Internet vendors. In addition, long-term care insurance is much more complex and at the least requires two visits from an experienced agent to discuss the product.

CHAPTER 14

Dos and Don'ts

- Ask questions and more questions. Take your time.

- Do not buy long-term care insurance out of fear. Investigate the entire situation and make a rational decision, not one based on sales hype or emotional blackmail.

- Don't buy a long-term care policy from a relative. Any adverse underwriting decision that results from your medical history could cause irreconcilable differences in long-standing family relationships.

- Investigate all your long-term care options, including Medicaid, self-funding, reverse mortgages, and help from your family. You may not need to buy long-term care insurance.

- Shop around. Long-term care insurance policies are not all the same.

- Examine all options in a policy including the daily benefit, duration of benefits, deductible, inflation coverage, home health care features, bells and whistles, and any escape hatches.

- Do not replace a policy purchased before December 31, 1996. Policies issued prior to that date are likely to contain benefits not available in current plans. If you do have a policy issued before that date and feel you need additional coverage, it is in your best interest to contact the agent who wrote that policy prior to December 31, 1996. If he or she is no longer in the business, try to find an agent in the same company. If that doesn't work, consider your other options.

- As difficult as the decision may be, make a decision whether to buy long-term care insurance; once you make that decision, stick with it.

- Understand all of the benefits available for long-term health care insurance under Medicare. Do not confuse the distinct differences between Medicare and long-term care insurance.

- Make sure that you realize that long-term care health insurance premiums are subject to increase. There are no yearly premium-paying policies available for sale that contain lifetime premium guarantees.

- If you decide to purchase coverage, have available a complete list of medications and the names and addresses of any physicians or facilities from whom you have received treatment.

- Don't drop a high-priced indemnity Medigap plan and replace it with an HMO senior plan just to use the premium savings to buy a long-term care policy. If you find that you must use that money to buy long-term care insurance, check with your doctor first. Ask how you will be affected if you change from your indemnity health care coverage to an HMO. In particular, ask whether your doctor's treatment decisions will be changed if you change to an HMO and whether your shift will have an impact on the doctor's income.

- Do not buy multiple long-term care insurance policies; one policy is enough. Multiple policies mean multiple paperwork.

- Consider having premiums automatically deducted from a bank account. If you become ill or forget to make payments, your coverage will not lapse.

- Consider the financial stability of the insurance company you choose. Evaluate several companies and agents, and purchase insurance from a highly rated quality insurer.

- In making your long-term care insurance decision, spend at least as much time exploring the options available as you did in the purchase of a TV, VCR, automobile, or your first home. All of those items cost you less than the dollar benefits that could be available under any long-term care insurance policy you might purchase.

- Don't pay any agent in cash. Write a check for any premium to the insurance company whose application you sign.

- Write down the name, address, and telephone number of the agent and the insurance company. You may be able to remember, but other people also need the information.

- If your policy doesn't arrive within 60 days, call the company and the agent.

- Don't go behind a parent's back, and without their informed consent, to try to determine their eligibility for coverage through discussions with an agent. Parents are very perceptive and can still teach their children a lesson or two.

- Don't use the premium a friend or relative pays for long-term care insurance as your standard for comparing the policies you are considering. Your premium will be based on your age and health, and on the amount and duration of the benefits you choose.

- Tell someone where the policy is and what the basic benefits are. If you suddenly need to go on claim, this person may have to call the insurance company for you.

- Take advantage of the free look period. You can cancel most policies within a set period of time, usually 30 days. If you decide against keeping the policy, send it back with a letter asking for a refund. Use certified mail and keep a copy of your letter.

- Don't be impressed or misled by slick newspaper, radio, and TV advertising starring celebrity endorsers. These endorsers are paid; as a general rule they are not insurance experts and are only interested in their self-interest.

- Be leery of any cards or envelopes concerning long-term care insurance you receive in the mail that are designed to seem to come directly from the federal government. They could be coming from a mail house that specializes in seeking out the long-term care insurance prospects that insurance companies are looking for.

- Avoid giving personal information about any of your insurance policies, including Medicare, to a stranger on the telephone. The individuals calling you may be accumulating a database that they will then sell to long-term care insurance marketers.

- Don't take the word of an insurance agent about tax consequences of your long-term care insurance policy. Talk to a tax expert.

- Don't apply to two different companies with two different agents at the same time. Your doctor won't like doing duplicate reports. If you desire to shop around, it is in your best interest to select a trustworthy agent or broker to do the shopping for you.

- Don't accept a current practice used in setting claims as assurance that any future claim you might have will be handled in the same manner. Unless your policy spells out the specific practice, your insurer may change the practice at any time.

- Don't alter your lifestyle to pay the premium for a policy.

- If possible, have a relative or friend sit in on any sales interview for long-term care insurance. A second ear always helps.

CHAPTER 15

Two Letters

A Letter to My Fellow Seniors

You have been on my mind since I began writing this book. You're still there as I finish it.

These questions are tough ones. But there is no way around them. As you've read this book, you've probably considered most of these issues.

Think now, plan now, and talk to your family now, while you are not under pressure, so that you will enjoy a dignified and independent old age.

- Will I qualify for Medicaid coverage?
- Do I understand what Medicare covers?
- Do I have the assets to pay for any long-term care I might need?
- Will my retirement savings be enough to pay for my spouse's needs and my own long-term care expenses?
- Where will I be willing to live in my very old age?
- Am I likely to pass the medical and cognitive underwriting screenings for long-term care insurance?
- How much can I afford to spend for premiums?
- How much will I feel comfortable spending for premiums?
- What realistic assumptions can I make about my long-term health? Does

my family history or a current medical condition suggest I might need care later in life?

- Am I willing to accept the possibility of catastrophic long-term expenses if my spouse or I am diagnosed with a degenerative disease such as Alzheimer's or Parkinson's?
- Am I willing to accept long-term care from my children?
- Am I willing to spend my children's inheritance on my own long-term care?
- Am I willing to sell my assets, such as a treasured family retreat or an antique, to pay for my long-term care needs?
- Where do I most want to spend my health care dollars, for my indemnity Medigap policy or for long-term care insurance?
- Am I able to talk rationally about an insurance policy that benefits me only if I am sick or disabled?
- Will long-term care insurance make sense for me if I can't afford to purchase inflation protection?
- Can I afford to keep paying for my long-term care insurance policy if the premiums go up?
- What professionals do I feel comfortable listening to? My financial adviser? My lawyer? My banker? My stockbroker? My life insurance agent? My casualty insurance agent?
- Will I be able to take action even if some or most of these advisers disagree on what I should do in terms of long-term care coverage?
- How much do I value the amenities in my life, including the helper who has been coming to my house for 30 years to help me maintain it?
- Is the price of long-term care insurance worth the peace of mind it might provide?
- If I am not used to managing my own affairs because my spouse always did so, do I have the confidence to figure out long-term care insurance options?
- Will I be welcome and able to move into my children's home if I feel the need for security or assistance?
- Should I discuss the buying of a long-term care policy with my children?
- Should I get advice about long-term care options from my friends or go it alone?

A Letter to the Children of My Fellow Seniors

I hope you realize by now that this book wasn't written just for seniors and that you recognize that when a parent needs long-term care, the entire family is affected. Even the best of relationships, between parent and child, spouse and spouse, sibling and sibling, is changed—not always for the better.

I've suggested that your parents think hard about what they want for themselves and what they expect from you. Now I invite you to do the same.

It takes honest introspection and truthful dialogue to arrive at a long-term care solution that pleases everyone. If you think first about what is involved, you'll be better prepared to help your parents. They will thank you for it.

In addition, you, yourself, will be better equipped to make your own long-term care choices sooner rather than later.

Join your parents: Start the thinking and the talking now:

- Will I be comfortable seeing my parents supported in a Medicaid facility in their frail final years?

- Will I be willing to help my parents think about and then decide on a long-term care insurance policy?

- Will I be willing (and able) to sit in when the agent pitches a long-term care policy to my parents?

- Will I be willing (and able) to pay for the long-term care insurance premium if my parents need that help?

- Will I be willing (and able) to pay out of my pocket for my parents' care?

- Will I be willing (and able) to interrupt my job to be a caregiver to my parents?

- Should I talk to my siblings before approaching my parents about the subject of their long-term care?

- If one of my parents is unisurable, will I offend the other by bringing up the subject of long-term care insurance?

- Will I be willing to forgo my inheritance so that my parents can remain in their own home?

- If my parent is in a second marriage, what is my obligation to that spouse?

- Will the second spouse assume responsibility for my parent's care?

- Will my parent assume responsibility for his or her second spouse's care?

- Can my own family manage if I shift our savings to the care of my parents?

- Will my spouse be willing to sacrifice time and resources for my parents? Will I be willing to sacrifice time and resources for my spouse's parents?

- Should I encourage both my parents to consider long-term care insurance?

CHAPTER 16

Epilogue

This is a very important book because patients and their families are clearly confused by what is available and are clearly frightened by the prospects of dependency.

—John Goodson, M.D.; physician, Massachusetts General Hospital; associate professor of medicine, Harvard Medical School

For everything there is a season, but the season for needing long-term care can happen at any time in our lives. Nonetheless, our concern for the most priceless assets we have, our independence and dignity, lasts far beyond the slow turnings of time.

My mother, an adult during the Great Depression, had no ambivalence about what she expected in her very old age. She told me, loud and clear, when she was 93 years old and beginning to falter after a series of falls and episodes of forgetfulness.

She expected to remain in her own home until she died and did not see why she should have to pay someone to live with her.

And why not? She knew the value of a dollar. In my mother's day, a Hershey bar cost a nickel, the daily paper was two cents, and a gallon of gasoline was 14 cents. My mother's independence, however, was beyond price. If she could have managed it, she would have lived alone until she died. She preferred to risk her well-being rather than compromise her dignity. And I had too few options for helping her achieve that goal.

Now, our new millennium brings an array of choices and opportunities, as well as a more complex set of obligations.

The gen-X adult says to her mother, "Mom, I love and honor you, but I live thousands of miles away. If I could, I would quit my profession to drive you to your doctor's office, to lay out your medications and be sure your refrigerator is well stocked. My husband would postpone his retirement for you, and my children would willingly fund their education through loans. But, Mom, we need to talk about other alternatives, Medicaid funding, partnership programs, long-term care insurance, and reverse mortgages."

And what does Mom say to her child? "I will not burden you with the responsibility of caring for me when I am older and more frail. My dignity means too much to me. Instead, I am planning now so that our time together will be joyful, not burdensome. I assert my independence now to protect our loving, long-term future as a family."

Independence and dignity. We've come full circle.

In the end, we are all responsible for the long-term well-being of our frail population, those in their very old age and those not yet there. Whether this population is physically disabled or cognitively impaired, we owe them the chance to live out their lives in whatever setting they prefer. We owe them careful attention, comfort, and a sense of self-worth.

We need to stand behind the disabled patient and the frightened, often bewildered family. The lawmakers seeking our votes, the insurance company seeking our money, and the medical professionals who deliver our care must each play a part.

Let me tell you what those parts might be.

First, the Doctors

We must support the reinvigoration of primary care values through such groundbreaking initiatives as the John D. Stoeckle Center for Primary Care Medicine at Massachusetts General Hospital. That's why I am donating all proceeds from this book to the Marjorie E. Lipson Fund at the Center.

As I explained in the Preface, the focus of the Stoeckle Center, according to its director, Dr. John D. Goodson, is "on the decision-making process" of physicians "with the clear and explicit mission of guaranteeing that each and every decision is in the individual patient's best interest." This is what we used to call traditional doctoring.

Why emphasize the role of the primary care physician?

Often this physician is the only practitioner to really know the level of medical care that the patient needs. He or she understands the language of Medicare and knows about long-term care benefit triggers. The primary care practitioners know their job. We must give them time and money to do that job well. If we do, patient, family, and society will be winners.

Patients want a connection with their doctors, but they can't make one. Thanks to managed care, capitation, and the financial and occupational need to change medical plans, it is difficult for a patient to establish an ongoing, caring relationship with the same physician. Meredith Beit Patterson, an elder care consultant, says, "There are some physicians who put themselves out as particularly interested in elders."[1] But we do not have enough geriatricians and we have many more elders! What happened to the good old family doctor?

There aren't many left, and barely a few like Dr. Stoeckle from Mass General. Instead, burdened by growing overhead, health care bureaucracy, and HMO gatekeeping, physicians feel forced into huge, multispecialty practices. Their allocated 15-minute office visits often take less time even though, as Patterson says, "It can take some people the 15 minutes to get undressed for the examination."

During the medical exam, there is scant laying on of hands. Technology has replaced conversation as a diagnostic strategy. If the patient's primary care doctor isn't in the office, it's no big deal; one of 20 partners will take over.

I'm not naively yearning for the good old days. I know that the growth in technology has dramatically altered the practice of medicine. How many of us would want to return to the time when many cancers were untreatable, when structural defects could not be repaired surgically, or when diagnosis depended on chest thumps and blood pressure alone?

These advances have also complicated decision making and caused medical care to be much more expensive. CAT scans, MRIs, and blood workups are sophisticated and valuable. Patients demand them. Prescription medications have fewer side effects yet cost so much that some uninsured seniors must choose between buying food and paying for their pills.

Those patients fortunate enough to have insurance often find their best interests and their doctor's treatment plans in conflict with the decision-making process of a bloated insurance company bureaucracy driven by the profit motive.

Health care has not always functioned this way. Many people over 50 remember when their pediatrician or family practitioner stopped by the house if they were sick, took their temperature, listened to their hearts, and reassured their families; all this, and often without a charge. If you are sick today, the doctor sends you to the emergency room. Your adult child needs to leave work for hours to keep you company in the ER waiting room, as you await treatment for a condition easily manageable at home—and easily avoided with the proper medical care.

Today we must locate the practice of medicine between the old-time general practitioner and the overburdened HMO primary care doctor.

Dr. Stoeckle's concern for his patients was so powerful an example that Massachusetts General Hospital wanted it to continue beyond his retirement. The Center is meant to be "a beacon, proclaiming the importance of doctoring skills."

More health care institutions should follow this example and remind every doctor that the best way to "care for the patient is by caring for the patient." This is the way Dr. Stoeckle practiced his craft.

Next, Prospective Patients and Caregivers

That includes all of us—perhaps caregivers now, maybe patients later, determined to preserve the independence and dignity of our old age.

What should we do? First of all, just what you have done by reading this book. Gather your information. Think rationally and logically about your long-term care choices. My colleague at the *Boston Globe*, syndicated personal finance columnist Charles A. Jaffee, reminds us that long-term care planning must be "financial and not emotional." We must approach the buying of long-term care insurance as carefully and rationally as we would any purchase, saying, "Here's what I have, here's what I am trying to protect, and here's why."[2]

We must trust our individual judgments. Jaffee stresses the importance of "peace of mind" in any financial decision. If buying long-term care insurance will give you peace of mind, buy it. If you must change your standard of living to pay for it, think twice. But once you've made up your mind, live with the decision, knowing you've arrived there after sufficient information gathering.

Finally, we must informally support our informal caregivers, those uncounted people who are the backbone of long-term care in this country. These are the spouses, children, and grandchildren of our frail population who labor with the barest nod of recognition. Charities, churches, and community organizations need to rally to keep the caregivers going before they also need long-term care. We have Welcome Wagons to greet new neighbors, we encourage child care cooperatives—let's do more of the same for the informal caregiver who feels just as isolated and unsupported as a new resident or a new mother.

Current caregivers must take care of themselves, too. They need to accept help from the community and the family and not martyr themselves in the task of caring for their loved ones.

The Lawmakers

Legislators and members of congress proclaim that caring for our frailest citizens is a shared social responsibility. Informal caregivers simply can't do it all by themselves. No matter how dedicated and how loving, the caregiving child or spouse must have help, or else the caregivers will themselves require costly long-term care.

While I would not advocate increasing the federal deficit or encouraging dependence, it is clear that the government must step in now.

Make long-term care premiums deductible for all consumers the way they are for many types of businesses. The short-term cost of above-the-line deductibility for all premiums paid by all consumers will be more than repaid by the relief for the Medicaid program.

Medicare must be expanded to cover prescription drugs. This fact is incontrovertible; the need is desperate. Without prescription medications, seniors will become sicker, their risk of disability larger, and society's long-term care costs greater.

Medicare must also be expanded to help people who discover, unexpectedly and out of the norm, that they are suffering from a degenerative disease that makes them uninsurable. Although these patients may now be functioning well despite their Parkinson's or multiple sclerosis, they face the potential need for long-term care and cannot buy insurance to cover it. The young Alzheimer's patient confronts the same dilemma. Federal entitlement programs need to acknowledge this real and growing need by making some sort of long-term care coverage available for all patients, despite their condition, and without forcing them to impoverish their families to manage their care.

The federal government must push forward with the Patient's Bill of Rights. Much of the current discussion, as of this writing, focuses on after-the-fact litigation. Encouraged by lobbyists, lawmakers seem mostly interested in figuring out ways a patient can redress grievances, not how to prevent them.

Granted, the citizen needs to be able to advocate successfully against the giant health care insurers. The patient must have a strong voice to be heard over the polished, crafted speech of the managed care organizations, which have too often been able to keep us from the medical and psychological interventions we pay for in premiums and which we are owed.

But let's move the discussion of patients' rights to where it really belongs: before the point where the patient ever needs to sue. The Patient's Bill of Rights must focus on making access to quality health care and adequate treatment easier for every patient. Once the treatment has been denied, litigation won't solve many problems.

State and federal governments, lastly, must educate the public about their long-term care possibilities and options. We trust government agencies to give us an unbiased, unemotional, unterrifying view of what we can expect.

Finally, the Insurance Industry

The insurance industry has done the frail elderly in this country a valuable service. It has educated us by telling us about the risks that we face in our old age. It has developed products to cover these risks.

But the insurance industry can do much, much more:

It should tell us about the risks that cause long-term care, but not frighten us with them. For starters, the companies must admit that half of all adults over 65 will not be in long-term care. And that more than 50 percent of these nursing home stays are for less than one year.[3]

They should talk to us in clear language, without jargon-loaded abstractions. We need to know exactly what we are buying. If we can use modern technology, we can understand how an insurance benefit works, what will trigger it, and what we are getting for our dollar. Make it easier for us, and we'll be less likely to blink, pause, and say no.

Insurance companies must use their multibillion-dollar resources to support public/private initiatives for long-term care coverage. If there is a short-term cost to letting the federal government dictate and interact with the company, there will be a vast long-term gain in public confidence and public purchases of long-term care insurance.

The industry is appropriately developing new long-term care insurance models. They need to make these improved policies worth the increased cost. Insurers must train their agents so that they can explain the variations in indemnity coverage, the nature of joint policy and different waiting periods, the way that enhanced home care benefits work, the purpose of broader waiver of premium features, the variations of survivorship coverage.

We also know what we want the insurance industry to do:

Establish the necessary reserves to pay for our long-term care benefits when we need them. Don't simply raise premiums.

Keep managed care out of the long-term care arena. Whether in employer-sponsored plans or individually purchased ones, don't force us to select from a certified list of providers that doesn't include those we really want in our homes.

Although the disabilities of aging, including Parkinson's and Alzheimer's, may become more common, don't limit our benefits. We need the payments even more in these cases, because life may last beyond the ability to enjoy it.

Don't make underwriting even more restrictive. We can't afford surcharges for specific illnesses or more additions to the automatic decline list.

Don't eliminate competition by increasing the number of mergers and acquisitions. Without competition, the consumer pays more and probably gets less.

A Last Word and Five Wishes

Now you have the tools to make your own long-term care plans. It's your turn now. Get out your pencils and figure out your lifestyle alternatives. Be thoughtful and take your time.

Meanwhile, I leave you with these five wishes:

1. May you never need long-term care.
2. If you do, may you have the prudent plans in place to protect your independence and maintain your dignity in your very old age.

3. May lawmakers remember that their job is to strengthen Medicare and Medicaid to help our frailest citizens who might otherwise be ineligible for long-term care coverage.

4. May the insurance industry remember that we are paying the bill and demand clear talk.

5. May the medical professionals remember the old days of primary care and connect with their patients the way those earlier doctors did.

Our founding fathers taught us that if we have the will to wish for noble accomplishments, we have the power to make them happen.

We have been provided a legacy that we must perpetuate during our lifetimes for the sake of those who follow us. To do anything less is unacceptable and a breach of trust to those who came before us.

Endnotes

1. Meredith Beit Patterson, letter, July 16, 2001.
2. Interview with Charles A. Jaffee, June 14, 2001.
3. A Massachusetts Guide. Massachusetts Division of Insurance. *Your Options for Financing Long-Term Care:* December 1999. p. 2.

Do I Need Long-Term Care Insurance?: Steps in the Process of Making a Decision

I.   **Do I foresee an eventual need for long-term care?**
   A. **What is my personal health appraisal?** (*See Chapter 1.*)
      What is my health right now?
      Am I currently getting adequate health care?
      What is my personal health history?
      What is my family's health history?
      What is my best guess about my long-term medical prospects?
   B. **If I do need long-term care, how long might it last?** (*See Chapters 5 and 7.*)
      Do I have any chronic conditions that might cause long-term disability?
      Do the people in my family live to very old ages?

II. **What is the best way for me to fund the long-term care I might need?**
   A. **Will I qualify for Medicaid or other public assistance programs?** (*See Chapter 2.*)
      Will I have to spend down my assets to receive Medicaid?
      Are there other programs such as veterans' benefits that will help me?
   B. **Do I have the assets to cover long-term care costs in my old age?** (*See Chapter 2.*)
      Do I have enough savings/pensions/other income?
      Can I tap into my real estate equity?

Can I use my life insurance?

Can I buy a partnership policy?

C. **What help can I reasonably expect from family or other people?** (*See Chapters 2 and 11.*)

Will my children have the willingness and means to help?

Are there other people who might help me?

D. **Will this help be financial, informal caregiving, or through living arrangements?** (*See Chapters 2 and 11.*)

Will my family pay the cost of my long-term care?

Will my family or anyone else help take care of me?

Will my family or anyone else provide housing for me?

III. **If I need long-term care, what location and what setting do I prefer?** (*See Chapters 1 and 3.*)

At home.

Continuing care retirement community.

Assisted living.

Nursing home.

IV. **If I need to be in one of these settings right now, in the area I prefer, what would it cost?** (*See Chapter 3.*)

At home, with alterations.

Continuing care retirement community.

Assisted living community.

Local nursing home.

Local certified home care provider.

Local uncertified home care provider.

V. **If I choose to buy long-term care insurance, what should I consider?**

A. **Will I qualify medically for long-term care insurance?** (*See Chapters 5, 6, and 7.*)

Do I have any preexisting physical conditions that might disqualify me?

Do I have any cognitive impairment?

B. **Can I afford the premium without changing my lifestyle?** (*See Chapter 2.*)

C. **What professionals should I speak to about long-term care insurance?** (*See Chapters 8 and 9.*)

Agent.

Broker.

Banker.

Stockbroker.

Other financial advisers, including lawyer, financial planner, or C.P.A.

Affinity group.

Employer-sponsored plan.
Internet sales.
D. **What benefits do I want?** (*See Chapter 3.*)
Reimbursement or indemnity model.
Daily benefit amount.
Length of benefit period.
Inflation protection.
Settings.
Elimination period.
Certified or uncertified caregivers.
Other benefits.
E. **What disabilities should trigger the benefit payments?** (*See Chapters 2 and 3.*)
F. **Do I want a tax-qualified plan?** (*See Chapter 4.*)

VI. **What should I look for in an insurance company?** (*See Chapter 10.*)
Should I trust the rating firms?
How important is service?
How important is the insurer's experience?
Might I find a better price/benefit ratio with another company?

Use this worksheet to record information when investigating which agencies and facilities provide long-term care services in your area (or in the area where you would be most likely to receive care) and what the costs are for these services.

Home Health Agency

Name of *one* Home Health Agency
you might use _____

Name of *another* Home Health Agency
you might use _____

_____

_____

Address _____

Address _____

_____

_____

_____

_____

Phone number _____

Phone number _____

Contact Person _____

Contact Person _____

Check which types of care are available and list the cost

❑ Skilled Nursing Care
  Cost/Visit $_____

❑ Skilled Nursing Care
  Cost/Visit $_____

❑ Home Health Care
  Cost/Visit $_____

❑ Home Health Care
  Cost/Visit $_____

❑ Personal/Custodial Care
  Cost/Visit $_____

❑ Personal/Custodial Care
  Cost/Visit $_____

❑ Home Care Services
  Cost/Visit $_____

❑ Home Care Services
  Cost/Visit $_____

FIGURE A.1 Availability and Cost of Long-Term Care
Source: Massachusetts Division of Insurance.

Nursing Facility

Name of *one* Nursing Facility

_____

_____

Address _____

_____

_____

Phone number _____

Contact Person _____

Name of *another* Nursing Facility

_____

_____

Address _____

_____

_____

Phone number _____

Contact Person _____

Check which types of care are available and list the cost

❑ Skilled Nursing Care
   Cost/Month $_____

❑ Personal/Custodial Care
   Cost/Month $_____

❑ Skilled Nursing Care
   Cost/Month $_____

❑ Personal/Custodial Care
   Cost/Month $_____

Other Facility

Other Facility or Service you might use
(e.g. adult day care center, assisted living, etc.)

Address _____

_____

_____

Phone number _____

Contact Person _____

What services are available? _____

_____

_____

What are the costs for these services?

_____

Other Facility or Service you might use
(e.g. adult day care center, assisted living, etc.)

Address _____

_____

_____

Phone number _____

Contact Person _____

What services are available? _____

_____

_____

What are the costs for these services?

_____

FIGURE A.1 *Continued*

I. FEDERAL TAX/STATE MASSHEALTH (MEDICAID) EXEMPTIONS

This Individual/Group Policy is Intended to:	Yes/No[3]
1. Qualify for **Federal Income Tax** Deductions/Exemptions under Federal Law*	
2. Qualify for **MassHealth (Medicaid)** Exemptions under Massachusetts Law*	

*These laws are subject to change at any time. These exemptions might not apply to this policy at a future date. Read *Your Options for Financing Long-Term Care: A Massachusetts Guide* for more information.

II. THIS POLICY COVERS THE FOLLOWING LONG-TERM CARE SERVICES

Type of Service	Daily Benefit[1]	Max Benefit ($/Days)[1]	Type of Service	Daily Benefit[1]	Max Benefit ($/Days)[1]
1. Nursing Home			5. Home Care		
2. Assisted Living			6. Adult Day Care		
3. Home Health Care			7. Respite Care		
4. Personal Care			8. Other		

III. BENEFIT LIMITS[2]

$_____ per day/month/year for _____ days/months/years **OR** $_____ per lifetime

IV. BENEFITS BEGIN AFTER:

____ Days **OR** $ _____ Deductible

V. EXCLUSIONS AND LIMITATIONS

Type	Yes/No[3]
PREEXISTING CONDITIONS	
OTHER:	

VI. TO BE ELIGIBILE FOR BENEFITS

You must need supervision due to a cognitive impairment OR
You must need **hands-on help/standby help** with ___ of the following Activities of Daily Living: eating, transferring, bathing, dressing, toileting, continence due to a loss of physical capacity or severe cognitive impairment.

VII. OTHER BENEFITS

Yes/No	Type	Terms	Premium
	Inflation Protection		$
	Nonforfeiture Benefit		$
	Other		$

VIII. ANNUAL PREMIUM

Terms and Conditions	Total
	$

IMPORTANT: This is a brief summary of proposed coverage. It is not a policy. If you choose to purchase a policy, please read and review your policy carefully to verify that the coverage you have purchased is the coverage you intended to purchase.

FIGURE A.2 Long-Term Care Insurance Policy Illustration Form
Source: Massachusetts Division of Insurance.

ADDITIONAL INFORMATION

[1] These benefit amounts usually are not cumulative. For example, if your policy provides a total of 730 days of coverage and you use 100 days to pay for home health care services, you will have 630 days of coverage left to apply to other services such as nursing home care.

Further information about the benefits covered by this policy:

[To be completed by carrier.]

[2] Long-term care insurance usually does not cover the full cost of long-term care services. According to the most recent *Your Options for Financing Long-Term Care: A Massachusetts Guide*, the **average cost** of private nursing home care in Massachusetts was $191 per day and the **average stay in a nursing home** lasted 511 days. The average cost of home health care services in Massachusetts was $45 per day.

Inflation is likely to have increased these average costs by the time you need long-term care services. Inflation protection coverage will help protect the value of your benefits:

[To be completed by carrier.] INFLATION PROTECTION ILLUSTRATION demonstrating graphically how inflation and inflation protection option could affect policy benefits over 20-year period. If necessary, a separate page may be attached to the Policy Illustration Form that includes an illustration of the policy's inflation protection.

[3] Further information about the **exclusions or limitations** contained in this policy:

[To be completed by carrier.]

[4] **Level premiums** are designed to stay the same for the life of the policy, although they can be changed for an entire class of policyholders. **Guaranteed premiums** never can be increased. Some premiums are subject to **discounts** (for example, spousal discounts or a first-year-only discount).

Prepared For: [Name]   **Date:**
Agent: [Name, Address, Phone]

FIGURE A.2 *Continued*

The purpose of this worksheet is to help you evaluate one or more life insurance policies with accelerated benefit riders that may be used to pay for the cost of long-term care services. Fill out the form so you can compare your options. In addition you should complete Appendix D regarding the long-term care benefits provided by the policy.

Insurance Company Information	Policy 1	Policy 2
1. Name of the insurance company		
Agent's name		
2. Is the company licensed in your state?	Yes / no	Yes / no
3. Insurance rating service and rating (Refer to page 28)		

Policy Information

	Policy 1	Policy 2
4. What kind of life insurance policy is it:		
Whole life insurance?	Yes / no	Yes / no
Universal life insurance?	Yes / no	Yes / no
Term life insurance?	Yes / no	Yes / no
5. What is the policy's premium?	$	$
6. How often is the premium paid:		
One time / single premium?	Yes / no	Yes / no
Annually for life?	Yes / no	Yes / no
Annually for 10 years only?	Yes / no	Yes / no
Annually for 20 years only?	Yes / no	Yes / no
Other?		
7. Is there a separate premium for the accelerated benefit in the life policy?	Yes / no	Yes / no
If not, how is the premium paid:		
• Included in life insurance premium?	Yes / no	Yes / no
• Deducted from the cash value of the life insurance policy?	Yes / no	Yes / no
8. How many people will the policy cover?		
9. Will the payment of long-term care benefits decrease the death benefit and cash value of the policy?	Yes / no	Yes / no
Will an outstanding loan affect the long-term care benefits?	Yes / no	Yes / no
Did you receive an illustration of guaranteed values?	Yes / no	Yes / no
If yes, do the policy values equal zero at some age on a guaranteed midpoint basis?	Yes / no	Yes / no
If so, at what age?		

FIGURE A.3 Accelerated Benefit Riders to Life Insurance Policies
Source: Massachusetts Division of Insurance.

For use after you buy a long-term care policy. Complete this form and put it with your important papers. You may want to make a copy for a friend or a relative.

1. **Insurance Policy Date**

   Policy Number _____

   Date Purchased _____

   Annual Premium _____

2. **Insurance Company Information**

   Name of Company _____

   Address _____

   Phone Number _____

3. **Agent Information**

   Agent's Name _____

   Phone Number _____

   Address _____

4. **Type of Long-Term Care Policy**

_____	Tax-qualified	_____	MassHealth (Medicaid)
_____	Nursing home only	_____	Home health care only
_____	Comprehensive (nursing home, assisted living, home and community care)		

5. **How long is the waiting period before benefits begin?** _____

6. **How do I file a claim?** (Check all that apply)

_____	I need prior approval	_____	Contact the company
_____	Fill out a claim form	_____	Submit a plan of care
_____	Doctor notifies the company	_____	Assessment by company
_____	Assessment by care manager		

7. **How often do I pay premiums?** _____ Annually _____ Semi-annually _____ Other

8. **The person to be notified if I forget to pay the premium:** _____

   Address _____ Phone number _____

9. **Are my premiums deducted from my bank account?** _____ Yes _____ No

   Name and address of my bank: _____

   Bank account number: _____

10. **Where do I keep this long-term care policy?** _____

    Other information _____

11. **Friend or relative who knows where my policy is:** _____

    Address _____

    Phone number _____

FIGURE A.4 Facts about Your Long-Term Care Insurance Policy

Uninsurable Conditions

AIDS

Alzheimer's disease

Amyotrophic lateral sclerosis (ALS)

Cirrhosis of the liver

Dementia

Demyelinating disease

Esophageal varices

Hemochromatosis (bronze diabetes)

HIV

Huntington's chorea

Mental retardation

Multiple myeloma

Multiple sclerosis

Muscular dystrophy

Nephrosclerosis

Neurogenic bladder

Organic brain syndrome, dementia

Paraplegia

Parkinson's disease

Polycystic kidney disease

Polymyositis

Postpolio syndrome

Schizophrenia

Temporal arteritis

Medications Commonly Associated with Uninsurable Conditions

UnumProvident provides all brokers of its individual long-term care insurance policies with the following list of medications commonly associated with uninsurable conditions. The broker uses the list to recognize those applicants who are likely to be uninsurable so that these clients do not waste time or effort filling out an application or undergoing medical underwriting.

However, while every long-term care insurer has such a list, the use of the medications may be handled differently. Some insurers will consider an applicant if he or she has stopped taking the medication for at least three months because the medical condition is fully resolved. Some insurers note that a medication may be taken for a medical condition other than that listed, as, for example, methotrexate, which is prescribed for both cancer and rheumatoid arthritis. In these cases, insurers will accept applications.

When you look through this list, then, remember that there may be circumstances in which your use of a listed medication will not automatically disqualify you from coverage. Talk to your insurance representative about your individual circumstances.

Acyclovir (AIDS)

Adriamycin (cancer)

Alkeran (cancer)

Antabuse (alcoholism)

AZT (AIDS)

Baclofen (multiple sclerosis)

Betaseron (multiple sclerosis)

Butazolidin (severe arthritis)

Cogentin (Parkinson's, antipsychotic, mental disorders)

Cognex (Tracine) (dementia)

Compazine (Parkinson's, cancer, AIDS)

Cytoxan (cancer, severe arthritis)

Deltasone (steroid)

Depo-Medrol (steroid)

Depo-Provera (cancer)

DDI or DDL (AIDS)

DES (cancer)

Ditropan (neurogenic bladder)

Ergoloid (dementia)

Gold (rheumatoid/severe arthritis)

Hydrea (cancer)

Hydregine (dementia)

Imuran (arthritic/inflammatory conditions)

Interferon (hepatitis)

L-dopa (Parkinson's)

Laradopa (Parkinson's)

Leukeran (cancer)

Levodopa (Parkinson's)

Lupron (cancer)

Medrol (severe arthritis)

Medroxyprogesterone (cancer)

Methotrexate (cancers, severe arthritis)

Myleran (cancer)

Navane (psychotic disorders)

Parlodel (Parkinson's)

Plaquenil (severe arthritis)

Prednisone (steroid)*

---

*Steroids (taken on an ongoing basis for any condition other than steroid inhalers for asthma) are considered uninsurable.

Sinemet (Parkinson's)

Solganal (severe arthritis)

Symmetrel (Parkinson's)

Testolactone (cancer)

Welleferon (HIV)

Zifovudine (AIDS)

Zovirax (AIDS, viral infection)

Physical Impairments and Medical Risk Selection Guide

Underwriting policy is an area of significant competition in the long-term care insurance business. See Chapter 6 "Underwriting for Physical Impairments: Changing the Odds in Underwriting Roulette," if you doubt that.

Here are UnumProvident's responses to a series of questions I asked several major insurance companies about their underwriting policies.

Competitors who look at UnumProvident's responses may argue that they are self-serving. These other companies will go to great lengths trying to prove that in selected situations their underwriting policies may be more liberal. In some cases, these companies are correct. Nevertheless, UnumProvident makes its underwriting guide available to brokers, and similar guides are available from other insurers. Any underwriting policy is subject to change.

Here are the questions I asked the major insurers and UnumProvident's answers:

What are the advantages and disadvantages of your underwriting policy?

We consider our underwriting criteria and risk assessment to be fair and consistent. Our philosophy is to seek opportunities to expand the market while protecting the integrity of the business. We have the advantage of being in this market for over 10 years and the ability to leverage Unum's past experience with disability insurance in creating and refining our underwriting risk rules. To date, we have not had an in-force policy rate increase and part of that can be attributed to prudent risk selection at the time of underwriting.

A disadvantage may be the perceived view by some producers that we are conservative underwriters. While criteria vary from carrier to carrier, this perceived disadvantage could actually be considered as an advantage when it comes to maintaining the integrity of our block.

How are rated cases treated?

Certain medical conditions by themselves, or in combination with other conditions, will sometimes warrant an additional premium rating. In these situations we have two ratings: a Class II (25% load) and a Class III (50% load). There are certain maximum plan limitations on cases that receive a Class II or Class III rating:

- Six-year benefit duration with inflation.
- If an applicant applies for lifetime without inflation, we will consider it.
- No Total Home Care benefit greater than 50% on Advantage I, or 60% on Advantage Plus.
- No monthly benefit greater than $4,000.

How often is the company underwriting policy reevaluated?

We have a Macro Risk and Medical Department that is charged with reviewing our underwriting criteria on a regular basis. They will review our claims experience, the latest medical information, and competitors' guidelines in order to evaluate our underwriting criteria and make changes as necessary.

What are your major underwriting concerns?

1. *Cognitive Impairment (Dementias, Alzheimer's, Short-Term Memory Loss).* These claims can be long in duration, especially in the absence of any real physical problems. Any mention of memory complaints in a doctor's records will usually render the applicant uninsurable.

2. *Strokes/Transient Ischemic Attacks (TIAs).* Strokes can vary in severity from fatal to mild. Some strokes that are not fatal can be very debilitating, and TIAs are an indication of a higher than average stroke risk. Multiple small strokes can eventually lead to dementia.

3. *Atrial Fibrillation.* This is an arrhythmia that has a high stroke risk.

4. *Diabetes.* This is a progressive condition that affects the circulatory system. Complications from this disease can lead to stroke, vision problems, nerve damage, and circulation problems including amputation.

Once a home office underwriter has available your application, details of your medical history, doctor's statements, and medical regimen, an assessment is made of your risk to determine whether you will be offered anywhere from the best (lowest) rate the company has for your age up to the highest rate—or even whether you will be declined.

Within those classes there are other underwriting designations applied that will increase your premium above the one charged as a preferred risk, or there could be a postponement, which indicates that after a certain period of time the company will reconsider your risk, provided there has been no deterioration in the interim.

UnumProvident translates this underwriting philosophy into its current field underwriting guide, as follows.

P20 – Acceptable Preferred with Underwriter Approval
CI – Class I Standard Rates
CII – Class II 25% Rating (see pg. 14 for plan design limitations)
CIII – Class III 50% Rating (see pg. 14 for plan design limitations)
PP – Postpone
D – Decline

A

Condition	Underwriting Action
AIDS, (HIV Positive, ARC)	D
ALCOHOL DEPENDENCY OR EXCESSIVE USE/DRUG DEPENDENCY	
■ *Completely alcohol/drug free - 36 months*	CI
■ *Ongoing use or complications (i.e. abnormal lab/testing, hospitalization)*	D
■ *Illicit drug use*	D
ALZHEIMER'S DISEASE	D
AMBULATION (i.e. Unsteadiness, shuffling, instability)	D
AMPUTATION	
■ *Due to trauma, now completely stable and independent*	CI
■ *Due to disease, (i.e. Diabetes, Atherosclerosis or co-morbid factors)*	D
AMYOTROPHIC LATERAL SCLEROSIS (ALS) (Lou Gehrig's Disease)	D
ANEMIA	
■ *Mild/moderate - asymptomatic*	CI
■ *Severe, chronic or undetermined cause*	D
ANEURYSM	
■ *Cerebral*	
■ *Status post aneurysm repair 12 months*	CI
■ *Not surgically treated*	D
■ *Residual limitations*	D
■ *Abdominal, Aortic, Thoracic*	
■ *Status post successful aneurysm repair 12 months*	CI

FIGURE C.1 Medical Risk Selection Guide
Source: UnumProvident Corporation. *Underwriting Guide*, July 2001.

Condition	*Underwriting Action*
■ *Residual limitations*	**D**
■ *If not surgically treated will consider*	**CIII**
■ *If size is greater than 6 cm or surgery recommended*	**D**

ANGINA
■ *Asymptomatic for 6 months*	**CI**
■ *Status post heart attack, stable and controlled angina after 12 months*	**CI/CII/CIII**
■ *Symptomatic*	**D**

ANXIETY
■ *Mild, situational, stable, treated w/Rx and/or counseling*	**P20**
■ *Chronic, stable w/ongoing medication (i.e. Xanax, Valium)*	**CI**

ARRHYTHMIA/IRREGULAR HEART BEAT (except Atrial Fibrillation)
■ *Asymptomatic, no treatment required*	**CI**
■ *Management with oral medication, no underlying pathology for 6 months*	**CI**
■ *Co-morbid factors (i.e. Cardiomyopathy, Valvular Disease, Diabetes, Vascular Disease)*	**D**

ARTHRITIS: See Rheumatoid, Osteoarthritis or specific joint

ASTHMA/BRONCHITIS
■ *Mild, seasonal, medication as needed*	**P20**
■ *Chronic, treated with medications, stable*	**C1**
■ *Complicated, multiple hospitalizations, steroid use above limits, chronic nebulizer, or heart condition*	**D**

ATAXIA
	D

ATRIAL FIBRILLATION
■ *Under age 65, no cardiovascular (hypertension, coronary artery disease, etc) or cerebrovascular (prior stroke, circulatory disorders) risk factors, stable for 6 months*	**CII**
■ *Over age 65 with effective anticoagulation therapy, no prior stroke*	**CIII**
■ *Over age 65 without effective anticoagulation therapy, no prior stroke*	**CIII with 3 yr. Benefit Period**
■ *Any age with effective anticoagulation therapy, stroke > 3 yrs. ago*	**CIII with 3 yr. Benefit Period**
■ *Over 65 without effective anticoagulation therapy History of stroke*	**D**
■ *Uncontrolled, Unstable or Complicated*	**D**

B

BACK DISORDERS (Spinal, Disc, Spondylothis-thesis, Spondylosis, Spinal Stenosis, Sciatica, Radiculitis)
■ *No functional limitations. Stable - 12 months*	**CI**
■ *Status post laminectomy, diskectomy, spinal fusion stable - 12 months*	**CI**
■ *Chronic pain, multiple surgeries, compression fractures, progressive muscle weakness or wasting, daily narcotic use, functional limitations*	**D**

BARRETT'S ESOPHAGUS
■ *Stable, controlled, negative work up for cancer*	**CI**

FIGURE C.1 *Continued*

Condition	*Underwriting Action*

BASAL CELL CARCINOMA · P20

BLINDNESS
■ *Progressive sight loss, co-morbid factors or with limited activities* · D

BRAIN DISORDER, ORGANIC BRAIN DISORDER · D

BRONCHITIS: See Asthma

C

CANCER
■ *Breast Cancer*
  - ■ *In situ - 0 months* · CI
  - ■ *Stage I - 12 months OR 0 months with 180 day EP** · CI
  - ■ *Stage II - 24 months* · CI
  - ■ *Stage IIIa, IIIb - 36 months* · CI
  - ■ *Evidence of active disease, Stage IV, or metastasis* · D

■ *Colorectal Cancer*
  - ■ *Stage A, Grade 1 or 2 - 12 months OR 0 months with 180 day EP** · CI
  - ■ *Stage A, Grade 3 or 4 - 24 months OR 12 months with 180 day EP* · CI
  - ■ *Stage B1, B2 - 36 months OR 24 months with 180 day EP* · CI
  - ■ *Evidence of active disease, Stage C or greater, or metastasis* · D

■ *Lung Cancer*
  - ■ *In situ - 24 months OR 12 months with 180 day EP** · CI
  - ■ *Stage I - 36 months OR 24 months with 180 day EP* · CI
  - ■ *Stage II - 48 months OR 36 months with 180 day EP* · CI
  - ■ *Stage IIIa, IIIb - 60 months OR 48 months with 180 day EP* · CI
  - ■ *Evidence of active disease, smoking, Stage IV, or metastasis* · D

■ *Malignant Melanoma Cancer*
  - ■ *Clark Level I - 0 months* · CI
  - ■ *Clark Level II - 12 months OR 0 months with 180 day EP** · CI
  - ■ *Clark Level III - 36 months OR 24 months with 180 day EP* · CI
  - ■ *Clark Level IV - 48 months OR 36 months with 180 day EP* · CI
  - *Or*
  - ■ *Breslow System <.5mm invasion into basal lamina (in situ) - 6 months or 0 months with 180 day EP* · CI
  - ■ *Breslow System <.76mm invasion into basal lamina - 12 months or 0 months with 180 day EP* · CI
  - ■ *Evidence of active disease, Clark Level V or Breslow System > 3mm invasion, positive lymph nodes, local recurrence within 3cm of primary site, or metastasis* · D

*EP refers to Elimination Period
These time frames are from date of last treatment and do not reflect a history of metastasis, node involvement, complications or multiple cancers. For information regarding the more advanced stages of these cancers or other cancers, call your UnumProvident representative.

FIGURE C.1 *Continued*

- *Malignant Lymphoma*
  - *Disease and treatment free - 60 months*   CIII
  - *Evidence of active disease or progression in lymphoma grade*   D

- *Prostate Cancer*
  - *Stage A1 - 0 Months*   CI
  - *Stage A2, B1, B2, B3 - 12 months OR 0 months with 180 day EP**   CI
  - *Stage C1 - 36 months OR 24 months with 180 day EP*   CI
  - *Evidence of active disease, Stage C2 or greater, Grade 3, Gleason Score 8 or greater, seminal vesicle involvement, or metastasis*   D

- *Uterine Cancer*
  - *Stage 0, I with Grade 1 or 2 - 24 Months*   CI
  - *Stage I, II - 48 months*   CI
  - *Evidence of active disease, Stage III or greater, pelvic or aortic lymph node involvement, or metastasis*   D

CARDIOMYOPATHY   D

CAROTID ARTERY DISEASE / STENOSIS
- *Asymptomatic, not requiring surgery, (less than 70% stenosis) or 6 months from Endarterectomy*   CI
- *Symptomatic, >70% stenosis, TIA, or Stroke*   D

CATARACTS   P20

CATHETER USE   D

CEREBRAL PALSY
- *Demonstrated stability, no co-morbid factors, < 60 years of age*   CI
- *Decrease in muscle strength or functioning*   D

CHOLESTEROL
- *Stable, controlled, no co-morbid factors*   P20

CHOREA, HUNTINGTON'S   D

CHRONIC OBSTRUCTIVE PULMONARY DISEASE: See Asthma

CIRRHOSIS OF THE LIVER   D

COLITIS/IRRITABLE BOWEL SYNDROME/ULCERATIVE COLITIS
- *Normal weight maintenance **0 months***   CI
- *Ostomy with independent management **6 months***   CI
- *Use of Azulfadine/Rowasa **12 months***   CI
- *Active*   D

*EP refers to Elimination Period

These time frames are from date of last treatment and do not reflect a history of metastasis, node involvement, complications or multiple cancers. For information regarding the more advanced stages of these cancers or other cancers, call your UnumProvident representative.

FIGURE C.1 *Continued*

Condition	Underwriting Action

COPD/EMPHYSEMA
- *Seasonal, short term steroid use, stable PFTs (Pulmonary Function Tests)* — **CI**
- *Recent hospitalizations* — **PP 12 Months**
- *Multiple hospitalizations, complicated and/or with smoking, daily use of steroids above limits, chronic nebulizer, heart conditions* — **D**

CONGESTIVE HEART FAILURE
- *Stable for 12 months, no functional limitations* — **CII**
- *Stable for 12 months, with mild functional limitations* — **CIII**
- *Multiple episodes, uncontrolled, restriction of IADLs or ADLs, or on > 80 mg/day of Lasix (Furosemide)* — **D**

CORONARY HEART/ARTERY DISEASE
- *Asymptomatic, no co-morbid factors* — **CI**
- *Status Post Myocardial Infarction, Angina, Angioplasty, By-pass - 6 months* — **CI**
- *Evidence of unstable Angina, Congestive Heart Failure, Co-morbid factors (Significant obesity, hypertension, heart disease, diabetes, peripheral vascular disease or smoking)* — **D**

CROHN'S DISEASE
- *Stable and medically managed for 24 months* — **CII/CIII**
- *Complicated, multiple surgeries or steriod use above limits* — **D**

D

DEFIBRILLATOR USE — **D**

DEMENTIA — **D**

DEPRESSION
- *Recent onset, start-up therapy session, changes in medications* — **PP 12 months**
- *Hospitalization for depression, < 12 months, resolved* — **PP 24 months**
- *Situational, 12 months, resolved* — **P20**
- *Chronic, compliance with medication, no limits to lifestyle* — **CI**
- *Complicated, multiple hospitalization, suicidal ideation or ECT* — **D**

DIABETES
Stable, controlled, Glucose readings <200, HbgA1C <9.0%, no complications (neuropathy, retinopathy, peripheral vascular disease, organ damage) or co-morbid factors (significant obesity, heart disease, hypertension, peripheral vascular disease or smoking) regular follow-up and
- *Age 50 or older at time of diagnosis, diagnosed <10 years ago, oral medication or diet controlled* — **CI**
- *Onset between ages 35 and 50, diagnosed <10 years ago, oral medication, diet controlled or <60 units Insulin/day* — **CII**
- *Onset after age 50 or diagnosed <10 years ago, <60 units Insulin/day* — **CII**
- *Onset under age 35 or diagnosed >10 years ago, oral medication, diet controlled or <60 units Insulin/day* — **CIII**
- *Complicated, Uncontrolled, or >60 units Insulin/day* — **D**

FIGURE C.1 *Continued*

Condition	Underwriting Action

DIALYSIS — D

DISABLED APPLICANT
- Applicant receiving disability payments, i.e. LTD, SSDI, etc. — D

DIZZINESS
- Benign, Positional, Stable - 6 months — CI
- Etiology unclear — PP
- Co-morbid factors, i.e. falls, neurological symptoms, cardiac condition — D

DRUG ABUSE: See Alcohol/Drug abuse

E

EMPHYSEMA: See Asthma

ENDOCARDITIS
- Fully recovered 24 months — CI
- Active, symptomatic, cardionecrosis, history of cardioversion — D

EPILEPSY/SEIZURES
- Controlled for 12 months, no complications — CI
- Uncontrolled, without firm diagnosis — D

EQUIPMENT USE
- Straight Cane, no co-morbid factors — CI
- Quad Cane (four prong cane), crutches, walker, wheelchair, commode, hoyer lift, etc. when related to an acute condition, temporary use — PP
- Quad Cane (four prong cane), straight cane, crutches, walker, wheelchair, commode, hoyer lift, etc. when related to a chronic or age related condition, frailty, osteoporosis or falls — D

EYE DISORDERS (Retinal Detachment, Vascular Retinopathy, Macular Degeneration, Retinitis Pigmentosa)
- Completely independent, stable for 24 months — CI
- Evidence of progressive sight loss, co-morbid factors — D

F

FALLS
- Multiple or recent, (irrespective of injury sustained); with dizziness, syncope, cerebrovascular disorder, osteoporosis or gait disturbance — D

FIBROMYALGIA
- No functional limitations, stable for 12 months — CI
- Chronic pain/fatigue that interferes with every day life, depression, hospitalizations — D

FRACTURES
- Single episode, fully recovered 6 months — CI
- Multiple falls, compression fractures, underlying condition (i.e. osteoporosis) — D

FIGURE C.1 *Continued*

Condition	*Underwriting Action*

G

GERD (Gastroesophageal reflux disorder)	**P20**

GLAUCOMA
- *One medication, stable pressure in both eyes, normal visual acuity and visual field* **CI**

GOUT
- *No functional limitations, well controlled with Medications* **P20**
- *Status post joint replacement, stable 6 months* **C1**
- *Chronic, Active with complications* **D**

H

HEAD INJURY
- *Stable condition with no residual paralysis or cognitive deficit for 12 months* **CI**
- *Existing functional or cognitive impairment* **D**

HEART ATTACK (MYOCARDIAL INFARCTION)
- *Status post single episode 6 months, no limitations* **CI**
- *Status post multiple episodes, with Co-morbid factors (See Coronary Artery Disease)* **D**

HEART TRANSPLANT	**D**

HEMOPHILIA
- *Mild* **CI**
- *Moderate* **CII**
- *Severe* **D**

HEPATITIS
- *Alcoholic: Fully recovered, no use for 5 years, or longer* **CI**
- *Alcoholic: Present* **D**
- *Hepatitis A, Fully recovered* **CI**
- *Hepatitis B, Fully recovered - 24 months* **CI**
- *Hepatitis C, Treated, Negative Viral RNA Load - 24 Months* **CI**
- *Hepatitis C, Treated, Positive Viral RNA Load* **D**

HIP DISORDERS / REPLACEMENT
- *No functional limitations, status post hip surgery/replacement 6 months* **CI**
- *Fracture/hip replacement with persisting pain, restricted activities, unsteady gait* **D**

HIV POSITIVE	**D**

FIGURE C.1 *Continued*

Condition	Underwriting Action

HODGKINS DISEASE
- Fully recovered from therapy 5 years - Stage I/II — **CI**
- Fully recovered from therapy 5 years - Stage III/IV — **CIII**
- Active disease — **D**

HYDROCEPHALUS (including shunted and normal pressure) — **D**

HYPERTENSION
- BP ≤140/90 all ages — **CI**
- BP >140/90 and ≤ 160/90 45 and under — **CII**
- BP >140/90 and ≤ 160/90 46 and over — **CI**
- BP >160/100 and ≤ 180/110 all ages — **CIII**
- BP >180/110 or severe/resistant — **D**

  (Tobacco use moves the applicant down a class rating)

I

INCONTINENCE
- Mild urinary or stress incontinence — **P20**
- Bowel incontinence — **D**

K

KIDNEY/RENAL FAILURE
- Renal failure or insufficiency, acute more than 12 months from recovery (APS) — **CI**
- Renal failure or insufficiency - current, acute or chronic — **D**
- Kidney transplant, Dialysis — **D**

KNEE REPLACEMENT
- 6 months after surgery — **CI**
- Multiple surgeries and/or on-going pain — **D**

L

LEUKEMIA
- Chronic Lymphocytic Leukemia (CLL)
  If diagnosed less than 3 years, Stage 0, I or II — **CI**
  If diagnosed more than 3 years, Stage 0, I or II — **CIII**
  If diagnosed more than 3 years, Stage III — **D**
- Acute Lymphocytic Leukemia (ALL) 5 years from diagnosis — **CI**
- Acute Myelogenous Leukemia (AML) 5 years from diagnosis — **CI**
- Chronic Myelogenous Leukemia (CML) w/bone marrow transplant,
  5 years from diagnosis — **CIII**
- Multiple Myeloma, Hairy Cell Leukemia — **D**

LOU GEHRIG'S DISEASE (Amyotrophic Lateral Sclerosis) — **D**

FIGURE C.1 *Continued*

Condition	Underwriting Action

LUPUS
- *Discoid, not SLE, stable - 6 months*   **CI**
- *Systemic Lupus Erythematosis if in remission 5 years*   **CIII**

LYMPHOMA
- *All types, disease, and treatment free - 5 years*   **CIII**
- *All types, disease free - 10 years*   **CI**

M

MEMORY LOSS	**D**
MENOPAUSE, WITH OR WITHOUT HORMONE THERAPY	**P20**
MENTAL RETARDATION	**D**
MULTIPLE MYELOMA	**D**
MULTIPLE SCLEROSIS	**D**
MUSCULAR DYSTROPHY	**D**
MYASTHENIA GRAVIS	**D**

O

OBESITY (As defined by our Height/Weight guidelines on pages 253-254.)	**D**
ORGAN TRANSPLANT	**D**
ORGANIC BRAIN SYNDROME (OBS)	**D**

OSTEOARTHRITIS
- *Mild, over the counter medications and consistent with age*   **P20**
- *Stable, prescription medication, no function limitations*   **CI**
- *Functional limitations, surgery recommended*   **D**

OSTEOPOROSIS
- *Mild*   **CI**
- *Moderate, no limitations*   **CII/CIII**
- *Severe, Compression fractures, or falls*   **D**

OSTOMY (See specific condition)	
OXYGEN USE	**D**

P

PACEMAKER
- *Asymptomatic for 6 months*   **CI**

FIGURE C.1 *Continued*

Condition	Underwriting Action
PAGET'S DISEASE OF BONE	
■ *No limitations, stable, in remission 24 months*	CI
■ *Symptomatic, extensive or history of compression fractures*	D
PANCREATITIS	
■ *Stable, normal weight maintenance - 12 months*	CI
■ *Evidence of active pancreatitis*	D
PARALYSIS	
■ *Longstanding and new onset paraplegia or paraparesis*	D
■ *Quadriplegia*	D
PARKINSON'S DISEASE	D
PEPTIC ULCER DISEASE (Gastric, Duodenal, Esophageal, Jejunal, Stomach)	
■ *Normal weight maintenance, well controlled*	CI
■ *History of GI bleeds, hospitalization, evidence of weight loss*	PP 12 months
PERIPHERAL NEUROPATHY	
■ *Mild, non limiting, non progressive*	CI
■ *Neuropathy without confirmed diagnosis*	PP 24 months
■ *Progressive, painful, uncontrolled or complicated*	D
PERIPHERAL VASCULAR DISEASE	
■ *Asymptomatic, no co-morbid factors*	CI
■ *Functional limitations, restriction of daily activities, co-morbid factors (Significant obesity, heart disease, diabetes or smoking)*	D
POLIOMYELITIS (POLIO)	
■ *No functional limitations*	CI
■ *Clinical evidence of post polio syndrome, change in muscle strength or functioning, increased fatigue*	D
POLYCYSTIC KIDNEY DISEASE	D
POLYCYTHEMIA VERA	
■ *Stable 24 months, treatment with Phlebotomy*	CIII
■ *Surgery required, abnormal lab values, weight loss, complications*	D
POLYMYALGIA RHEUMATICA	
■ *No limitations, stable, in remission - 24 months*	CI
■ *Symptomatic or complications*	D
POST POLIO SYNDROME	D
PROGRESSIVE MUSCULAR ATROPHY	D

FIGURE C.1 *Continued*

Condition	Underwriting Action

PROSTATIC HYPERTROPHY, BENIGN (BPH)

■ *PSA <10, regular follow-up, asymptomatic*	P20
■ *PSA <10, regular follow-up, mild symptoms and/or history of TURP*	CI
■ *PSA >10, regular follow-up, negative biopsy, medical explanation not suggestive of cancer*	CII

PULMONARY FIBROSIS | D |

R

RHEUMATOID ARTHRITIS

■ *No functional limitations, stable - 12 months, use of non steroidal anti-inflammatory drug*	CI
■ *Chronic steroid use, use of Enbrel, history of compression fractures, multiple joint replacements*	D

RENAL FAILURE/RENAL INSUFFICIENCY | D |

S

SARCOIDOSIS

■ *Mild, single-site sarcoid, stable, no limitations - 6 months*	CI
■ *Multiple site sarcoidosis - 12 months*	CI
■ *Active, current treatment, symptomatic, smoker*	D

SCHIZOPHRENIA | D |

SCLERODERMA | D |

SEIZURES | See Epilepsy |

SJOGREN'S SYNDROME | D |

SLEEP APNEA | P20 |

SMOKING/TOBACCO USE

■ *Tobacco use, no co-morbid factors (significant obesity, heart disease, hypertension, peripheral vascular disease, diabetes or smoking*	CI

STEROID USE

■ *Prednisone, Deltasone > 10mg/day*	D

STROKE (CVA, TIA)

■ *Single episode, 10 years out, no residuals or co-morbid factors*	CI
■ *Single episode, 3 years out, no residual weakness*	CIII
■ *Multiple strokes or TIAs, persistent co-morbid factors (i.e. cardiovascular disease, valvular disease, carotid stenosis)*	D

SYNCOPE (FAINTING, PASSING OUT)

■ *See specific condition*	CI
■ *Unconfirmed diagnosis*	D

FIGURE C.1 *Continued*

Condition	*Underwriting Action*

T

TEMPORAL ARTERITIS	D

THROMBOCYTOPENIA	
■ *Idiopathic, platelet count > 80,000, stable - 24 months*	CI

THROMBOPHLEBITIS/PHLEBITIS	
■ *Superficial, fully recovered*	CI
■ *Deep, single episode, fully recovered - 6 months*	CI
■ *Co-existing condition (i.e. Recurrent venous ulcers, Diabetes, Coronary Artery Disease)*	D

THYROID DISEASE (Hyper/Hypothyroidism)	
■ *Controlled with medication or by surgery*	P20

TRANSIENT GLOBAL AMNESIA	
■ *Single episode, confirmed diagnosis, no complications co-morbid factors, stable and normal cognitive function - 24 months*	CI

TRANSIENT ISCHEMIC ATTACK (TIA) See Stroke	

V

VALVULAR HEART DISEASE	
■ *Mitral Valve Prolapse, mild, asymptomatic*	P20
■ *Mild or moderate Aortic/Mitral Disease, asymptomatic, no-comorbid factors*	CI
■ *Moderate to severe Aortic/Mitral Disease, asymptomatic, no-comorbid factors*	CII
■ *Severe Aortic/Mitral Disease, asymptomatic, no-comorbid factors*	CIII
■ *Severe symptomatic, unstable or with co-morbid factors (Significant obesity, heart disease, hypertension, peripheral vascular disease, diabetes or smoking)*	D

VERTIGO	
■ *Benign, positional with successful treatment, stable - 6 months*	CI
■ *Unclear etiology*	PP
■ *Evidence of co-existing condition, neurological symptoms, demyelinating disease, tumor, stroke*	D

W

WEIGHT (See guidelines on pages 253-254.)	

WILSON'S DISEASE	D

FIGURE C.1 *Continued*

Height and Weight Charts

Females ages 18 and Over				
Height	Under Weight	Average Weight	Preferred Range	Standard Range
4' - 8"	78	111	94 - 163	164 - 191
9"	79	113	96 - 166	167 - 195
10"	80	115	97 - 170	171 - 199
11"	82	117	99 - 174	175 - 203
5' - 0"	84	120	102 - 178	179 - 208
1"	86	123	104 - 182	183 - 213
2"	88	126	107 - 186	187 - 218
3"	90	129	110 - 191	192 - 223
4"	92	132	112 - 196	197 - 229
5"	94	135	115 - 200	201 - 234
6"	97	139	118 - 205	206 - 239
7"	99	142	120 - 210	211 - 245
8"	102	146	125 - 215	216 - 251
9"	105	150	127 - 221	222 - 257
10"	108	154	131 - 228	229 - 264
11"	111	159	135 - 236	237 - 272
6' - 0"	115	164	139 - 244	245 - 282
1"	118	169	143 - 252	253 - 291
2"	121	174	148 - 260	261 - 300
3"	124	179	152 - 268	269 - 309
4"	127	184	156 - 276	277 - 318

Note: An applicant weighing less than the weight indicated in the 'Underweight' column or greater than the high–end of the 'Standard Range' will be uninsurable.

FIGURE C.1 *Continued*

Height and Weight Charts

Males ages 18 and Over				
Height	**Under Weight**	**Average Weight**	**Preferred Range**	**Standard Range**
5' - 0"	92	131	111 - 180	181 - 213
1"	94	134	114 - 184	185 - 217
2"	96	137	116 - 188	189 - 222
3"	99	141	120 - 193	194 - 227
4"	102	145	123 - 198	199 - 232
5"	104	149	126 - 203	204 - 238
6"	107	153	130 - 208	209 - 244
7"	110	157	133 - 214	215 - 250
8"	113	161	136 - 220	221 - 257
9"	116	165	140 - 226	227 - 264
10"	119	170	144 - 232	233 - 271
11"	122	174	148 - 238	239 - 278
6' - 0"	125	179	152 - 244	245 - 285
1"	128	183	155 - 251	252 - 292
2"	132	188	160 - 258	259 - 299
3"	135	193	164 - 265	266 - 307
4"	139	199	169 - 272	273 - 315
5"	143	204	173 - 279	280 - 323
6"	147	210	178 - 286	287 - 331
7"	151	216	183 - 293	294 - 339
8"	155	221	188 - 300	301 - 347

Note: An applicant weighing less than the weight indicated in the 'Underweight' column or greater than the high–end of the 'Standard Range' will be uninsurable.

FIGURE C.1 Continued

Glossary

Accelerated death benefit   A feature of a life insurance policy that permits the use of some of the policy's death benefit prior to death. Certain policies may allow this benefit to pay for long-term care services.

Activities of daily living (ADLs)   Everyday functions and activities individuals usually do without help. ADL functions include bathing, dressing, eating, toileting, transferring, continence.

- *Bathing*—Washing oneself by sponge bath or in either a tub or a shower, including the task of getting into or out of the tub or shower with or without equipment or adaptive devices.
- *Dressing*—Putting on and taking off all items of clothing and any necessary braces, fasteners, or artificial limbs.
- *Eating*—Feeding oneself by getting food into the body from a receptacle (such as a plate, cup, or table) or by feeding tube or intravenously.
- *Toileting*—Getting to and from the toilet, getting on and off the toilet, and performing associated personal hygiene.
- *Transferring*—Moving into or out of bed, chair, or wheelchair with or without equipment such as canes, quad canes, walkers, crutches, grab bars, or other support devices including mechanical or motorized devices.

- *Continence*—The ability to maintain control of bowel or bladder function; or when unable to maintain control of bowel or bladder function, the ability to perform associated personal hygiene (including caring for catheter or colostomy bag).

Acute care   Short-term medical treatment for a serious injury or illness; should not be confused with chronic care, which is ongoing long-term care in either a home or a skilled nursing facility.

Adult day care   Social or dementia day care for adults, usually at senior or community centers.

Advanced age   Refers to the inability to perform an ADL or the presence of cognitive impairment because of frailty or debilitation resulting from the aging process.

Alternate care provision   A benefit available in some individual long-term care insurance policies that may cover unspecified treatments or services if agreed to by the insured, the insurer, and the insured's health care practitioner.

Alzheimer's disease   A progressive, degenerative form of dementia that causes severe intellectual deterioration.

Assessment   An interview done by a designated representative of an insurance company to assist in the determination of one's insurability at the time of application, or the determination of disability at the time of a claim.

Assisted living facility   A residential living arrangement that provides individualized personal care and health services for people who require assistance with activities of daily living.

Bed reservation   If you are confined to a nursing facility and have the need to leave temporarily for a hospital stay you will be reimbursed up to the number of days provided in the policy for the cost of guaranteeing your bed or room is reserved when you return.

Benefit triggers   Term used by insurance companies to describe when the policy will begin to pay benefits.

Caregiver training   When an informal caregiver—perhaps a friend, relative, or someone you live with—needs training to help care for you at home and is reimbursed for that training subject to a lifetime maximum as provided in your policy.

Care management services   A service in which a professional, typically a nurse or social worker, may arrange, monitor, or coordinate long-term care services.

Chore care   Nonmedical services that are provided in the insured's home and are designed to maintain the insured's home so that it remains habitable, including at a minimum: vacuuming (including the moving of furniture), washing floors and walls, defrosting the freezer, cleaning the oven, cleaning the attic and basement to remove fire and health hazards, changing storm windows, performing heavy yard work, shoveling snow, and making minor home repairs.

Chronic illness   An illness with one or more of the following characteristics: permanency, residual disability, requirement of rehabilitation training, or requirement of a long period of supervision, observation, or care.

Cognitive impairment   A deficiency in a person's short- or long-term memory; orientation as to person, place, and time; deductive or abstract reasoning; or judgment as it relates to safety awareness.

Community-based services   Services designed to help older people stay independent and in their own homes.

Custodial care (personal care)   Care to help individuals meet personal needs such as bathing, dressing, and eating. Custodial care is not medical care and may be provided by someone without professional training.

Daily benefit   The amount of insurance benefit in dollars a person chooses to buy for covered long-term care expenses.

Deductible   A flat dollar amount that an individual must pay for covered services before the insurance company will begin to make payments.

Dementia   Deterioration of intellectual faculties due to a disorder of the brain.

Disabled   Unable to perform without substantial assistance from another individual at least two activities of daily living, or requiring substantial supervision by another individual to protect a person or others from threats to health and safety due to severe cognitive impairment.

Elimination Period   A type of deductible; the length of time the individual must pay for covered services before the insurance company will begin to make payments. The longer the elimination period in a policy, the lower the premium.

Group policy   A policy sold through an employment-based group, association, or special group insurance trust. Individuals receive certificates of coverage from the group policy. These policies are not subject to most state insurance requirements.

Guaranteed renewable   Policy feature guaranteeing the insured's right to continue a policy. The company cannot change the coverage or refuse to renew the coverage for other than nonpayment of premiums (including health conditions and/or marital or employment status); however, the company can revise the rate subject to the approval of the state commissioner of insurance.

Health Insurance Portability and Accountability Act (HIPAA)   Federal health insurance legislation passed in 1996 that allows, under specified conditions, long-term care insurance policies to be qualified for certain tax benefits.

Home care services   Household services done by someone other than yourself, because you're unable to do them. Services include, but are not limited to, shopping, planning menus, preparing meals, home-delivered meals, laundry, and light housecleaning and maintenance, including vacuuming, dusting, dry mopping, dishwashing, cleaning the kitchen/bathroom, and changing beds.

Home health care   Services for occupational, physical, respiratory, speech therapy, or nursing care. Also included are medical, social worker, and home health aide services.

Incontestability clause   A provision in every long-term care policy that after a specified period of time, usually for a policy in force less than six months, the insurer may contest the policy upon showing a misrepresentation that is material to your acceptance of coverage. For a policy in force at least six months but less than two years, the insurer may contest the policy upon demonstrating a misrepresentation that both is material to your acceptance of coverage and pertaining to the conditions of your disability. In some states, after two years from the policy's effective date only fraudulent misstatements in your application can be used to contest your policy.

Individual policy   A policy sold directly by a company to an individual without requiring the individual to be a member of an employment-based group, association, or special group insurance trust. These policies usually are sold by insurance agents and brokers but sometimes are sold through direct mail or phone solicitations.

Inflation protection   A policy option that provides for increases in benefit levels to help pay for expected increases in the costs of long-term care services. Applicants usually have the choice of automatic increases or periodic special offers to increase plan benefits.

Instrumental activities of daily living   Telephoning, bill paying, grocery shopping, cooking, doing laundry, taking medicine, and housekeeping.

Lapse   Termination of a policy when a renewal premium is not paid.

Licensed health care practitioner   Any physician, and any registered professional nurse, licensed social worker, or other individual who meets such requirements as may be prescribed by the Secretary of the U.S. Treasury.

Maximum benefit amount   The total dollar amount of benefits that will be paid under the policy. It includes the combined dollars paid out for nursing facility and assisted living facility benefits. The maximum benefit amount is shown in the policy schedule. If the policy schedule shows that the maximum benefit amount is "lifetime," the maximum benefit amount will be adjusted to include any inflation protection option increases, if applicable.

Medicaid   A joint federal/state program that pays for health care services for those with low incomes or very high medical bills relative to income and assets.

Medicare   The federal program providing hospital and medical insurance to people aged 65 or older and to certain ill or disabled persons. Benefits for nursing home and home health services are limited.

Medigap insurance   A private insurance policy that covers many of the gaps in Medicare coverage.

Monthly benefit amount   An insured person's monthly nursing home benefit amount or monthly assisted living facility benefit amount shown in the policy schedule.

National Association of Insurance Commissioners (NAIC)   Membership organization of state officials supervising insurance. One of its goals is to promote uniformity of state regulation and legislation related to insurance.

Nonforfeiture benefits   A policy feature that provides a specified paid-up benefit or returns at least part of the premiums to a person who cancels a policy or lets it lapse.

Nursing home   Facility that is primarily engaged in providing nursing care and related services on an inpatient basis under a license issued by the department of public health or the appropriate licensing agency of the state in which it is located.

One-time elimination period   Once the elimination period or the deductible is satisfied it no longer applies during a policy's lifetime.

Outline of coverage   A form provided by an agent or broker in connection with the sale of a long-term care policy that gives the purchaser an overview of the coverage purchased.

Respite care   Services to temporarily relieve family caregivers of the stresses and demands of caring for a person with a chronic illness or cognitive impairment. In addition to home care, personal care, and home health care, respite care services may include but are not limited to short-term placement in adult foster care, nursing facilities, or rest homes.

Restoration of benefits   A provision offered by some long-term care policies which restores the policy's full benefit if no money is paid out for a specified period of time.

Rider   Addition to an insurance policy that changes the provisions of the policy.

Severe Cognitive Impairment   A severe deterioration or loss, as reliably measured by clinical evidence and standardized tests, in short- or long-term memory; orientation as to person, place, and time; or deductive or abstract reasoning. Such deterioration or loss requires substantial supervision by another individual for the purpose of protecting oneself. Such loss can result from a disability, Alzheimer's disease, or a similar form of dementia.

Skilled nursing care   Daily nursing and rehabilitative care that can be performed only by or under the supervision of skilled medical personnel. The care received must be based on a doctor's orders.

Spend down   To use up most of one's income and assets to meet Medicaid eligibility requirements.

Substantial assistance   Stand-by assistance without which someone would not be able to perform an ADL safely and completely.

Tax-qualified long-term care insurance policy   A policy that conforms to certain standards in federal law and offers certain federal tax advantages.

Third-party notice   A benefit that lets the insured name someone whom the insurance company would notify if coverage is about to end due to lack of premium payment. This can be a relative, friend, or professional such as a lawyer or an accountant.

Underwriting   The process of examining and accepting or rejecting insurance risks, and classifying those selected in order to charge the proper premium for each.

Waiver of premium   A provision in an insurance policy that relieves the insured of paying the premiums while receiving benefits.

Index

About the Author

For more than two decades, Ben Lipson has been a consumer advocate and newspaper columnist known for his work on patient rights, senior health care issues, and long-term care insurance. He is also an independent insurance broker who has been actively involved in the insurance industry for 50 years.

Benjamin Lipson is the founder and president of Just for Seniors Insurance, Inc., Chestnut Hill, Massachusetts, and edits the "Just for Seniors" newsletter. For the past 20 years, his columns and opinion pieces on health-related insurance issues have appeared in the *Boston Globe*.